Philosophic Foundations of Education

Philosophic Foundations of Education

S. SAMUEL SHERMIS
Purdue University

VAN NOSTRAND REINHOLD COMPANY

New York   Cincinnati   Toronto   London   Melbourne

ACKNOWLEDGEMENTS

The author would like to express his gratitude to the following persons who, in many ways, were instrumental in the writing of this book:

Professor Donald Kline, Idaho State University, who encouraged the author and provided assistance in duplicating earlier versions of this work.

Professor V. James Simms, education department, Ball State University, who read and criticized Chapter 1.

Mr. and Mrs. William McHugh, Pocatello, Idaho, who read various chapters and provided helpful suggestions.

Dr. Robert Dettloff, counselor at Idaho State University, Counseling and Testing Center, who criticized the section on existentialism and gave the author many insights into the position.

Robert Emerson, M.D., and his wife, Marilyn, who provided assistance and interpretation on a number of illustrations involving the biological sciences.

The students in Education 401, Philosophy of Education, at Idaho State University, who acted as guinea pigs for the first half of this book and who were most helpful in providing criticism and suggestions.

Professor B. Robert Butler, Educational Curator of the Idaho State University Museum, who gave the author many insights into archaeology and who helped him clarify his thinking on the scientific method.

Professor William Shunk, head of the Educational Foundations section at Purdue University, who read and made suggestions for the section on idealism.

Professor Arnold Lazarus, Department of Education, Purdue University, for kindly reading and making suggestions on Chapter 8.

Professors Morris Bigge and Maurice Hunt, Fresno State College, and Eldon Field and Ernest E. Bayles, The University of Kansas, whose classes provided an indispensable background for this book.

Mr. Duke Brannen, graduate assistant, Purdue University, who assisted so ably in reading the manuscript.

The author's wife, Lulla, who was active in every stage of this work, from inception to conclusion. There is no adequate way of thanking her.

Preface

Philosophic Foundations of Education is designed for use in basic courses of philosophy of education or educational foundations. Its purpose is to make the prospective teacher aware that underlying every educational judgment, attitude, practice, is a philosophical assumption, and that stemming from each judgment are broad intellectual and practical implications. It is our hope and deep concern that the future educator, in *examining* the quality of his judgments, will *improve* that quality.

The text is organized around traditional philosophical categories, so that the student will gain familiarity with central concerns in metaphysics, epistemology, axiology, and social philosophy as they apply specifically to educational considerations. In each instance we have focused first on the educational issue—curricular, administrative, financial, or methodological. We have then turned to the historical and cultural context of the problem. What antecedents does it have in the history of social development and educational thought? And, finally, we have focused on philosophical analysis: What view of the world does a given educational approach or practice presuppose? Does that view support or contradict other practices engaged in at the same time? Which consequences tend to flow from one philosophical premise and which from another?

While we have a clearly defined philosophical position of our own, we have not here attempted to persuade the reader of its rightness. Our overriding aim has been to move the student toward insight into the meanings and implications of the philosophical positions he already holds.

We have not assumed the student to be well grounded in philosophy. For this reason, we have provided a systematic introduction to the major philosophers who have concerned themselves with education, particularly Plato, Aristotle, St. Thomas Aquinas, Dewey, and selected contemporary thinkers. Technical terms have been kept to a minimum and, when introduced, are defined and illustrated. Where repetition seemed not only useful but essential, a concept was introduced successively into several different problem areas.

Care has been taken to make the book readable. It is hoped that the numerous examples help clarify data and points of view. It is hoped, too, that the briefly annotated suggested reading lists at the ends-of-chapters will encourage students to read and study further. End-of-chapter questions are of two types—those to review and "set" concepts, and those to give the student practice in applying intellectually what he has learned.

S. S. S.

Contents

Philosophic Foundations of Education

1

What Is
Philosophy
of Education?

What Is Philosophy?

The word *philosophy* refers to a certain method of thinking. As with all thought, philosophy arises out of an attempt to solve a problem—to make sense out of a confusing situation or to explain an inadequacy. But unlike most kinds of thought, philosophy has no immediate object. That is, philosophy is concerned not so much with solving a confronting problem as with finding the deeper meaning of problems.

We can obtain an insight into the differences between philosophy and other modes of thought by contrasting an everyday problem and a philosophical analysis of that problem. Imagine three situations: a physician attempting to save the life of a patient who has a serious disease; a young man planning the best way to ask a girl for a date; an archaeologist and a layman viewing the bones and artifacts that constitute archaeological evidence.

The physician's duty is to arrange the most effective combination of medical techniques so that the patient will either recover or be relieved of symptoms. This simple statement of the physician's aim is based on certain philosophical assumptions about which he has probably thought little. He is probably assuming, for instance, that a human life is worth saving at all costs. If we probe somewhat more deeply in an analysis of his assumptions, he is also assuming, in all likelihood,

1

that life is good—that life on any terms is better than the alternative. These statements are philosophical assumptions. They cannot be proved by evidence, for no amount of evidence can demonstrate the truth or falsity of the proposition that life *per se* is indeed good.

There are a variety of philosophical assumptions concerned with the importance of life. One is that life is a gift from God, which He alone has the right to take away. Another is that being alive is so intrinsically pleasurable that it is always to be preferred to death. On the other hand, it will be remembered that before Socrates drank his cup of poison he said, "The hour of departure has arrived and we go our ways—I to die, and you to live. Which is better God only knows." [1] That is to say, it is not possible to assert definitely that life is truly better than death. Another assumption, not usually entertained by most, is that under certain conditions death is to be preferred to life. Romeo committed suicide because he preferred no existence at all to one without his beloved Juliet.

Turning to the second example, the young man who is planning his dating strategy is operating on the assumption that it is "good" to have pleasurable experiences, an assumption so obvious that few would even think about it, let alone debate it. But philosophical problems arise. We may ask, "How pleasurable?" And this question suggests another one: "What is the meaning of true pleasure?"

To the Hedonists, a school of philosophers in ancient Greece, the answer to the latter question was that pleasure springs from satisfaction of desire—regardless of the nature of the desire.[2] But many ancient Christian theologians would have denied this and asserted that true pleasure is found, not in the satisfaction of desire but in repressing desire and in rejecting the sin-ridden and deceptive world. Indeed, one philosopher went so far as to assert that the world of things which most of us assume is both necessary and good is actually the source of sin and suffering.[3] By contrast, some philosophers belonging to a school known as "naturalism" have asserted that what is "natural" is good.

Though our hypothetical young man is not likely to be exploring these philosophical positions while he is making his dating plans, it is fairly certain that sometime during his life he—and most of the rest of us—will have to deal with such questions as: "What kind of pleasure do I really wish?" "Is one kind of pleasure better than another?" "What

[1] From Plato's *Apology*.

[2] A brief discussion of Hedonism is in Wilhelm Windelband, *A History of Philosophy* (New York: Harper and Row, 1958), Vol. I, p. 85.

[3] This is the position of an ancient philosopher named Plotinus who is generally called a neo-Platonist. See Windelband, p. 247: "Matter is for him absolute negativity, pure privation . . . complete absence of Being, absolute Non-being."

kinds of pleasure should I choose or avoid?" That is, sooner or later, most of us are faced with philosophical problems relating to pleasure, value, and desire.

As for the archaeologist and the layman contemplating the artifacts, assume for a moment that the archaeologist has analyzed them and decided that the evidence points to the existence of a tribe of men that lived some 100,000 years ago. He arranges the artifacts behind a glass showcase in a museum, where they are viewed by a woman, who reads the explanation thoughtfully provided for the lay public. Her reaction is "What nonsense!" The artifacts, she knows, do not point to any 100,000 year old culture, for there could have been no men alive at that time. Genesis states clearly that the world was created by God in six days—and there is certainly no mention of any 100,000-year-old tribe.

The difference in interpretation of the "same" evidence suggests a rather ancient problem concerned with knowing and knowledge. What, precisely, does it mean to "know"? Are there different modes of knowing? And if so, is one method more valid than another? On analysis, it is seen that the archaeologist has employed the scientific method of knowing, which is rooted in observation of *empirical events* —that is, he is utilizing knowledge based on sensory evidence, things which can be felt, touched, weighed, seen, and measured. The woman has accepted as valid knowledge said to have been revealed by God to man and contained in a book taken to be infallible.

These three examples—none of them farfetched—suggest a number of characteristics of what we call philosophy. First, they illustrate the difference between a problem and a philosophical problem. A philosophical problem is an abstract analysis, not only of the here-and-now, but of the underlying beliefs and barely verbalized feelings of people as they make assertions, ask questions, express preferences, plan for the future, appreciate beauty, and condemn evil. *Philosophy is the formulation of what human beings mean—at the deepest level of meaning—when they think, discourse, and act.*

Second, the illustrations suggest that philosophical problems are only slightly removed from "everyday" happenings. Indeed, they indicate that as soon as one begins to reach beyond the obvious confronting situation, he finds himself face to face with philosophical analysis.

Third, it would seem that in our society there is an extremely wide range of philosophical positions from which one can choose. Thus both Hedonism, with its emphasis on sensuous pleasure as the highest good, and the ancient Christian belief that true goodness lies in renouncing sensuous desire are viable alternatives. Hedonism may be found in the emphasis on the pleasures of food and drink in advertising; eroticism has been almost institutionalized in the movies, literature, and popular magazines. On the other hand, a young person can still get into trouble with school authorities for "violating standards of decency and propriety."

A final fact in relation to philosophy is that it is most difficult to avoid philosophical positions of some sort. One may be blind to one's position, as in fact most persons are. One may conceal them from himself. The positions may be mixed and contradictory. Or they may be held on a purely unconscious level. It is even possible to deny that one is operating with any philosophical assumptions (as is done by a rather large number of scholars in various fields). But it is difficult not to conclude that philosophical positions are inescapably part of existence.

The Origins of Philosophy

Although we cannot be certain about the origins of philosophy, an imaginative reconstruction of the past—with help from scholars in different fields [4]—can provide at least a plausible explanation of how and why men came to philosophize. Apparently philosophy arose from the first crude, magical explanations of primitive man as he confronted a world which was, in the highest degree, awesome and terrifying. Without reliable information on why and how nature operated, primitive man apparently provided an explanation which was at first based on magic, then on religion, and only later on philosophy and science.

That some men caught animals and some were eaten by them was obvious. But why? The volcano that suddenly erupted smoke, flame, and burning rock must have inspired awe—and still does, even to scientists. The landslide that unaccountably buried a family beneath tons of rock must also have evoked fear and a feeling of helplessness. Birth and death were also mysteries, of course.

To the primitive mind these events could be explained only by the presence of mysterious entities, invisible powers, which somehow "caused" all things, and which inhabited both animals and inanimate objects. Apparently primitive man's first response to the mysterious world involved magic, a kind of collective, sympathetic, emotional association between himself and what we designate the non-human and inanimate world. [5] Eventually primitive man began to label, define, and

---

[4] Such as archaeology, anthropology, comparative religion, and psychology.

[5] The present belief is that primitive man did not make the same, clear-cut distinction between "animate" and "inanimate" that we do.

describe these mysterious powers. His classification produced a host of powerful spirits, some friendly to man and some hostile. One beneficent spirit made the wood burn, but a malevolent one warned the deer of a hunter's presence or caused the spear to miss its target.

Thus in time man created a rather complex but convincing and emotionally satisfying world, in which everything could be attributed to the actions of the spirit world. Since primitive man apparently did not distinguish between what we could call the "natural" world and the "social" one, the invisible world of spirits was seen as having a direct bearing on man's social relations, on his behavior, and on "good" and "evil." For instance, the ancient Hebrews believed that in each man were lodged two spirits, the *yetzer ha tov*, or spirit of good, and the *yetzer ha ra*, the spirit of evil. When man's behavior was good, the spirit of good was dominant; but when he committed an evil act, he did so at the prompting of the spirit of evil.

At a certain stage of this early history, it occurred to man that, although he could not understand the exact nature of the spirit world, he could affect the actions of the spirits. By chanting certain prayers in the correct manner, presenting sacrifices, and propitiating the spirits he could influence them to do his bidding. He could please the spirit of rain, who would send moisture, or he could propitiate the spirit of the harvest, who would make plants grow bounteously.

Since his actions had a direct bearing on the spirits' good will, and since their good will was necessary for group survival, all behavior took on great significance. Some behavior was bad, for it clearly endangered the cohesiveness or safety of the group. Other behavior was good, for it appeared to protect the group. Perhaps in such a manner, out of a magic-religious concern for group survival, men came to make distinctions between "necessary," "desirable," "good," and "evil."

In primitive times man did not make the distinctions we now make among such terms as "science," "magic," "religion," and "philosophy." At a certain stage in prehistory, all these were somehow combined in an attempt to understand and control the natural and social world by explaining events and by creating codes of behavior to bring about desired results.

Although the later agricultural civilizations that grew up in the Middle East must have modified the original character of the magical explanations of the universe, the essence of primitive man's explanation of the universe did not change substantially. The ancient Egyptians, Greeks, Romans, Hebrews, Sumerians, and others who have left some kind of record reveal an explanation quite similar to that offered by their ancient ancestors. The world was inhabited and directed by spirits (the Hebrews substituting one spirit for a large number of them) and, while these spirits were essentially beyond understanding, it seemed clear that certain actions would ensure their good will.

With the invention of writing, many ancient cultures recorded their perceptions of the world and their codes of behavior. Perhaps the Old Testament of the Hebrews is the best known record of one culture's religion and philosophy. There is in the Old Testament a *cosmogeny,* an explanation of the origin of the universe. The Lord created the world and all that was therein, in much the same way that a potter creates a vase. There are also complex regulations in the Old Testament establishing the correct relationship between man and God and man and man. In addition to detailed requirements for correct rite and ritual, prayer and sacrifice, there is much said about ethics and morality. The Lord indicated precisely what kind of behavior was acceptable to him and what would result in famine, captivity, or even destruction.

There is in the Old Testament an *eschatology,* the philosophical term for the study of the final, ultimate end. Although man's earthly days must come to an end, for those who obeyed the Lord's will there was a promise of life eternal, perhaps even a continuation of the life they knew in this world. We see in the Old Testament, a religious document which is also a record of an ancient mode of philosophizing.

There are some striking parallels between the Hebrew Sacred Scriptures and the early Greek mythological explanation of man, his creation, and desirable behavior. Unlike the Hebrew system, however, the Greek mythological system was not formulated as a creed; and unlike the Hebrews, the Greeks were polytheistic. The essential similarity was that the Greeks accepted a super-natural world, peopled by spirits who had created this world and who laid certain requirements on man.

During the eighth century B.C. there arose a school of thinkers who attemped to formulate an explanation of the origin and nature of the universe in terms very different from the mythological explanations earlier accepted as valid.[6] These thinkers—known as the Milesian school, from the name of the Greek city in which they lived—asked

[6] Despite the Milesians' rejection of polytheism and magic, and despite their attempt to offer a rational explanation of the world, Professor Cornford asserts that their explanation was still rooted in ancient mythological thought. See Francis M. Cornford, *From Religion to Philosophy* (New York: Harper and Row, 1957); see also Bronislaw Malinowski, *Magic, Science, and Religion* (New York: Doubleday Anchor Books, 1954).

the traditional questions: What is the world really like? Whence did it originate? Of what is it made? Although we would not consider their explanations "scientific," in a sense they were. They tried to account for the nature of the universe in rational, empirical terms. In place of a magical explanation that the world was created by spirits, the Milesians attempted to explain the universe as made up of elements, physical things which were arranged in an orderly way and which were essentially understandable and explainable.

Eventually this kind of speculation led to further attempts to explain man's behavior. They asked such questions as: Why do men behave as they do? What is evil? Is man's life controlled by blind chance, or is there some purpose and order which can be understood? What is the relationship (until then apparently not sensed) between man's behavior and the physical universe? Again, the Greeks attempted to explain man's social relationships not in purely magical terms, but in terms which were—at least to them—rational.

From the eighth century to the birth of Jesus, Greek philosophy became increasingly more complex and subtle. In the Hellenistic phase of Greek history,[7] Greeks came into contact with many other cultures. The differences among behavioral codes were striking, and it became clear to some Greek thinkers—known as Sophists—that what is deemed "good" behavior in one place is not so considered elsewhere.

The welter of conflicting Greek philosophies formed the basis of modern philosophy. Theirs was apparently the first recorded attempt to explain the world of man and nature in a self-conscious, non-mystical, non-magical manner. Here the word "self-conscious" is used deliberately, for it is one thing to make a judgment or offer an explanation and quite another to be *aware* that one is judging or explaining. It is the latter which is at the root of philosophizing—that is, philosophizing as a rational, systematic thing. As was noted, primitive man's magical explanation of the world constituted a certain mode of philosophizing, as did the Hebrew explanation. But neither can be considered philosophy in the sense of a rational explanation for the *basis* or *ground* of something. A magical explanation is not capable of rational explanation. The Hebrew cosmology, cosmogeny, and ethical account of the universe is based on revelation, and revealed wisdom must be accepted at face value, for it, too, is inherently mysterious. It is only when one seeks to provide a self-conscious, systematic, logical inquiry into the world that he can talk of the grounds for knowledge,

[7] By "Hellenistic" is meant that later phase of ancient Greek history in which the Greeks attempted to export their culture to other parts of the world.

or the basis of value judgments or statements about reality and existence.

The reason for the foregoing explanation of the origins of philosophy is to indicate that while modern philosophy, as we would define the term today, came into existence with the Greeks, its origins lie much further back—in the realm of primitive magic and religion. Furthermore, as will become apparent, present philosophical speculation which is technical, subtle, and highly complex is by no means without vestiges of its primitive origins.

What Is Education?

If it is difficult to define "philosophy," it is even harder to define "education"—not for the layman, of course, who knows that education obviously means "learning." The trouble with this definition is that it defines one rather high-level abstraction, "education," with another, equally high-level abstraction, "learning." To define education as learning does not tell us much about either term.

For the serious student of education—presumably the teacher—it is necessary to go beyond the layman's superficial view. It is critically important to understand the meaning of the word "education"—or, more accurately, to understand the meanings different people have ascribed to the term. Why this understanding is critical is easily stated: one's conception of what education is has much to do with how he is going to teach.

Although there are many definitions of education, a brief look at four widely used meanings will reveal, first, why education is a subject of controversy today, and second, why teachers need to study philosophy of education.

Consider the classical definition of education. To the Greeks and Romans, education meant the forming of a child into a harmonious, well-balanced adult. Such an adult was ideally a perfect balance of moral, intellectual, and physical components. He would be sober, wise, courageous, temperate, possessed of pleasing manners, conscious of his civic and social obligations, fluent in expressing himself, and physically well developed.[8]

The young Roman or Greek aristocrat was educated carefully from boyhood to manhood to acquire those characteristics which would form him into the ideal. No one aspect of his life was to be overdeveloped or emphasized at the expense of another. The finished

---

[8] You can obtain a good insight into what were considered aristocratic virtues from Marcus Aurelius, *Meditations*.

product of such an education would resemble stereotypes neither of the feeble intellectual of today nor the dense, musclebound athlete. For though his education was largely intellectual, he was expected to study the arts of war, engage in gymnastics, and participate in the complex political and social life of his time. He was trained to appreciate his musical and literary heritage by early and prolonged exposure to instrumental and vocal music and to the writings of Homer, Hesiod, and other literary heroes. While the core of his education was centered around language study—grammar, rhetoric, and literature—it also included music, philosophy, mathematics, and gymnastics. He was to emerge from this education a representative of the classical ideal—*mens sana in corpore sano,* a sound mind in a sound body.[9]

So powerful has this view of education been that after 2,000 years many still consider it a valid, relevant conception. Not only has the curriculum of American education—at least up until rather recently—reflected this classical conception in its emphasis on verbal and literary subjects, but its advocates, who are literate and intelligent, are persuaded that it should still be the model of American education. Whether or not these educational philosophers are beclouded with nostalgia and are hopelessly out of tune with modern times is beside the point. The idea that schools exist to mold a child into a well-developed and harmonious adult is still considered valid.

The classical conception, however, does not constitute the only legitimate educational philosophy in this country or in Europe. Originating with the Hebrews in ancient Palestine is the belief that education exists to form an individual who is to grow into a likeness of God. Here education is conceived as essentially a moral and not exclusively an intellectual enterprise, and its goal is the creation of a "good" human being, one who not only *knows* what is right but *does* what is right.

The ancient Jews were most clear about what was "right." Right behavior and the good life, they held, were neither automatic nor accidental. One did not become good by chance; one *learned* to be good. The Old Testament, called the "Torah" by Jews, was seen as the divinely inspired word of God, and in it was to be found the course of study for children, young men, and even adults. In the Sacred Scripture was found the key to right living—in minute detail, from instructions on ceremony to an interpretation of the very meaning of existence. Without long and arduous study of the holy word,

[9] A good treatment of classical education, although quite detailed, is H. I. Marrou, *A History of Education in Antiquity* (New York: Mentor Books, 1956). See Part II.

one would not know how to live correctly. And living correctly—that is, understanding the difference between good and evil and always preferring good—was absolutely essential for salvation.[10]

The conviction that the purpose of education was to insure proper morality and salvation was transmitted into Western civilization through Christianity. It was reiterated forcefully during the sixteenth-century Protestant Reformation and in the seventeenth century in New England. Both Calvin and Luther stressed the dogma that salvation was available through faith alone. But faith was not automatic; it could be reached only through careful study of the source of faith—the Old and New Testaments.

Hence the Protestant Revolution gave rise to an educational system throughout Europe which was devoted to teaching literacy skills and ancient languages, to the end that the student should be able to read and interpret the Bible and thereby secure his salvation. In colonial America the Puritans continued to stress the relationship between education and the Bible and salvation. It is not an overstatement to say that the sole educational aim of seventeenth-century Calvinists was to educate people for salvation.

Obviously, this conception of education is still held by many today. Parochial education, which includes about 10 percent of the total number of children in schools today, still emphasizes the study of God's word and the formation of good character. The shocked outcry when the United States Supreme Court and several state supreme courts declared an officially composed school prayer and mandatory Bible reading unconstitutional attests to the continuing strength of the belief that education means moral training. Even individuals who may not be especially religious often express their hope that schools will teach the values of tolerance, kindness, charity, honesty, social concern, and other heritages of the distant Hebrew past.

A more recent conception of education is that of the twentieth-century behavioristic psychologists.[11] These psychologists have attempted to put the study of human behavior and education on a rigidly scientific basis. Education and psychology should be patterned after chemistry and biology—that is, the more education becomes like a science, the more reliable the knowledge of the educative process

---

[10] By "salvation" is not meant the Christian concept of an afterlife. The Jews were—and still are—quite vague as to an afterlife.

[11] This school includes the earlier John B. Watson and Edward Lee Thorndike and the contemporary B. F. Skinner. The term "conditioning" is properly attributed to Ivan Pavlov, the Russian psychologist and advocate of the "conditioned reflex."

will be and the more efficient the system will become. Although there are differences among different behaviorists, it is fair to designate their conception of education as "conditioning."

The assumption behind education as conditioning is that human beings are similar to machines. Like machines, human beings are ultimately "explained" by mechanical laws. What teaching should consist of is the presentation of certain "stimuli" designed to evoke desired "responses." The desired response is "rewarded"—B. F. Skinner uses "reinforced"—and correct learning consists of making the appropriate responses. Learning, then, consists of "conditioned" responses.

Although most teachers do not live up to the expectation of either the earlier or the contemporary behaviorists, they are still sufficiently— if unwittingly [12]—imbued with behavioristic psychology to talk about efficient and scientific teaching, responses, rewards, and reinforcements and other terms from the vocabulary of the behaviorists.

Translating this conception of education into classroom practice involves considerable drill and repetition. The teacher may present the stimulus, such as the flash card so popular a few years back; or the set of stimuli may be the programmed questions and answers of a teaching machine. Whatever the nature of the stimuli, this conception of education is a highly mechanical one, ultimately reducible to the formation of desired habits. Education as conditioning is not well understood by the general public, but it is a way of looking at education which has found considerable favor among American teachers in this century.

The three conceptions of education just discussed are open for considerable debate. But one meaning of education that does not usually evoke argument is the social scientist's definition of education as the transmission of the cultural heritage. Anthropologists and sociologists have formulated a definition of education which goes about as follows: All people have a culture, which consists of their learned behavior. This learned behavior includes both the tangible and the intangible: tangible objects, such as tools, clothing, and shelters; and such intangibles as language, beliefs, aspirations, attitudes, and religion.

Education is the passing on of this culture. Therefore, according to this definition, an American child who is learning through television "Westerns" to regard Indians as irrational savages is being "educated"

[12] "Unwittingly" because most psychologists and psychology textbooks no longer distinguish between different schools or families of psychology.

in precisely the same sense as when he learns that two and two equal four. Both the attitude toward American Indians and arithmetic are aspects of our cultural heritage. Whether the transmission is done formally or informally is immaterial.

The significance of this approach is that education is not confined to what takes place in classrooms. Any action designed to insure that a person learns some aspect of his culture is, by this definition, education. We are being educated constantly, for we are, almost without cessation, acquiring attitudes, values, and beliefs from many sources. Whatever serves to transmit the cultural content—whether we are consciously aware of it or not—is education in the anthropological sense of the term.

Analysis

These four definitions of education—and there are many others— illuminate the problems of communicating meaningfully about schools, learning, curriculum, goals, teaching methods, or anything else that can fall under the rubric of education. If we accept the semanticist's conviction that language functions as a kind of road map, a device to paint a picture of reality, then the point of this discussion about different conceptions of education is obvious: in the same way that an unclear and inaccurate road map is likely to get us into trouble on a trip, a set of conflicting and inaccurate directions is likely to cause trouble in the planning of any important enterprise.

Consider the plight of the teacher who accepts parts of two conceptions of education—as conditioning and as the formation of a well-proportioned human being. How, in any consistent and effective manner, is he to go about choosing appropriate curricula or teaching methods? Or consider the school administrator who conceives of education as something reducible to efficient technique: how is he to understand the art teacher who believes that art education is an enterprise characterized by freedom, joy, and spontaneity? Finally, consider American society, which embraces all four conceptions—and many others. What is the quality of communication with regard to educational matters? What kind of planning is possible when there is an enormous gulf between the perceptions of education by laymen, by teachers, by administrators—and of course, by students?

The different conceptions of education reflect, of course, different conceptions of values, knowledge, reality, and other philosophical categories we are now ready to discuss.

What Is Philosophy of Education?

If philosophy consists of an abstract analysis of man's beliefs about himself and the universe in which he lives, and if education is—at least by one definition—the transmission of knowledge, skills, and values of a culture, then seemingly we should be able to define "philosophy of education" by combining both definitions. We can, of course, do just this. But it may be better to approach this problem inductively, by considering what philosophy of education actually does.

First let us examine the antecedents of educational philosophy. In one sense, philosophy of education is an ancient subject. In another sense, it is quite modern. In the sense that there were thinkers in antiquity who theorized about education, it is a venerable subject indeed. Hebrew sages recorded in the Old Testament and in the *Talmud*—the commentaries on the Old Testament—many of their beliefs about teachers, students, learning, discipline, and the goals of education. Plato's *Republic*, ostensibly a treatise on a utopian society and on justice, contains a description of a complete educational system. Philosophers during the intervening 2,000 years have recorded their thoughts on almost every phase of education.

But the first study of educational philosophy that called itself just that was John Dewey's *Democracy and Education*.[13] *Democracy and Education* was a systematic analysis of education from the standpoint of pragmatic philosophy, a school of philosophy that Dewey helped create. Dewey's analysis was challenged by thinkers from other schools. Herman Horne's *The Democratic Philosophy of Education* [14] was only one of many works which attempted to rebut Dewey's position. By 1941 there was enough dialogue between different educational philosophers to warrant the creation of a scholarly society, the Philosophy of Education Society.

Unfortunately, philosophy of education—as is typical of young disciplines—is plagued by symptoms of immaturity. The field itself has not been clearly delimited. There are still persons who have not had adequate training in the subject but who continue to write about and teach educational philosophy at the college level. Philosophers in the older fields, such as logic, metaphysics, and aesthetics, are apt to be distrustful of those who call themselves "philosophers of education." Despite these obvious stumbling blocks, there clearly *is* a field known as philosophy of education.

[13] John Dewey, *Democracy and Education* (New York: Macmillan, 1916).
[14] Herman H. Horne, *The Democratic Philosophy of Education* (New York: Macmillan, 1932).

What is the content of the field? Again, it is not always clear precisely what constitutes the subject matter of educational philosophy. It seems unlikely that all educational philosophers would accept or agree upon any one description of the field, but here is a classification of what appear to be the concerns of those in educational philosophy:

Metaphysics

Metaphysics is the name for the study of the grounds of being, existence, or reality. It asks such questions as: What does it mean to exist? What kinds of reality are there? In what sense can we say that something is or is not? These questions may sound abstract and irrelevant but we should remind ourselves that before one can deal with any aspect of his life, he must first be convinced that it is, in some sense, real. It is the phrase "in some sense" that is the concern of metaphysics. Literature teachers deal with something called "beauty" and physiology teachers talk about the function of endocrine glands. Both are convinced that beauty and endocrine glands exist. It is obvious that endocrine glands are real enough, but what about "beauty"? In what sense does "beauty" exist? Not, apparently, in the same sense as endocrine glands, whose reality can be seen and verified. One who believes that God commanded man to obey certain rules and regulations believes that God exists and is not merely a figment of his imagination. But in what sense does God exist? In the same sense as "beauty," or as endocrine glands? Or perhaps in a completely different sense?

The child who spells "cat" k-a-t really believes that cat is spelled with a "k." Now if this is the child's reality, and if the teacher is interested in promoting correct spelling, it behooves him to know something about the child's perception of reality. Hence an ancient but now somewhat neglected [15] area of philosophy, metaphysics, seems to be appropriate for those who wish to understand what teaching is about.

Knowledge

That education is somehow concerned with knowledge and its transmission is fairly obvious. But there are some unsolved and persistent problems with regard to knowledge. Is all knowledge probable,

[15] There are many philosophical journals in this country, but only one specifically devoted to metaphysics, *The Review of Metaphysics,* and it has been published only since 1947.

or is some knowledge certain? How do we go about obtaining what we call "knowledge" from the world around us? Do we "discover" knowledge or do we "invent" it? Is all knowledge of equal value or is some knowledge worth more than other knowledge, and if so, how can we be sure? Is there one method of knowing or many?

This last problem, in particular, has been a stumbling block for teachers. Consider the statements "I know that two and two are four" and "I know that mosquitoes undergo a four-stage metamorphosis." Both statements use the word "know," but it seems obvious that one knows each in a different way. We know something about mosquitoes by watching them; we can see a mosquito egg change from a larva to a pupa and then to an adult. But has anyone seen a "2"?

Another question, reemphasized with particular clarity by the nineteenth-century English philosopher Herbert Spencer, relates to the worth of knowledge. What knowledge, he asked, is of the most worth? [16] Whereas most people would agree that knowledge of safe-cracking is not generally valuable and knowledge of reading is, agreement seems to end with such obvious contrasts. It is extremely hard to reach consensus on the value of knowledge in this society. For every person who feels that it is "important" to know about mathematics and literature, there are others who feel, just as strongly, that it is worth more to study wood-working. Behind the acrimonious debates in popular journals about curriculum stand certain assumptions about what knowledge is of the most worth.

Another long-standing problem that creates ill will, largely because it is completely unrecognized, is the question "What use can one make of knowledge?" It is held by many that knowledge is worth having for its own sake—that it is, in and of itself, good and needs no justification. But many Americans believe that only knowledge yielding something "useful" or "practical" ought to be taught in schools. Thus bookkeeping is good to know, for one can make a living from it; and home economics is good to know, for one can learn to make omelettes. But we can make no practical use of ancient history or rhyme schemes. Frequently the defenses that teachers make of subject matter go right over the heads of their students. The students often operate on the assumption that "good" knowledge is "practical," while the teachers feel that knowledge is good to have, not for what you can do with it, but for what it can do for you. Perhaps the enormous amount of for-

[16] His answer, destined to have a great effect on the twentieth century, was that scientific knowledge is of the most worth. His essay on the subject may be found in Robert O. Hahn and David B. Bidna, *Secondary Education: Origins and Directions*, A Book of Readings (New York: Macmillan, 1965), pp. 108–117.

getting of subject matter is linked with the fact that often students do not place much value on what they are supposed to.

Values

The last statement leads to the next philosophical consideration: What is of value? Educational philosophy is concerned with what people judge to be good, bad, or in between, and why and how they defend such judgments. Philosophers ask such questions as: What is a value? What are the sources of values? How do the valuing and the knowing processes relate to each other? How does one justify a judgment of value? Such questions are related to education, which, few would deny, is a value-laden process.

Teachers generally believe it possible to teach values to students, by which they seem to mean that we can and should teach students to like what they should like. On the other hand, teachers also feel that indoctrination is an unacceptable teaching technique and must be avoided, particularly in a democracy. Yet "teaching students to like what they should like" is scarcely distinguishable from indoctrination. And it is by no means clear that it is even possible to teach values in a classroom—even though this is one of the most commonly held assumptions about education in our society.

Nor can it be shown in any convincing manner that teachers deal with what philosophers call the *grounds* of a value judgment. They tend to rely, as do most parents, on their more advanced age, on their larger size, or on the authority given them by the state. Thus, should a student inquire, "Why should I like (or do) this?" the answer is often a simple "Because if you don't you will get into trouble," or the even simpler, "Because I say so." That such answers are unconvincing is clear when one considers that, despite the fact that most children are taught to like "good" literature, they read very little of such literature after they get out of school. Or despite the exposure to civics—which seems to amount to getting students to be loyal to the democratic form of government—the number of citizens who participate in government (even to the limited extent of voting) is discouragingly limited.

Another paradox is that the most frequent value problem—learning to choose between two different goods—is totally ignored by schools. The choice between good and evil is, despite strong feelings to the contrary, not really a major problem. The real problem is the choice between what is perceived as two goods or two evils.

The recent scandal at one of the military academies is a case in point. The many dozens of students involved were dismissed, not for cheating, which is almost universally regarded as "bad," but for not reporting their comrades who did cheat. While the honor code at the military academies requires that cadets report evidence of dishonesty, it is also true that most young people believe it is not "good" to tattle or report the misdeeds of their peers. The choice between observing the honor code, which is perceived as "good," and being a "good" guy —not being a "stool pigeon"—is a choice between two goods. This seems to have escaped the academy officials, as it has escaped most.

There are other problems in the area of value theory, but perhaps these examples will indicate why it is "good" to understand and study values.

Human Nature

Without more than half realizing it, most people entertain some conception of what philosophers call "human nature." It has been widely believed that some characteristics are "natural"—that is, inherent, born into all human beings. Aristotle believed that men naturally desire to know. Supporters of capitalism feel that men are naturally self-centered and are concerned first with their own good. Those within certain religious traditions hold that human nature is innately depraved and wicked, a belief reflected in the popular bromide that "People are no damn good."

Each of these assumptions about human nature carries certain implications for education. If people naturally desire to know, then one can infer that education should "cooperate" with this natural tendency. Teaching should simply be directed at fulfilling this natural drive. If, on the other hand, people are motivated toward self-interest and gain, then teaching should strive to cooperate with this innate desire—as teachers do when they make use of spelling bees, letter grades and awards. If people are innately depraved—as the Judeo-Christian tradition has held—then education should be a matter of reforming the naturally "evil" instincts and replacing them with acquired "good" traits.

All these assumptions about human nature may be found within our society, and often within the thinking of the same person. It seems reasonable to conclude that these contradictory assumptions are translated into contradictory teaching methods. Because there is a direct relationship between theories of human nature and teaching, educational philosophers are concerned with attempting to trace this relationship.

Social Theory

Educational philosophers deal with social philosophy because education is a social process. What a given society holds to be true about social relations, government, economic practices and theories, and other social concepts has a decided influence on what takes place in its classrooms. In a democracy, with its emphasis on decision-making, one expects to find schools trying to improve the quality of students' choices. A dictatorship, on the other hand, would attempt to inculcate the habit of unquestioning obedience to higher authority.

In a culture in which technology is highly complex, schools are expected to prepare students to deal with this technology. Thus, there has recently been increasing emphasis on mathematics, science, and subjects dealing with technology. And—although counselors may deny this—one of the purposes of testing programs is to enable students to be guided to "appropriate" occupations. It becomes increasingly risky, in a technologically complex society, to try to fit round pegs into square holes.

Another aspect of social theory involves what is known as the "social" or "cultural lag." Since the technology of a given culture tends to advance much faster than the values, habits, outlooks, and social philosophy of the people in that culture, we find schools transmitting values and knowledge more appropriate to a previous historical period.

Since culture is learned, to a considerable degree, unconsciously, and since the problems and paradoxes of the culture are not apt to be realized, one of the major functions of educational philosophy is to reveal the philosophical implications of our social heritage.

Goals and Aims

A goal is a value, often a supreme value, which directs behavior in certain channels or directions. If one's supreme goal in life is to make money, this means that it has precedence over all other goals—that whatever conflicts with making money will take second place. A goal or aim of education is the value we consider highest, the end toward which we educate. Our culture has many goals. We do not, as we did in seventeenth-century New England, educate toward one end; we tend to educate toward a variety of ends, many of which are or seem inconsistent with one another. It is simultaneously believed that the goal of education is the inculcation of moral goodness, that the goal of education is the creation of good citizens, that the goal of education is the fulfillment of each person's capacities, and recently, that the goal of education is keeping up with or surpassing Russia. The problem is that multiple goals do not direct an activity in one direction.

For some reason, stating the problem this way irks Americans. The idea that one cannot logically hold a wide variety of conflicting, inconsistent, or unharmonious goals strikes Americans as an undemocratic infringement of their freedoms.

If goals direct practice, and different goals direct practice in different directions, it follows that a teacher with multiple goals is apt to be directed in several directions at once. How, it may be asked, is one to operate with the goal that education exists to prepare children for eternal salvation and *also* that the goal of education exists to develop their decision-making capacities?

The bland unawareness of this problem and the persistent refusal to acknowledge it suggests that our culture is uniquely indifferent to philosophical thought, and perhaps also that philosophical analysis is a tool that teachers very much need.

The Modus Operandi of Educational Philosophers

What do educational philosophers do when they "philosophize" about "education"? In the first place, most educational philosophers seem to accept one statement made by the late Alfred North Whitehead, that "in order to understand any one fact, one must understand an infinity of facts." What Whitehead seems to be saying is that there is such a complete interrelationship between all phases of knowledge that understanding any one item of knowledge requires understanding all knowledge. This is obviously a rather tall order. But the spirit of the proposition seems to have permeated educational philosophy, for educational philosophy touches on every other field of knowledge.

One may find educational philosophers dealing with art, literature, and music, areas usually designated as aesthetics. Others prefer to concentrate on exploring the link between educational philosophy and science. Or their primary concentration may lie in the relationship between schools and the social sciences, especially anthropology and sociology. Certain educational philosophers emphasize the relationship between psychology, philosophy, and education. Others prefer to deal with industrial arts, home economics, and what many have chosen to call the "practical arts." One can continue almost indefinitely. The point is that educational philosophers have constituted themselves a sort of intellectual link between education and almost every other human endeavor.

One can now ask, "How does educational philosophy treat these areas?" Briefly, and probably too simply, educational philosophers perform two tasks: analysis of meaning; and suggestions for action. The first task is an explanatory, descriptive one. Here educational philosophers attempt to explain what a given position means—that is, they try to lay bare the logic of a philosophical system. They explore the problems involved in translating certain theoretical concepts into practice, as a number of educational philosophers have done recently with regard to creativity. They attempt to trace the implications of a given value, such as democracy, for classroom practices. They may concentrate on one concept, or their analysis may involve an entire philosophical system.

The other function is less *descriptive* than *prescriptive*. This means that educational philosophy has tried to provide guidance for particular aspects of the educational enterprise. The aim is to indicate what someone takes to be the preferable course of action. It may involve making schools less authoritarian and more democratic, as Dewey suggested in *Democracy and Education.* Or it may involve persuading teachers to try to make students more sensitive to beauty. Or it may be to try to make teachers more intelligent in their understanding and use of psychology.

Of course, the descriptive and prescriptive functions are not usually separated. Most educational philosophers try to join them, first indicating what something means, why it is desirable or inadequate, and then suggesting what might be done in some specific situation.

With this bare description of a field that is so comprehensive that it almost defies description, let us turn our attention to why it is especially relevant for prospective teachers to study educational philosophy.

QUESTIONS FOR DISCUSSION

1. What implications are there in the assertion that philosophy is not entirely free from its early magical origins?

2. Would you agree that all of us operate with some philosophical assumptions? What evidence is there to support this? What evidence is there that many do not acknowledge their philosophical premises?

3. The text gives a brief definition of philosophy. Compare it with other definitions in textbooks on philosophy or philosophy of education. Are there differences in emphasis? Are there qualitative differences?

4. In what sense does one's conception of education influence his daily classroom teaching?

5. Why is the word "mechanistic" or "mechanical" used to describe the theories of Pavlov, Thorndike, Watson, and Skinner? Why do supporters of these psychologists usually deny that they are "mechanists"?

6. If one combined a mechanistic conception of education with a classical one, how would he teach? What might be the results?

7. In what sense may jokes about the foibles of the President or Congress be considered educative?

8. Ask half a dozen teachers about their goals of education. Did they have difficulty answering the question? How many goals did they mention? Would these goals, as stated, actually be capable of guiding education?

SUGGESTED READINGS

CORNFORD, FRANCIS M. *From Religion to Philosophy*. New York: Harper and Row, 1957. A scholarly essay on the transition from religion to philosophy, with particular emphasis on the difference between magico-religious and rational speculation.

ORLICH, DONALD C., AND SHERMIS, S. SAMUEL. *The Pursuit of Excellence: Introductory Readings in Education*. New York: American Book, 1965. See Part II, Educational Goals, for a number of essays on conflicting goals in American education.

ROBINSON, JAMES HARVEY. *The Mind in the Making*. New York: Harper, 1921. This work, a classic in its field, discusses the history of man's attempt to understand his world.

SMITH, T. V. *From Thales to Plato*. Chicago: U. of Chicago Press, 1956. This book of readings contains selections from pre-Socratic philosophers, with appropriate comments.

TITUS, HAROLD H. *Living Issues in Philosophy*. Fourth Edition. New York: American Book, 1965. The first chapter, "Philosophy and the Contemporary Scene," is an excellent summary of definitions of philosophy and its application and relevance.

2

Why Study
Educational
Philosophy?

It is by no means self-evident that educational philosophy ought to be studied. A course in teaching methods, psychology, or curriculum recommends itself immediately by providing information that obviously will be of use in teaching situations. But, given the abstract nature of philosophy, what practical value does it have for teachers?

To be sure, theories of knowledge and metaphysics are interesting in their own right, and many enjoy grappling with abstract issues without consideration for the utility or practicability of a subject. But for Americans who have always been concerned with the down-to-earth, "interesting" subjects *per se* do not usually recommend themselves. For college students majoring in education, a course needs to justify itself by claiming some utility.

Without lamenting this cultural trait—and to many it is extremely lamentable—let us consider the reasons why educational philosophy plays an important role in teacher preparation. Our discussion will be in three parts: an exploration of the meaning of *theory*, with special emphasis on the words *practical* and *practice;* a consideration of the anthropological concept of *culture;* and some attention to the complex relationship among theory, culture, practice, and educational philosophy.

Theory

We shall define *theory* as an abstract body of concepts that serves as a basis for practice. This definition reflects an attitude toward theory not widely subscribed to. The American people have almost always exhibited contempt for or indifference to theory. In casual conversation the expression "ivory tower" is often coupled with "theory," as if theory were simply the idle speculation of a mind out of touch with actual events. For this attitude there are historical reasons with which we cannot deal at length,[1] but we do need to treat some of them briefly.

First, as the American historian Oscar Handlin points out, the colonists found themselves without a dependable body of theory to deal with the wilderness.[2] Many of the theories they did possess, though sanctioned by hundreds of years of experience, simply broke down in the completely novel situations of the New World. Social class theory, which stipulated that gentlemen did not engage in manual labor, needed to be radically altered to meet the demand for work imposed by the raw frontier. Colonists were forced to modify their established theories of warfare, since Indians persistently refused to line up in neat rows, as was dictated by European traditions. Even some theories relating to hunting, fishing, and agriculture had to be ignored. Agricultural methods of Europe did not work very well in New England soil, as the first colonists found to their immense unhappiness. With breathtaking rapidity, frontier conditions forced abandonment of a broad range of theories—social, political, administrative, legal, and religious. Colonists were forced to create, innovate, invent, improvise. From this, we can apparently trace the American tendency to be somewhat suspicious of all theory.

In addition, the practice of theorizing had been carried out traditionally by a class of persons known as intellectuals, who were often linked either with the established Church or with the aristocracy. Theorizing was an activity that belonged to a ruling class. In a country that was soon to pride itself on having no classes, what eventually emerged was rejection by most people of *both* the upper class *and* its activities—music, poetry, belles-lettres, philosophy, and painting. To this day, those who engage in writing, philosophizing, or painting are regarded by many as people with nothing better to do.[3]

Theorizing, therefore, is often looked on as not very useful, as mere speculation, out of touch with what is actually going on. What has counted in this country is practice. Indeed, it has often been assumed that the simple, untutored man is more able to deal with a knotty situation precisely because his mind is uncluttered by theories.

[1] See Richard Hofstadter, *Anti-intellectualism in American Life* (New York: Knopf, 1963).

[2] See Oscar Handlin, "Shaped in the Wilderness," *Atlantic Monthly*, 311 (June, 1963): 94–106.

[3] For some interesting interpretations of the status of intellectuals in this country, see Part VI, "Intellectuals in Various Countries," Section D, in *The Intellectuals, A Controversial Portrait*, edited by George B. de Huszar (Illinois: The Free Press of Glencoe, 1960).

Henry Ford, for instance, referred to history as "bunk" and boasted that he did not read books because he didn't want to clutter up his mind. It is the technological innovators like Henry Ford and Thomas A. Edison who are respected; most adults know that Edison invented the electric light bulb but few can name any of the men whose theories made this invention possible. The American folk hero is still the man who breaks new ground, who creates practical innovations to meet the needs of a new situation.

The result of rejection of theory has yielded practice without theoretical guidance. One decides what has to be done and, without prolonged study, goes ahead and does it. This procedure is of mixed value. On the other hand, it may well be that the great flexibility in American society is the result of not having a heavy load of rigid, sometimes obsolete theories. By not being encumbered with theories which absolutely dictate what must and must not be done, Americans have felt freer to experiment, discard, shift, modify, and innovate on a grand scale. The New Deal is perhaps the best example of our tendency to adopt a free-swinging, unstructured, experimental style— when the situation seems to require it. But the rejection of theory has also resulted in confusion and conflict—as well as enormous difficulty in judging and evaluating results; for it is difficult to judge unless one has a standard, a theory, against which to judge.

In education, for example, the tendency of Americans to reject theory in favor of unguided practice has led us to ignore what has been found out by the experimental sciences. Teachers seemingly are unaffected by the theories propounded in journals and by professorial and scholarly bodies. They generally tend to teach in about the same way they were taught. Most teachers claim to have profited little by classes in educational theory—in curriculum, methods, philosophy, administration, and psychology. One hears teachers say, for example, "I know I shouldn't punish a child this way, but it's the only thing that seems to work." That is, when confronted by a problem that could be helped by the insights of the behavioral sciences, teachers tend only to experiment and innovate, to keep on trying until they find something that "works."

What Is Theory?

If theory is defined as we have defined it above, its relevance to education may be somewhat more apparent.[4] If we define theory as an

[4] An excellent treatment of educational theory and its relation to practice is H. Gordon Hullfish and Philip G. Smith, *Reflective Thinking: The Method of Education* (New York: Dodd, Mead, 1961).

abstract body of concepts which serves, in some sense, to guide practice, then it is relevant to ask: How does theory guide practice—that is, what can theory *do?*

First, theory can describe a given situation. In this sense, theory acts as a map. Maps are valuable to the degree that they indicate clearly and accurately what the terrain is like. By the same token, theory ought to describe what the situation is like—not what it ought to be like, not what one wishes it were like, not as it would be under ideal circumstances, but what one can reasonably expect to find. Much educational theory does not distinguish between the circumstances as they are and as they should be. Texts often deal with discipline, for instance, as if students were all normal, willing, highly motivated, middle-class children. When a novice teacher discovers the many apathetic or maladjusted children in his class, he has reason to depreciate theory designed for a non-existent situation.

Second, theory can indicate what values are involved. Theory often says, "This is desirable" or "This is bad" or "This is less desirable than that." When theory deals with value judgments, it is most useful if there is a justification, a rationale, for the judgment—that is, "This is good *because* . . . ." Without some kind of underlying reason for a particular value, one does not usually know *why* something is desirable or undesirable; and without a sufficient understanding of what is involved, value judgments are likely to be shallow.

Theory may also indicate what one is to do and, conversely, what one is not to do. Theory may say that one *must* do this, one *might* do this, or one *can* do this. Thus theory not only describes the behavior but often indicates the degree of necessity involved. Or theory may describe the goal and the possible means by which it may be reached. For instance, one may say, "In order to reduce anxiety, a therapist may allow the patient to verbalize freely about whatever is on his mind." On a less serious plane: "In order to enjoy as much scenery as possible, it is always best to see this area in the early spring." It may seem strange to see the latter classed as theory, but it is, albeit a fairly low-level theory. Theory may be high-, medium- or low-level.

Theories often contain standards—means by which results may be evaluated. Standards are derived from objectives, statements of a goal to be reached. One may say, for instance, that the goal of a reading class is to teach one to read with a certain degree of speed and understanding. Certain methods are employed and, if they are successful, the person learns to read with the requisite skill. One constantly checks progress against an assumed set of standards for performance. The problem in much of teaching is that we lack means by which to evaluate performance. It is quite possible to evaluate physicians and salesmen against a hypothetical standard, but it is difficult at present to say who is and who is not a good teacher.

Theory also acts to clarify meanings and interpret results. If we apply the theory correctly, we know what a given situation is likely to mean. Quite typically, a physician uses his theory to explain what a particular set of symptoms means. That is, his theory clarifies, helps him interpret a particular set of conditions.

An important factor is that theory be capable of modification. If the actual practice indicates that the theory is not quite as stated, then the theory should be enriched and improved by knowledge of the new practice. That is, theory and practice should be related in such a way that theory directs practice, and awareness of what the practice means can help one improve the theory. It is for this reason that most of us prefer a skilled physician to an interne. Not that the interne is necessarily incompetent or incapable, but that the more experienced physician has a richer fund of theory by which to diagnose cases, note exceptions, spot faint symptoms, or vary possible treatments. By "richer fund of theory" we mean that his practice has enabled him to augment, correct, and modify his theory.

If this description of theory is valid, then several judgments follow. What is called educational theory consists, to a very large extent, of a mixture of high level abstractions not clearly related to existing practice and low level, rule-of-thumb prescriptions. The former is apt to be removed from the real situation; the latter, because it is based on the experiences of one individual, is likely to be as limited as the experience of that individual. What education is apparently in need of is not less theory, as is so often held, but more theory which knows what it is about. The milennium will have arrived when teachers no longer say, "That's good theory but poor practice," for it will be realized that good theory is the most practical thing in the world.[5]

Culture: Definition and Relevance

Among educators it is axiomatic that education always takes place in a particular social matrix.[6] The kind of social matrix in which a group of people live is perhaps the key factor in deciding who is educated, what is learned, who teaches, and what uses are made of the transmitted knowledge. For this reason it is important that prospec-

[5] This analysis owes much to the writings of Boyd Bode, an associate of John Dewey. See Bode's *Conflicting Psychologies of Learning* (Boston: Heath, 1929).
[6] A recent treatment of this is George D. Spindler, *Education and Culture, Anthropological Approaches* (New York: Holt, Rinehart and Winston, 1963).

tive teachers understand some basic assumptions made (by social scientists) about society and culture. It is also important that teachers have a good idea of the most important characteristics of American culture.

First, the word itself. *Culture* is often used to designate something equivalent to the fine arts, to advanced education, or to refined taste. In this sense, one who speaks in a cultivated voice, who "appreciates" good music, who knows something of literary movements, and so on, is "cultured." But this is a common use of the term, not what social scientists mean by it.

For the anthropologist, *culture* refers to all the learned ways of behaving of any given group of human beings. The distinction between *culture* and *society* is that, whereas *society* refers to a group of people, *culture* refers to the ways they behave. It is important to note that culture is learned; as far as we know, it is not inherited.

The study of culture, which has been carried on by anthropologists for nearly a century, has revealed knowledge that is most unsettling to "common-sense" understanding. First, perhaps, is the fact that cultures differ considerably. The ways of one culture may be shockingly different from the ways of another. Having been brought up in one culture—the anthropological term is "enculturated"—people tend to believe that what they see around them is natural and that anything sharply different is alien, strange, queer, perhaps perverted. So thorough is the learning of a given culture that other cultural traits frequently do not make sense.

Second is the fact that cultures are nevertheless to a considerable degree very similar. Apparently there are cultural universals, institutions which are shared by all cultures throughout the world. These universals include clothing, shelter, music, art, tools, literary tradition, language, sexual mores, religion, family, and some form of government. Apparently all cultures possess each of these universals. But the structure and function of these institutions take different forms. Thus while Americans and Tierra del Fuegans (at the tip of South America) both have a governmental structure, that of the United States is a complex, highly developed, intricate affair, and that of the Fuegans is so loose as to be scarcely discernible.[7]

Or, again, while the technology of the United States is extremely sophisticated, that of the Australian Bushman involves only a very few articles—a bowl, a spear, and a spear thrower. The Bushman,

[7] This point is made by Kaj Birket-Smith, *The Paths of Culture,* A General Ethnology (Madison: The U. of Wisconsin Press, 1965). See Government and State in Chapter 6, "Social Organization."

however, has a fantastically complex set of kinship regulations, far more complex than those of the United States.

Cultures possess "patterns," which are organized ways of behaving or particular arrangements.[8] One American cultural pattern is for people to shake hands on being introduced. In parts of Asia the correct pattern is to bow. Eating patterns of this country usually involve "three squares" a day, but people in some other societies eat four times and in others they eat whenever they are hungry. All cultures have numerous cultural patterns, and "to learn" means, in part, to learn the patterns of one's society.

With these basic anthropological concepts, we are able to generalize about our own culture. Cultural patterns within the United States tend to be mixed, indistinct, conflicting, and usually in process of undergoing rapid change. Patterns regarding the consumption of alcohol will serve as example. Alcohol may be regarded as proper for one age group but not another. Alcohol may be regarded as immoral under any circumstance. Heavy drinking may be regarded as proper for males but not for females. Alcohol may be seen as a necessary part of any celebration, or as so insidious that it must be smuggled in in a flask. Attitudes toward alcohol have changed through the years—approving, disapproving, and once more approving.[9]

Some cultural patterns are quite clear and distinct, and we usually have no trouble understanding them and behaving properly. But many important cultural patterns are similar to that of alcohol consumption. In important areas, it may be most unclear what we *should* do, *may* do, *can* do, or *must not* do. Values are blurred, and standards are shifting and confusing.[10]

In a preliterate tribe, by comparison, the cultural patterns have not been disrupted by constantly changing technology, improved communications, and constant contact with others. In a preliterate culture, religious ceremonies and taboos are usually well understood by all members. Religious rites and rituals are a part of the society, and everyone knows when the feast days are and what they symbolize. Everyone knows which gods are to be propitiated, how they are to be propitiated: what chants are to be sung, what dance steps are appropriate, what prayers must be said. In our society not only are there many different religious traditions, but no particular religious

---

[8] *Ibid.*, The Pattern of Culture, in Chapter 3, "Culture and Its Laws."

[9] See J. C. Furnas, *The Life and Times of the Late Demon Rum* (New York: Putnam's, 1965) for an amusing but perceptive history of the use of alcohol.

[10] This point is well developed in Maurice Hunt and Lawrence Metcalf, *Teaching High School Social Studies* (New York: Harper, 1955), in Chapter I, "Alternative Theories of Learning and the Democratic Ideal."

tradition is a necessary part of society. One may elect to belong to the Catholic, Protestant, Jewish, or other faith, each with a particular set of beliefs and practices. Or one may elect, of course, to belong to no organized religion. Within the Protestant or Jewish faiths, one may choose a particular emphasis—Episcopal, Baptist, Nazarene, Methodist, Congregationalist, and many others within Protestantism; in Judaism, there are three subdivisions. While there are similarities among the three major faiths, there are also considerable differences, and while we profess to cherish these differences, there is still considerable abrasion between Protestantism and Catholicism, or between Judaism and Christianity.

Nor is the situation different with regard to cultural patterns relating to government. We have a democracy organized along republican lines. But the meanings of "democracy" and "republic" are by no means clear. In practice, decision-making in a democracy is systematically denied to many qualified members. A republic, which is simply a form of representative government, ought to provide no difficulty in interpretation, especially in a culture which decided 175 years ago on the proper form of representation. However, as these words are written there is an unresolved constitutional question over proportional representation. Nor is there even unanimity as to the precise function of government. While many believe that the best government is that which governs least, the trend in the last half century is clearly toward expansion of governmental functions.

The cultural patterns concerning music are equally unclear. One may choose styles ranging from what is called classical, to folksongs, jazz, "pop" music, or "teenage" music. Even within each of these musical classifications there is enormous diversity: a classical music lover may prefer Baroque music (sixteenth- and seventeenth-century music), nineteenth-century romantic, or twentieth-century modern. A jazz lover may prefer New Orleans dixieland, or he may be a modernist and lean toward Gerry Mulligan or George Shearing. The degree of abrasion among music lovers is almost as extreme as between members of different religions. Typically, Baroque music lovers are contemptuous of, say Tchaikowsky, just as lovers of "pure" jazz often believe that pop music is trash.

What has been said of religion, government, and music applies to other cultural universals. There does not appear to be a cultural pattern that provides an unquestioned standard, understood and desired by all; rather, there is considerable conflict between patterns and within any given set of patterns. "Between" and "within" are important words here; we have been discussing the varieties of choice and conflict *within* a cultural pattern, but there is also conflict *between* cultural patterns.

For instance, a town in which the author used to live experienced a fair amount of conflict and ill will over the issue of Sunday horse-racing and gambling. While Sunday racing was advocated by some members of the community on the grounds that it would pump money into the local economy, it was opposed by others, who asserted that gambling in general is bad and gambling on the Lord's day completely immoral. Those who advocated gambling were premising their arguments on sound capitalistic doctrine. Gambling circulates more money, and this stimulates demand for products and services, creates jobs, and raises the standard of living. Those who opposed Sunday racing were doing so on theological grounds. Gambling was seen as an indefensible waste of money, and using Sunday for this purpose was desecrating an important Christian, American value—honoring the Lord on this one day of the week. It would be pointless to deny the validity of either argument for, viewed from the particular grounds which support them, they were both equally "correct."

One cultural pattern that has been in dispute since the first Quaker was hanged in New England involves that value known as civil rights.[11] For instance, it is a matter of long-standing agreement that any nation has the right to protect itself against internal or external subversion. It is also true that a democratic society extends to its members the widest possible range of freedoms—for example, of speech, religion, thought, publication, association. However, as a culture we have never known what to do with those forms of expression that appear to constitute a threat to the government. Is the Communist Party within its rights in advocating a radical change in our economic system, or do communists constitute a threat to our national security? In another area, are certain movies or books merely disgusting obscenity and pornography, or does an author or film-maker have a right to express what he considers not pornography at all but important artistic themes? To be sure, much depends on what we mean by such words as "subversion," "threat," "freedom," and "pornography," [12] but even if there were common agreement on the meaning

---

[11] See *The Annals of the American Academy of Political and Social Science, Civil Rights in America,* 275 (May, 1951). See especially Edward C. Kirkland, "Do Antisubversive Efforts Threaten Academic Freedom?"

[12] For one author's point of view on pornography and obscenity, see Chapter II, "Pornography Here and Now," in David Loth, *The Erotic in Literature* (New York: Julian Messner, 1961). For a philosophical analysis of obscenity, see Abraham Kaplan, "Obscenity as an Esthetic Category," in Sidney Hook (ed.), *American Philosophers at Work* (New York: Criterion Books, 1956).

of these terms, the problem would still not be solved, for what is involved is cultural conflict—conflict between two or more extremely important cultural values.

Implications for Education

Since our cultural heritage is a mixed one, it is always unclear first, what elements of the cultural heritage should be transmitted, and second, how a teacher may validly transmit them. There is no age, grade, or subject matter that does not reflect the conflict in our cultural patterns.

Who Is To Be Educated? In a preliterate society, all children are educated. In many traditional European societies, it has been customary to afford a literary education to a few members, usually on the basis of membership in a middle or upper class and, perhaps, possession of high verbal intelligence. The masses have received a basic education—that is, an introduction to reading and mathematical subjects, and training in some specifically vocational area.[13] Americans decided in the nineteenth century that such an arrangement was completely unacceptable in a democracy, which stresses equality and assumes that education is absolutely indispensable for success. Although this is part of the democratic creed, it has also been historically true that many Americans have been shortchanged in their educational opportunities or, in the case of Negroes, have been given training rather than education.[14]

Thus while there is one cultural value which stresses equal educational opportunity for all, there is another which has meant in practice shabby schools and inadequate education for certain racial minorities. Too, while teachers may verbalize a belief in the educability of all or most children, they avoid assignment to slum schools, are often unaware of the feelings of minorities, and are frequently hostile to lower-class children.

In brief, it is not yet clear who is to be educated. While the "official" democratic cultural pattern emphasizes equal educational opportunity for all, other patterns militate against such equality.

[13] This description is not entirely accurate in Europe today. European countries are rapidly moving toward universal, comprehensive education, American style, and are also extending opportunities for higher education. See the November, 1961 issue of *Phi Delta Kappan* for an up-to-date treatment of this situation.

[14] See the *History of Education Journal,* 7 (Summer, 1957) for two extensive articles on this topic. See also *Phi Delta Kappan,* 45 (May, 1964).

What Is To Be Taught? Another term for "what is taught in schools" is curriculum.[15] Narrowly defined, curriculum refers to subject matter—arithmetic, spelling, history, shop, home economics, art, and so on. Curriculum may be more broadly defined as "all the experiences for which a school is responsible." No matter how curriculum is defined, nothing seems to be more controversial than the question: What should schools teach? A random sampling of members of any community will reveal several attitudes. Some persons want more emphasis on courses designed for college entrance. They see schools as essentially preparatory institutions, designed to enable children to get ready for the next educational stage.

Some want more emphasis on vocational subjects. These persons argue that we are living in an increasingly complex technological world, and that schools exist to educate people to live in this world.

Some want more emphasis on what psychologists call "interpersonal relations" and what laymen call "getting along with others." They hold that the fourth "R" is "relations," and that schools ought to be responsible for developing sound, healthy personalities.

Others believe that only those subjects which train the mind constitute valid curriculum. These subjects are usually held to be history, languages, science, and mathematics. Concern with either vocationalism or personality development is seen as not the proper function of schools.

These attitudes toward curriculum—and they are only a small fraction of the number and kinds of attitudes that are held—are a good example of cultural conflict. In a preliterate culture there is no doubt about the cultural heritage to be transmitted. In our own culture there is extensive conflict about what portion of our cultural heritage schools should pass on to the young. Another way of saying this is that it is not clear what the school should be doing. As a consequence, schools usually do whatever a large or influential enough group wishes them to do.

Children are affected by the kinds of cultural conflict which result in lack of clarity about curriculum. For instance, one cultural pattern within our society stresses the value of music, art, and literature. This pattern is reflected in the many years children are required to study English and American literature. But another cultural pattern is to look on these subjects as effeminate. Thus, at about the age of ten or eleven, most boys begin to resent poetry. The teacher may

[15] See Chapter V, "Forces Shaping the Curriculum," in Donald C. Orlich and S. Samuel Shermis, *The Pursuit of Excellence: Introductory Readings in Education* (New York: American Book, 1965).

rhapsodize as much as she pleases, but all "normal" boys know that poetry is essentially "sissy stuff," suitable for girls and strange people —indeed, her rhapsodizing may be all the clincher needed! This feeling is intensified as the boy goes on to high school, providing discouragement for literature teachers and, eventually, considerable impoverishment of our culture.

Although history is taught, sporadically, in the elementary and secondary schools and is required in most colleges, there is a cultural pattern which militates against good history teaching. Most foreign observers, from Alexis de Tocqueville in the nineteenth century to Dennis Brogan in our time, have noted that Americans are singularly uninterested in history—their own or others. These observers often note that such antipathy is understandable when one takes into account the fact that most Americans locate their Golden Age not in the past but in the future. Of what good is it, many Americans feel, to be concerned about the doings of dead people when what really counts is what is going to happen tomorrow, next week, and in the next decade? [16]

What is true of literature and history is true in one way or another of all other elements of the curriculum. Mathematics, while seen as essential, is widely disliked by both students and teachers who must instruct in the subject. Biology is regarded as innocuous and is tolerated by many—until it happens to touch on such issues as sexual reproduction or evolution. Art and journalism classes are often seen as dumping grounds for children who cannot succeed in a curriculum designated as academic. Physical education is divided between pointless "group games" and intensive training for athletically talented boys. High-school girls tend to perceive physical education as unfeminine. One can adduce volumes of evidence to indicate that, quite literally, nothing that schools should do is clearly desired by all in the same way.

Method   Usually what is taught has been conceptually separated from how to teach it. "How to teach" is known as method.[17] Arguments over kinds of teaching methods have gone on for years. The sharpest differences in this century have been between Progressives and advocates of a more mechanistic approach. As we saw in chapter 1, a psychology known as Behaviorism assumes that man is a passive

[16] This point is developed in Clyde Kluckhohn, *Mirror for Man* (Greenwich: Fawcett, 1960), p. 182.

[17] Content and method are separated in certain traditional approaches to education. For another point of view, see Hunt and Metcalf, Chapters 9 and 10.

organism, and that teaching consists of the presentation of stimuli to an organism which makes the correct response.[18]

In more recent years, behavioristic psychology has turned to programmed learning, a method which makes use of many simple questions and explanations placed in strategic locations in a programmed machine or textbook. Programmed learning devices, popularly called "teaching machines," are based on the early theories of S. I. Pressey, but now rely on those of B. F. Skinner and Norman Crowder. Although advocates of programmed learning have varied their terminology—they talk about responses being "reinforced" or "confirmed" —they share the view toward man and the learning process of the original behavioristic psychologists: man is basically an extremely well-designed, clever machine, and learning is an additive affair, in which one simply builds correct response on correct response.

Since the introduction of Progressive Education in the late teens and early 1920's, a rather different approach to educational method has found its way into classrooms. The emphasis of Progressivism— an emphasis which, despite much harsh criticism, has apparently been permanent—was on expression: the construction of things, games, field trips, the utilization of play as a teaching technique—in short, what is called loosely an activity curriculum. All these techniques have become part of teaching method, though the extent of their use is extremely variable.

The mechanistic approach to teaching and learning may be traced to a particular cultural pattern in our society, one which stresses order, control, efficiency, and predictability. Progressive teaching methods reflect another cultural pattern, which stresses movement, freedom from restriction, creativity, and respect for individual differences. That these cultural patterns exist as alternatives is not usually recognized. Thus at any time a teacher can unconsciously select the pattern stressing order and control, and lecture on assigned topics, provide workbooks which require simple, short answers, and allow time for recitation—that is, questions and answers. Or the teacher can choose from the other pattern and structure the class rather loosely, with open discussion, field trips, and attention to student feelings and expression. The teaching methods actually employed in the classroom, therefore, depend not on what is consciously chosen as a better teaching method, but rather on the teacher's temperament, the feelings of the administrator, local tradition, and other poorly understood factors.[19]

---

[18] See Chapter 11, "What are the Two Major Families of Contemporary Learning Theory?" in Morris L. Bigge and Maurice P. Hunt, *Psychological Foundations of Education* (New York: Harper, 1962).

[19] Orlich and Shermis, "The Curriculum: Attitudes and Problems," p. 224.

Administration   The traditional conception of administration is changing. Traditional administrative theory has been premised on the assumption that decision-making power flows from top to bottom. In line with this assumption, it has been held that school boards at the state or local level should determine major educational policy. The administrator as an executive interprets this policy, and teachers carry it out. Of late, however, scattered groups of teachers and certain teachers' organizations are insisting that this theory of administration, sanctioned by well over a century and a half of use in our country, is not democratic. Their position is that teachers ought to have a part in making decisions relating to extracurricular load, salary, teaching assignments, and other conditions of work.

The administrative theory based on the assumption that decision-making power necessarily flows from top to bottom is an authoritarian one. It reflects an ancient cultural pattern, illustrated by European institutions such as the Church and the feudal social hierarchy. The second position flows from a democratic assumption that decision-making is best done by those who are directly affected by the decisions.

Both administrative theories are defensible—if one accepts the philosophical premises on which they are based. The philosophical premises are rooted in certain cultural values. Both the cultural values and the philosophical premises are largely unanalyzed. That they are unrecognized is probably a factor contributing to much teacher-administration conflict, dissatisfaction, harrassment, low morale, and high teacher turnover—to say nothing of poor teaching.

Generally, administrators operating under the older, more authoritarian theory tend to hire teachers who are docile, accept dicta from above without question, submit to administrator requests, and cause little trouble. Such characteristics, however, are not those which describe a highly intelligent and creative teacher. In brief, despite the extensive verbalizing about democracy and education, the lack of awareness that there are older, undemocratic cultural values has continued to perpetuate schools that are what John Dewey called them more than half a century ago: citadels of undemocratic values.

Teacher Organizations   In the same sense that there are cultural conflicts inherent in curriculum, methods, and other educational matters, there are philosophical considerations involved in the conflict in theories of teacher organization. At present there are two patterns of teacher organization. One is reflected by the National Education Association (N.E.A.). The N.E.A., which is over a century old, operates on the assumption that the aims and goals of teachers can best be realized by persuasion and continuous education of the public. Essentially a conservative organization, the N.E.A. has been dominated, at least until recently, by rural leadership and values. The N.E.A. has appealed to teachers who wish to affiliate with a professional body and want the respect usually accorded any middle-class profession.

The American Federation of Teachers, (A.F.T.), a newer organization, has consistently refused to emphasize middle-class respectability and has relied on certain proved labor union techniques to realize what they consider the goals and aims of teachers. This has come to mean recognition as an independent representative body, collective bargaining, and the threat of a strike if all other means fail.

The N.E.A. and its many state and local affiliates reflect several important cultural patterns and values. Traditionally this country has been middle-class oriented, and the professions have occupied a position of very high status. The A.F.T. also reflects certain important cultural patterns. Our country is characterized by an extraordinarily large number of pressure groups—churches, unions, agricultural organizations, scholarly bodies, professional groups, industrial associations, and so on. Such groups try to get what they want by the application of various kinds of pressure: propaganda, direct or indirect influence on legislators, threats to withhold or actually withholding service. The last technique, the strike, has been extremely effective in securing very important gains for labor unions. The A.F.T., very much aware of the uses of economic and political pressure, operates out of the cultural pattern which states that if one wishes something, he does not politely request it; he demands it and backs the demand with a threat.[20]

This conflict between the cultural pattern which stresses respect due to a profession and the pattern which indicates that improved working conditions and higher salary are obtainable only through pressure and threats has not yet been resolved. Both cultural patterns assume a number of values—and neither the values nor the cultural patterns are the objects of widespread discussion or awareness.

The Current Status of Educational Theory

The conflicting cultural patterns described above have rendered educational theory—primarily that aspect of theory which suggests courses of action—considerably less useful than it could be.

Much, or most, educational theory does not accurately describe situations in which teachers work. Instead of indicating what to do or

[20] *Ibid.,* Chapter VI, "The Profession of Education." See also Myron Lieberman, *The Future of Public Education* (Chicago: U. of Chicago Press, 1960).

what to avoid, much educational theory permits teachers to do anything. In place of a coherent theory of values, much educational theory says that everything is valuable: that order is good and that freedom is good, that spontaneity is desirable and that structured learning is essential, that democracy is valuable and that authority must be obeyed regardless of personal feelings, that a body of subject matter must be mastered by all and that the curriculum must be tailored to meet individual differences and needs, that schools should be controlled locally and that control must be shared by the state and the nation.

Nor does educational theory provide a clearly understandable means of evaluating results. Evaluation is essentially a matter of placing a value on something, and disagreements about what is valuable characterize educational theory. Because there is little agreement about what is good, many educational researchers have avoided evaluation and have contented themselves with gathering large quantities of factual data. Unfortunately, without criteria of goodness, all the factual information in the world does not add up to anything.

In this century, strangely enough, educational theory has not been vastly improved by observation of practice. First, there is no particular agreement about what constitutes desirable practice.[21] Second, much of the scholarly evidence from the fields of psychology and sociology has not been assimilated by educational practitioners, as a consequence of which the valid findings that do exist are simply not utilized in the classroom. The end result is that educational theory in curriculum, administration, finance, psychology, methodology, and other fields has little relationship to what teachers do. Much educational theory tends to be either technical analyses of concepts which most teachers are not prepared to understand, or "glittering generalities" which provide little guidance.

It should be emphasized once more that the conflict in educational theory reflects the conflict within our culture. Without some kind of stable core of values on which to base a recommendation for practice, everything is simultaneously allowed and rejected. While one may argue that there does indeed exist such a stable core of values in our culture, it is difficult to translate these core values into practice. One may enumerate such core values as respect for the rights of others, belief in the essential dignity of all human beings, shared effort toward a common goal, or tolerance for other points of view. Such

[21] For a complete discussion of the history of American educational theory and practice, see Charles Brauner, *American Educational Theory* (Englewood Cliffs: Prentice-Hall, 1964).

values, while they would probably elicit approval by most, are cultural ideals which are not clearly understood by all, and which, in fact, may be absent much of the time. Further, each of these values may at times be in conflict with other values. For instance, people who are working toward a common goal with dedication and enthusiasm often exhibit vast intolerance of those who do not accept that goal. Finally, while we may agree at a verbal level that all human beings possess innate dignity, it is quite another matter to translate this verbal agreement into operational agreement. The point is that, given the absence of clearly understood cultural values, education—which is inseparable from the social matrix—is left without effective guidance.

If the above analysis is valid, teachers in our culture have a more difficult task in ascertaining their precise role than teachers in other cultures. It is at this point that educational philosophy may be of considerable assistance. Educational philosophy may provide a person with the conceptual apparatus to evaluate and analyze the beliefs and practices in education to the end that he can enhance his ability to decide what should be done and how best to do it.[22]

Educational Philosophy as Theory

But what are these "intellectual" tools and to what use can one put them? The simplest and most direct way of answering this question is to see what it is that educational philosophers do. By analyzing the methods used by philosophers, we can see that educational philosophy can function as theory. That is, in the same sense that theory acts to guide practice, educational philosophy as theory can function to provide guidance for educational practice.

Here are a number of categories which may describe the procedures of philosophers of education. Please remember that other categories are entirely possible. These categories are separated from each other in order to provide an analysis; in actual philosophical thought they are not separate and discrete.

Interpretative   All philosophers attempt to interpret an infinite amount of phenomena. They classify, describe, and evaluate behavior, ideas, objects, or anything else they feel important. Plato attempted to provide an interpretation of what he considered the good life and the ultimate aim of the state. Kant interpreted the nature and limits of

[22] See Ernest E. Bayles, "Present Status of Educational Theory in the United States," *School and Society*, 87 (January 17, 1959): 5–7.

experience. Aristotle and Bacon interpreted the process by which we gain valid knowledge.

These philosophers provided interpretations by creating *categories of meaning*. They described related ideas, noting similarities and differences. For instance, Aristotle categorized two kinds of knowledge, the practical and the theoretical. Plato categorized three different levels of ability among human beings. John Dewey devised five categories to describe the scientific process. Without some kind of categorization it is impossible to "make sense" out of the bewildering mass of data which confronts us.

All of us function very much like philosophers: we try to group related things in what we take to be a reasonable and consistent manner. While we may not always be aware of it, we classify constantly: effective and ineffective teachers; cheap, reasonable and expensive goods; A, B, C, D, and F classwork; folksongs, pop music, jazz, and "longhair" or classical music. Since most of us tend to classify unconsciously, our categories and descriptions often lack the consistency and clarity we really wish. Educational philosophy can help teachers understand what a "category" is and how it functions. We can ask such questions as: Is "culturally deprived" an accurate category? What makes an "effective" teacher? Are there really objective criteria for determining grades? Do we mean "punishment" when we say "discipline"?

By becoming aware of the descriptive and categorizing functions of thought and by asking relevant questions, we can accomplish two goals: dissolve categories which confuse more than they classify; and improve the accuracy and effectiveness of those categories we do use. If philosophy did nothing more than this, it would be of practical value to education.

Clarification Clarification—the process of making things clear—is, of course, inseparable from interpretation. The difference is in emphasis. In clarifying, we strive to strip away irrelevancies, obscurities, linguistic confusion, and preconceived or erroneous notions. For instance, we have all heard teachers refer to the "fact" that two plus two equals four. This constitutes extraordinary confusion, for it is not a fact that two and two are four. This is a concept, a mathematical construct, and to treat it as if it were an empirical event is to miss the whole point of mathematics. To require people to clarify their thinking process with regard to this point is to get them to see the difference between a mathematical construct and an empirical event.

This means dissolving a widespread but erroneous notion about mathematics and replacing it with a more correct category of meaning.

One educational philosopher has devoted much of his time to clarifying the meaning of professionalism as it relates to teacher activities.[23] The term *professionalism* has been bandied about so often that it has all but lost its original meaning. Since many teachers can't distinguish between a professional and a nonprofessional activity, they do not know how to gain their heart's desire: the benefits of a real profession. Lieberman points out that most teachers consider withholding of service unprofessional. But, he asserts, under certain circumstances all professionals may withhold their services. By clarifying the meaning of *profession* and *professional,* teachers may be able to strip away the irrelevancies of rhetoric and emotion-laden verbalisms to see just how a profession operates.

Evaluative Related to both clarification and interpretation is an evaluative function. Evaluation attempts to determine the worth of anything. It is in essence a measure of the degree of goodness or badness. Once again it must be pointed out that all of us evaluate. We cannot humanly refrain from saying: "This is unacceptable behavior. You did a good job. Your stitching is sloppy. The oral report was too brief. Your committee functioned well. Your work is neat. You forgot to mention something important." However, most evaluations are made unconsciously, as it were, and because of this they are frequently inconsistent, arbitrary, inappropriate, or not substantiated. Conscious concern with the problems of evaluation may help us do a better job in making those judgments which we must make.

Educational philosophy, therefore, attempts to acquaint us with the components of an evaluation by raising such questions as: How do I know that something is good, true, bad, false? What should I do when evaluations differ? How does a description relate to an evaluation? What kinds of evaluations help students and what kinds hurt, and how can I tell the difference? In raising these questions about evaluation, educational philosophy attempts to make us more sensitive both to ourselves and to what we evaluate.

Prescriptive Frequently philosophers move away from analysis to say, "This is what you must do," or "This is what you must not do." This is a prescriptive function and involves indication of the most desirable line of activity. Prescription follows from evaluation, for it

[23] Lieberman, *The Future of Public Education.* See also Lieberman's *Education as a Profession* (Englewood Cliffs: Prentice-Hall, 1956).

says, "This is good and therefore you ought to do this." As with other philosophical functions, all of us engage in prescription: we make requests, give orders, submit demands, issue instructions, and at times employ force. Philosophy, as it applies to education, attempts to deal with prescriptions at a more sophisticated level than most of us reach in our everyday activities.

First, philosophy attempts to make our prescriptions dependent on a more adequate basis of evaluation. It attempts to point out *why* something is desirable or undesirable, how it got that way, or in what the value consists. Second, it attempts to relate the "you should" statement to the evaluation. As a classical example of this process we can cite Aristotle's *Politics*. First Aristotle describes the number and kinds of governments. Then he evaluates each by pointing out what he considers the ideal form of each type of government and what he considers the corrupt form of each. Then follows a series of prescriptions about how men should govern themselves.

What educational philosophy wishes to achieve is a more adequate relationship of the descriptions of our experience to the evaluations we make, and of the evaluations to the prescriptions we make. In place of saying, "Do this because I say so," or, "Don't do this because it is just not done," the goal is awareness of exactly what makes this piece of conduct desirable or undesirable. The goal of philosophy is to move from blind, unconsidered behavior to behavior that is more thoughtful. In place of unexamined motivation, educational philosophy attempts to have us relate our world of meaning to effective action.

Systematizing Although philosophical system-building is not as important now as it has been in the past, one can argue that a more systematic treatment of philosophical issues is still important. As we have seen, our culture tends to produce an eclectic approach toward almost every activity—that is, we tend to dispose of theory and approach each task without concern for keeping our practice consistent and harmonious. In view of the fact that our culture is a combination of greatly dissimilar cultural patterns, this is scarcely surprising. The result of the combining of values from dissimilar cultural patterns is an educational system in which democratic beliefs alternate with authoritarian ones, mechanistic psychology is mixed with religious idealism, respect for certain subjects is combined with indifference and even contempt for the same subjects, concern for individual differences exists side by side with repressive conformity, and emphasis is placed on both creativity and drill, on freedom and obedience to external authority—in short, everything is both allowed and rejected.

To prevent educational practices which tend toward inconsistency —and frequently poor learning—philosophy may be utilized in a number of ways. One can first become aware of the existence of competing philosophical systems. One can see that different philosophical systems yield different kinds of educational practice. Second, one may learn to think philosophically—that is, learn to appraise educational practices in the light of the philosophical categories just discussed.

Third—and perhaps most important—one can become conscious of those philosophical issues which have generated thought for thousands of years. Such problems as the relationship between freedom and order and between relative and absolute knowledge, or problems concerned with the meaning of the good life, or with the nature of human nature are as relevant today as they were when they originated in Milesia over two and a half thousand years ago. That these problems are relevant and important is evidenced by the fact that they are still at the core of most—if not all—controversies which men engage in today.

One may make two different uses of a philosophical system. One may build a system that will provide "final" answers for all situations. But in a culture as many-faceted as ours, such a purpose is likely to be self-defeating. More valuable, a coherent philosophical system may be used to provide a relatively dependable framework within which one can ask relevant questions, evaluate behavior, determine goals, establish priorities in value, select appropriate techniques—in short, create a basis for consistent, effective teaching.

Despite the lack of stable cultural guides, it is still possible— difficult as it may be—to provide such a basis for effective teaching. But before one can build an educational theory that generates good practice, the insights of philosophy are needed. Philosophy is, as Dewey said, the general theory of education.

QUESTIONS FOR DISCUSSION

1. Summarize briefly the reasons given in the text for studying educational philosophy.

2. How does "theory" as used in this chapter differ from scientific theory?

3. Offer a hypothesis to explain the apparent fact that schools persistently refuse to study or examine those cultural patterns about which there is most conflict.

4. Make an informal survey asking the following persons why English

should be studied: an English teacher; a high school principal; a business-man; a person in his thirties; a person in his sixties; a high school student; a college freshman. How much agreement is there in the answers?

5. Ask a professor of psychology who expresses some commitment to S-R learning theory whether his theory assumes a "mechanistic" theory of human nature. In all liklihood, he will say it does not. Why?

6. Look through any standard textbook in educational methods to see whether there are prescriptions—that is, orders, requests, "Do-it-this-way" statements. See if you can discover the rationale for these prescriptions. If there is no rationale, why not? If there is a rationale, what kind is it? That is, is it implicit, explicit, clear, or ambiguous?

7. Make a list of a number of value categories used by your peers. How many of these categories actually communicate, and how many of them are vague and emotive, like "cruddy" and "swell"?

SUGGESTED READINGS

BAYLES, ERNEST E. *Democratic Educational Theory*. New York: Harper and Row, 1960. Bayles' essays on democracy, philosophy, and theory are ex-cellent summations of the relativistic point of view.

BODE, BOYD H. *How We Learn*. New York: Heath, 1940. A brief discussion of different theories of mind. The author analyzes a number of theories and rejects them. His own candidate is a functional theory of mind, which he presents in the last few chapters.

DEWEY, JOHN. *Democracy and Education*. New York: Macmillan, 1916. This work, a classic in education, is Dewey's explanation of the relationship between democracy, education, philosophy, and culture. Although it is not easy going, it will repay your efforts.

HOFSTADTER, RICHARD. *Anti-intellectualism in American Life*. New York: Knopf, 1963. A Pulitzer prize winning essay on five sources of anti-intel-lectualism in our culture.

JOAD, C.E.M. *Philosophy*. New York: Fawcett World Library, 1962. Specif-ically designed for laymen, this is a most readable introduction to philosophy. See Chapters I and II, "On Reading Philosophy" and "Subject Matter and Scope."

KNELLER, GEORGE. *Foundations of Education*. New York: John Wiley, 1963. See Part I, "Theoretical Foundations," which is a good introduction to educational philosophy and theory.

3

Metaphysics: The Basis of Theory and Practice

The Problem

Whether something is "real," whether it exists and in what sense it exists, scarcely constitutes a problem for most people most of the time. However, when something is either unclear or in dispute, then the reality of a given thing or event is, indeed, the central issue.

Consider the conflicting versions of different witnesses in a law trial. Did X "really" signal a right turn? Was Y "really" going too fast? Does Z's behavior "really" constitute negligence? Or consider the judgments men make about religion and art. Does God "really" exist, and if so what is He like? Are Picasso's paintings "really" art? Behind all disputes about what should or should not be done are certain assumptions about what *is*. Given the character of American education, which has been a focal point of controversy, it is important for teachers to understand what kinds of metaphysical assumptions lie behind the curriculum, teaching methods, administration, and educational goals.

History of an Unpopular Subject

For many persons "metaphysics" is the epitome of useless subjects. It is often equated with mystical nonsense, a vestigial remnant of the Middle Ages. To many, metaphysics is a sort of mumbo-jumbo debate about how many angels can dance on the head of a pin.[1] It is believed that metaphysics has no relevance to anything important and that it simply reflects the regrettable tendency of academicians and intellectuals to confine themselves to ivory towers and inconsequential, hairsplitting arguments.

To others, however, the term has rich and manifold meanings. Those who are training for the ministry often spend years studying metaphysics, for they realize that a defensible religious position rests upon certain statements about the nature of reality. Those who explore scientific theory are also directly concerned with metaphysics, for—despite objections to the contrary—the entire scientific method rests on certain assumptions about what is or is not real. And the serious student of educational philosophy realizes that different claims about the superiority of teaching methods or administrative techniques are based on assumptions, usually not explicitly stated, about the nature of existence.

There are probably a number of reasons for the present indifference to metaphysics as a legitimate study. In the first place, it is an extremely difficult and abstract subject, requiring years of concentrated study. Second, there is a heritage stemming from the Protestant Reformation which may play a part in the widespread rejection of metaphysics. When the early Protestant leaders repudiated many of the practices of the Catholic church, they also repudiated the metaphysics of Aristotle and St. Thomas, which were at the heart of Catholic theology.

A third reason may have to do with the rise of the experimental sciences in the last two centuries. The position was developed, in both the "hard" sciences and the behavioral sciences, that science can dispense with any sort of speculative or metaphysical basis. Scientists, it has been held, simply record their observations of physical events. The process of data-gathering, inference, and construction of scientific "laws" has nothing to do with metaphysical assumptions. The story is told that when someone asked Conrad Roentgen what he thought when he saw the first X-ray picture of a key, he replied, "I thought nothing. I investigated." Newton said, *"Hypotheses non fingo"*—"I do not construct hypotheses." [2] What these two statements apparently meant is

[1] The angels-and-pins-illustration has been used so often, it is a cliché. Actually, this question was not at all as popular in the medieval world as is assumed. However, the question is by no means trivial: it would have been most important for medieval theologians to understand the nature of a supernatural being.

[2] Isaac Newton, *Mathematical Principles of Natural Philosophy*, Book III, "General Scholium." Furthermore, he states, ". . . hypotheses, whether metaphysical or physical, whether of occult qualities or mechanical, have no place in experimental philosophy."

that a scientist does not speculate about the philosophical basis of his theories or investigations: he simply records, measures, and analyzes what is "out there."

This anti-metaphysical attitude has also been characteristic of some of the social sciences, especially psychology. In the late nineteenth century, when psychologists were struggling to break away from their historical ties with philosophy, they tried to model themselves on the sciences of chemistry, physiology, biology, and physics. The feeling grew that a good psychologist neither speculated about his findings nor relied on unseen "mental" processes. All the psychologist could and should do was record observable behavior. From observable behavior one could then state conclusions that were simply accurate summaries of what was empirically verifiable. The American behaviorist John B. Watson said:

Psychology as the behaviorist views it is a purely objective experimental branch of natural science. Its theoretical goal is the prediction and control of behavior. . . . The time seems to have come when psychology must discard all reference to consciousness; when it need no longer delude itself into thinking that it is making mental states the object of observation.[3]

The repudiation of metaphysics by psychologists is reflected in one of the most common definitions of learning as a "change in behavior." Since the only thing deemed valid was observable behavior, "learning" was simply a form of "behavior." [4]

In recent years, however, one can discern a trend on the part of some physical, natural, and behavioral scientists to pay some attention to their own philosophical assumptions. Since the rise of relativistic physics and gestalt psychology in the twentieth century, a number of scientists have become aware of the particular metaphysical assumptions which underlie their constructs. However, in general, it would seem that most scholars and teachers in the sciences—and in education—are still indifferent to metaphysics.

Metaphysical Positions and Their Implications for Education: the Pre-Socratics

As indicated in our first chapter, the Milesian school of philosophers in the seventh century B.C. were the first known philosophers to

---

[3] "Psychology as the Behaviorist Views It," in Thorne Shipley (ed.), *Classics in Psychology* (New York: Philosophical Library, 1961), pp. 798–804.

[4] Most persons are hard pressed to see how some kinds of learning which are not observable can be classified as "observable behavior."

record their theories about the origin and nature of the universe. Some of them attempted to discover an ontological principle that would explain the structure of observable reality. Thus *ontology,* the philosophical term for the study of reality, was both philosophical speculation and early science.

These early philosophers created theories which are, in philosophical terminology, *monistic, dualistic,* or *pluralistic.* Monism is a belief that the ultimate, unchanging reality is reducible to one kind of reality. For example, Anaximenes regarded air as the first principle of reality, while Thales believed the ultimate reality to be water.

Xenophanes was a dualist—that is, he thought there were *two* essential principles of reality. "We are all sprung from earth and water." [5] Later the philosopher Empedocles expanded the number of elements to four; he is therefore classified as a pluralist. "Here first the four roots of all things: bright Zeus, lifegiving Hera and Aidoneus, and Nestis who moistens the springs of men with her tears." [6] These gods were the equivalents of fire, air, earth and water—the four elements that were to survive as scientific explanation until the late medieval period.

These ancient speculations are of significance, not because their positions are still considered valid, but because they cast the metaphysical problem into the mold which was to predominate for many centuries. The early philosophers' concern with the ultimate nature of reality, with opposites such as love and hate, and with the contrast between the world of change and the unchanging reality became the frame of reference for later Greek philosophers—in particular, Plato and Aristotle. Indeed, the assumptions of these ancient Greek philosophers were so thoroughly assimilated by Western civilization *that it is still almost literally impossible to think of reality in terms other than those given 2500 years ago.*

Briefly summarized, here are the assumptions about reality that can be derived from the pre-Socratics:

1. That reality—either as a principle or as a thing—is something which lies *beyond* the observable world. The feeling developed that beyond the changing and confusing world of perception must lie some *ultimate* reality. Eventually philosophers accepted the idea that this ultimate reality was more satisfying. Thus both some Pagan and certain Christian philosophers developed the position, which was transmitted into practice, that we ought to concentrate on the other world and disregard this one.

[5] T. V. Smith, *From Thales to Plato* (Chicago: U. of Chicago Press, 1956), p. 14.
[6] *Ibid.,* p. 28.

2. That reality can be known *in and of itself*. A rather longstanding philosophical issue is whether we can know things in and of themselves or only through our perception of them. If we can know things precisely as they are, the logical philosophical outcome is *absolutism*. Absolutes are characterized by permanence, perfection, and immutability. They exist without respect to any given individual's perceptions, awareness, feelings, or beliefs. Much—if not most—philosophical thinking has been characterized by reliance on absolutes. In education the practice has been to expose children to a world of knowledge which is assumed to be independent. This has come to mean that the job of teachers is simply to transmit the absolute content of reality and the job of students to apprehend it, preferably uncritically. In the training of teachers, many absolutes are often part of educational theory. Thus, "*Never* lose your temper in class."

3. That reality can be known by the unaided process of the mind. This is a description of what is known as *rationalism*. Rationalism, which has many variations, is characterized by the belief that true reality is not particularly dependent upon the world of perceived objects; that one can reason one's way to the ultimate truth. Thus Zeno, Empedocles, Anixamander, and later Socrates reasoned their way to the ultimate principle of reality. Their approach did not involve controlled inquiry—that is, hypothetical constructs, systematic data gathering, the use of experimental designs, quantification, and constant checking and re-checking. Rather, they logically inferred that which must necessarily be true.

To reason one's way to ultimate truth is another way of saying that the unaided mind has the power to know, with a high degree of certainty, what the senses cannot tell us. To know that if B is greater than A and C is greater than B, C must be greater than A is an example of such truth. Such knowledge, utterly independent of empirical evidence or example, can be applied to other kinds of reality. For instance, one can reason one's way to general laws of nature or even to important value judgments. The belief that *only* certain subjects can strengthen the mind is an example of reasoning one's way to truth. No empirical evidence exists to demonstrate that history, literature, or mathematics—usually the subjects designated as mind-strengthening—actually train the mind, but such a belief is widely held today, especially by many educational critics who wish to see high schools retain these subjects and eliminate all others.

4. That reality can be thought of as *dualistic*. A dualism is a statement in which reality is described in two opposite, irreconcilable terms. We employ "good" and "evil," "sacred" and "profane" as if the

members of each pair had completely opposite meanings. It is actually rather difficult to talk about many things in other than dualisms. One usually brackets "classical" *or* "popular" music, "democracy" *or* "social-ism," the "mental" *or* the "physical," and "thought" *or* "emotion" as if they were always antagonistic, mutually exclusive entities. In educa-tion, dualisms abound. It is popular to talk about teaching as *either* "subject matter" *or* "method"—that is, "what to teach" or "how to teach."

All the preceding ancient metaphysics was inherited by two Athenian philosophers of the fourth and third centuries B.C. Plato and Aristotle are regarded as highly original thinkers who created the matrix of Western thought for two thousand years. In a sense, this is true. But in another sense, they reworked materials already at hand. The tendency to think in dualisms, the belief that reality can be known in and of itself, the feeling that a higher reality lies beyond what can be sensed—all found their way into Platonic and Aristotelian thought.

No understanding of the intellectual life of two thousand years of history is possible without some comprehension of the thinking of these two giants of Greek philosophy. So extensive was the range of their thought that it anticipated almost all subsequent philosophy. Their theories about ethics, logic, aesthetics, political theory, education, and science formed the basis of subsequent philosophizing—even philosophizing which appears to be quite different from theirs. One commentator has even suggested that all philosophical thinking of the last two thousand years has been footnotes to Plato and Aristotle. To this day, philosophers who attempt to philosophize systematically usually must account for Plato and Aristotle, either by refuting them or agreeing with them.

We shall consider Socrates and Plato as a unity for the simple reason that we have no actual recorded writings of Socrates.[7] Plato expounded Socrates' thinking in a series of dialogues which are studied as both literature and philosophy. Aristotle, a student of Plato, did not make use of the dialogue form, but recorded his thinking in a series of essays and lectures that are as difficult to read as Plato's dialogues are pleasant.

Plato

Plato developed Socrates' metaphysical speculations in dialogues usually called by the name of one of the major characters, such as the

[7] Although some historians of philosophy do attempt to distinguish between the thinking of Plato and Socrates, their task is apparently extremely difficult. One historian of philosophy has commented that we might as well talk about "Plocrates."

Phaedrus, Theatetus, Phaedo, Timaeus, and *Philebus.* In the *Republic,* which is ostensibly a discourse on justice, Plato develops much of his theory of forms.

In the *Republic* there is an allegorical story which provides a part of Plato's ontology. Imagine, says Socrates, prisoners chained in a cave in such a way that they are facing the back of the cave. Behind them is a fire which casts shadows on the wall. The prisoners can see nothing but these dim shadows on the wall; they are unable to see the outside world in its bright, vivid clarity. Should they be released from their imprisonment and taken outside, they would not be able to comprehend such a world, so habituated would they be to their shadows. In some such way is reality related to us, not *as* reality, but as shadows on a wall.

What we take to be reality, the world of sensory impressions, is a deceptive kind of reality. The things we see, the objects of sense impressionism, are images projected from another source. The world as we perceive it, the sensible world that we can see, hear, feel, and touch, does not constitute the ultimate reality. It is a world of change and imperfection which we mistakenly believe to be reality for, like the prisoners in the cave, we are deceived by the *appearance* of reality.

But what *is* the world of ultimate reality? Ultimate reality is the realm of pure form, of absolute truth, justice, and beauty. In this world, says Plato, "... abides the very being with which true knowledge is concerned: the colorless, formless, intangible essence, visible only to mind, the pilot of the soul." Such true knowledge is not like that which "... men call existence." It is "... knowledge absolute in existence absolute." Plato paints a word picture of a realm of absolute existence in which are to be found forms or ideas, distilled, intangible representations of absolute truth. In such a realm lie absolute justice, absolute wisdom, absolute temperance. The world we see round us is a rather dim projection of this world of absolutes.

Such a realm of absolute truth is available only to the soul, the incorporeal, indestructible, immortal, self-moving spark which inhabits the bodies of men and which is the only source of truth and wisdom. As the soul leaves the body on death, it is allowed to return to this other world, where it briefly glimpses more or less of this "knowledge absolute." Some souls are fortunate enough to see much of the absolutes, and these souls inhabit the body of a "... philosopher, an artist or some musical and loving nature." [8]

In this manner, then, human beings are born into the world with a dim remembrance of the absolute knowledge they perceived in the

[8] The quotations are from the *Phaedrus.*

other, ultimately real world. By means of proper teaching, which is essentially skillful questioning, the dimly remembered knowledge is recollected. In Thut's words,

[K]nowledge of the good is acquired by bringing to consciousness the impressions received by the soul before it was introduced to this life. Developing the ability to bring to consciousness the knowledge hidden within the soul is what Plato assumed to be the main role of education.[9]

True knowledge, then, is not of sensory objects. It is rather of the nature of a conception, which is not primarily sensory but intellectual. In other words, true knowledge is not *per*ceivable; it is *con*ceivable. Bear in mind that one does not invent the conception, the idea. "[I]t is already there, it requires only to be delivered from the envelopes of individual experiences and opinions in which it lies hidden." [10]

Plato's ontological theory presupposes two realms of existence, two kinds of reality. The first is what we observe in everyday life. It is the world of perceptions, and, as is evident from the differences of opinion about this world, it is rather dim and illusory. It is in the realm of ideas—Plato uses "form" and "idea" as synonyms—that we can arrive at true, ultimate reality. But ultimate reality is of the nature of a pure idea. Since it is an idea, we apprehend it, not by careful attention to the world of sensory objects, but by an act of the intellect.

One obvious problem—as Aristotle was rather fond of pointing out—is that this ontological description is not clear about how the sensible world relates to the intelligible world, the world of forms. In some way, the sensory objects *participate* or *partake* of the idea of that object. There is, for example, an idea of beauty; *this particular beautiful statue* participates in that idea. Similarly, a given act which we call "just" is just only because, in some way, it partakes of the *idea* of justice. Perhaps it may help to see how Plato probably arrived at this formulation.

Assume that we are all young again and without an idea of what dogs are like. What we wish to do is build a conception of "dog." We must observe many dogs, compare our observations, and reflect upon what dogs have in common. No matter how our dogs differ, they possess certain traits in common. They are all mammals. They are all four legged. No matter how their hair differs, they all have hair. By

---

[9] I. N. Thut, *The Story of Education* (New York: McGraw-Hill, 1957), p. 61. See the chapter entitled "Learning to Recall Knowledge."

[10] Wilhelm Windelband, *A History of Philosophy* (New York: Harper and Row, 1958), Vol. I, p. 97.

sifting out those traits which are common to all dogs, we can arrive at a conception of "dog." We can see what it means to be a dog. In Plato's manner of speaking, we have arrived at the essence of dog.

What we now have is an idea of "dog." When we see an individual representative of this class, we designate it "a dog." At precisely this point, we can see what probably occurred in the thinking of Plato. Most of us would say that the class name "dog" is simply a general term describing spaniels, cockers, dachshunds, terriers, collies, and so on, and that, of course, there is no idea of "dog" apart from individual dogs. But, says Plato, not only is there a reality called "dog" apart from any and all individual dogs, but this reality is far more real than this or that individual dog. Further, the idea is actually the cause of the object. The idea precedes and, in a sense, creates the object. It may help to compare this theory with the Judeo-Christian concept of God. According to the Judeo-Christian belief, God is a creator who fashioned human beings in His image. By the same token, in Platonic theory, all material things are fashioned after the original idea. Material objects imitate ideas in much the same sense that human beings are imitations, although much inferior ones, of the Lord.

Another comparison with Judeo-Christian cosmogeny is relevant. Those who devised and those who still accept this cosmogeny would not say that they are "making up" a myth to explain what is otherwise inexplicable; the story in Genesis is to be taken literally. By the same token, Plato probably did not believe that he *created* his world of abstract ideas which, having an existence apart from objects, nevertheless created them. He probably believed that his explanation of the apparent difference between the real, permanent, and perfect and the illusory, perishable, and imperfect was the only true one.

This, then, is an interpretation of *how* Plato arrived at his ontology. It is also relevant to ask *why* he felt it essential to construct such a complicated world, peopled with eternal ideas which are impossible for us to know [11] but which, notwithstanding, we are told to contemplate.

Recall that Socrates and Plato were but two philosophers in a city full of competing philosophies. Cynics, Pythagoreans, Epicureans, Stoics, Sophists, and materialists competed with one another for approval of the Greek aristocrats, who ran Athens for their own pleasure and who had the leisure to engage in philosophical speculation.

Socrates was particularly anxious to rebut the Sophists, fluent and

---

[11] This may enable you to see the contradiction in Socrates' injunctions that we should know ourselves and that he (Socrates) was wise because he knew that he knew nothing.

clever debaters and teachers of rhetoric [12] in fourth-century B.C. Athens. The Sophists were committed to the idea that perceptions vary widely, and that, as a result, it is impossible to say anything objective about reality. That which is good, useful, or desirable is only that which *appears* to someone to be good, useful or desirable. Hence, goodness is relative only to an individual at a particular time.[13]

Against this conception of ethical worth, which is obviously a shifting and uncertain one, Plato tried to construct a theory that would provide an absolutely objective standard of goodness. Goodness, then, would not "depend" on anything; that which was good would be good permanently, absolutely, objectively, and unchangeably. Any such absolute standard of goodness would necessarily have to be supported by an absolute metaphysics. In the search for a standard of completely valid ethical judgment, what is obviously required is a completely valid, certain, and unchanging reality. Such a reality Plato thought he discovered in the realm of the *idea*.

The reason for seeking absolute reality in the realm of ideas can be explained in psychological terms. It is obvious that the world of everyday experience is characterized by vast imperfection—death, sin, error, confusion, ignorance, and injustice. Only if we leave this world of confusion and distortion and go to an inner world, a world of ideas, can we arrive at untroubled, unchanging, complete certainty. In the world of ideas, one need not be contradicted by ambiguous evidence from the outer world. In Dewey's words, "Experience itself, as such, is defective, and hence default is inevitable and irremediable. The only universality and certainty is in a region above experience, that of the rational and conceptual.[14]

Analysis

An assessment of what Plato meant and what influence his writings exerted on a later age is hazardous. His theories have always been

[12] In the first book of the *Republic,* Plato pours scorn on the Sophists in the person of Thrasymachus. He has Thrasymachus, who is purple with anger over something Socrates has said, fly into a rage and attack Socrates in most intemperate language. Socrates, of course, answers him gently and in a few pages Thrasymachus is left confused and speechless. Unfortunately, because of Plato's antagonism to the Sophists, most of us have a rather biased attitude toward them. Indeed, the word "sophist" is a synonym for one who invents likely excuses for doing as he wishes.

[13] This is essentially the argument of Protagoras, a Sophist. It has been called "relativism," but the reader is cautioned not to confuse this position, which is better described by the term "subjectivism," with the relativism of John Dewey. Dewey's position is discussed later in this chapter.

[14] John Dewey, *Reconstruction in Philosophy* (New York: Henry Holt, 1920), p. 81.

the subject of controversy. Even immediately after his death, Platonists were divided on what the master meant. We are no more certain today. Did he mean to provide a metaphysical basis by building on a fantastic theory of the transmigration of souls? Or, as Copleston posits, is his soul theory simply a mythological exercise and not to be taken seriously? [15] If we are not to take his world of "absolute knowledge in existence absolute" seriously, where do we locate this other world? And if we do not locate it in any geographical place, as Copleston insists that we do not, what is its relationship to the sensible world?

Despite the problems in interpretation of Plato, one may still make some observations about his influence on Western educational practice.[16]

Knowledge Plato's distrust of the empirical, the sensory object, and his exaltation of rationalism probably had much to do with the slight progress in the sciences for well over 1500 years. Science requires close observation of empirical events; Plato believed that empirical events were so deceptive and illusory that they could not form the basis for true knowledge.

Science also requires manipulation of things. One needs tools and measuring instruments, machines, experimental animals, recorded information, in order to carry out a scientific experiment. However, it was precisely tools and machines that were seen as unworthy of an aristocrat. One who wished to attain true knowledge did so by contemplation, by a process of dialogue, perhaps even by divination—not by building a machine, observing carefully, and recording observation. What, after all, were slaves for if not to do this sort of labor? The notion that science and technology were inherently inferior died very slowly. In the nineteenth century it was still possible to read the comment of a literary humanist who, on being told of a recent scientific invention, remarked that he would not walk across the street to see it.

Subject Matter Linked to distrust of sense perception is a hierarchy of subject matter which persists, in some degree, to this day.

[15] Father Frederick Copleston, S. J., is a renowned student of the history of philosophy. See his *A History of Philosophy,* Volume I, Part II (New York: Doubleday, 1962), "The Doctrine of Forms," pp. 188–231. See also Alban Dewes Winspear, *The Genesis of Plato's Thought* (New York: S. A. Russell, 1956), "The Philosophy of Plato," pp. 269–302.

[16] The reader is urged to keep in mind that Plato and Aristotle were transmitted to Western civilization largely through the Christian tradition. See Edwin Hatch, *The Influence of Greek Ideas on Christianity* (New York: Harper and Row, 1957), "Christianity and Greek Philosophy," pp. 116–138.

Following Plato's conviction that speculative subjects were more appropriate for study than those which depended on empirical observation, the tradition arose that subjects most fit for an education were speculative and theoretical—arithmetic, geometry, metaphysics, theology, and astronomy (provided one did not depart from the Ptolemaic theory).

For many centuries—and even in this century—the truly educated man was seen as one who could converse fluently about a broad range of matters. The expert, the one who knew a great deal about a limited subject, was little regarded, particularly if he were proficient in a technological subject. Essentially this conception of an educated man stemmed from Platonic assumptions.

Something of the hierarchical arrangement of studies can still be seen in secondary schools and universities, where some subjects are perceived (at least by professors and teachers) as inherently more worthwhile than others. For example, mathematics and literature are somewhere at the top of the hierarchy, while business and home economics are close to the bottom. Presumably the first two approach some kind of intellectual ideal, while the latter are merely practical. It does no good to defend them on the grounds that they are useful, for this is precisely what makes them inferior.

A most interesting, if frustrating, conflict arises when teachers attempt to argue that literature and grammar have practical value—hence the term "communications" for English classes—and that practical subjects can be treated abstractly. Making grammar useful is often taken to mean a unit called "Fun with Verbs" or "Our Helpers, the Adjectives." On the other hand, attempting to make a practical class theoretical often appears to involve simply more factual detail and more middle-level generalizations. Neither of these two modifications appears to be particularly successful. The entire problem seems to arise from a cultural discontinuity: unconsciously we still accept the Platonic definition of intellectual and theoretical, *but* utilitarian subjects are also perceived as good.

Teaching Methods The belief of Plato—and to some extent Aristotle—that one could arrive at knowledge by rationalistic processes and abstract reasoning has influenced modes of teaching. In higher education during the Middle Ages and the Renaissance, attention was paid to the form of an argument and to rhetorical devices and persuasive techniques. Minute distinctions were applied to the logical process. But scant attention was given to grounding statements on empirical observation. There is an account of a debate at Cambridge in the seventeenth century in which the disputants logically deduced how long a person could go without food! [17]

Although nothing would seem more reasonable than that all science courses taught in schools should be accompanied by laboratory experimentation and observation, many science classes have been taught "from the book." Much biology teaching, for instance, consists merely of memorizing technical terminology. These practices seem to be a hangover from an intellectual tradition in which subjects were valued in proportion to their removal from contact with empirical objects.

Evaluation   Recently an art teacher stated that he was attempting to get his students to approach an ideal in artistic production. The belief that there exists an "ideal" is essentially a Platonic position, for Plato's "ideas" also function as "ideals." If there is such an ideal, then it exists to be imitated. One is evaluated—graded—on the extent to which he approaches the ideal.

Americans have added a rather interesting modifier to this notion of the ideal. We apparently believe that the ideal exists in measurable degrees, beginning at 100 percent and going downward. Ideals are also held to exist in the area known as "citizenship," and those who most closely approximate them receive a good-citizenship award. The same seems to be true of good behavior, neatness, good sportsmanship, and the like. It is not usually held that one can be a good citizen in a variety of ways; rather, there is some "ideal" of citizenship, which few reach but which should be emulated nevertheless.

In a recent series of nationwide discussions concerning the revised Code of Ethics of the National Education Association, the following statement was often repeated: "The real value of this Code will be as a means of inspiration, an ethical ideal for all to strive for." The actual use of a code of ethics in a modern profession is not as an "ideal," but as a means of regulating and controlling the behavior of members. To see a code of ethics as an "ideal" would seem to be an expression of

---

[17] See William T. Costello, S. J., *The Scholastic Curriculum At Early Seventeenth Century Cambridge* (Cambridge: Harvard U. Press, 1958). Says the author, "How long a human animal can go without food is an empirical problem, yet the question seems to suppose that the integrity of the principle is prior to knowledge of the fact. . . . As a consequence of this 'metaphysicizing' and 'a-priorizing' the entire discipline became a hopeless jumble of proper speculation about the nature of the soul and the intellectual process with improper guesswork about the effects of too much sleep." This quotation and other relevant discussion is in the chapter entitled, "The Undergraduate Sciences," pp. 71–106.

the Platonic assumption that there exists an ideal, not attainable, but inherently capable of imitation.

Educational Aims In the immediate past, most students who have attended secondary schools (high schools in this country and gymnasiums or lycées in Europe) have been required to study a good deal of higher mathematics, especially geometry. There has also been extremely heavy emphasis on mastery of grammar. Any defense of these subjects on the grounds of their practical utility is weak: until rather recently, most students did not make use of their higher mathematics; and grammatical analysis has little to do with developing skill in communication. Apparently the emphasis reflects the Platonic belief that one can arrive at higher truth by manipulation of symbols. Mathematics and grammar involve such symbols. If language and mathematics were not taught for some specific use, it seems entirely possible that they were taught because of the cultural value placed on them. It is not too farfetched to conclude that the unstated aim of these two subjects has had more to do with reaching higher truth than with utility.

In sum, the conception of education and of an educated man, the emphasis on acquisition of verbal skills and mastery of symbols, exaltation of the theoretical and rejection of the empirical, seem to be the educational legacy of Plato's philosophy. Much more can be said —for instance, the practice of shuttling young boys off to boarding schools can be traced to Plato's *Republic*—but it is time to examine the writing of Plato's student, an equally important figure in educational philosophy.

Aristotelian Metaphysics

With Aristotle, Plato's student and assistant at the famous Academy, philosophy reached a new stage. In place of the mysticism, flights of poetic fancy, and fragmentary thinking that characterize the Socratics' or pre-Socratics' metaphysics, Aristotle provides a thorough, organized, systematized, almost overpowering attempt to state the grounds of *all* existence.

What is equally important, as we shall see, Aristotle's metaphysical position was directly related to his other works on art, literature, logic, and rhetoric. An understanding of this metaphysical framework, then, is a prerequisite not only to an understanding of Western thought and Western religion, but also of Western education.

Plato and Aristotle

Since Aristotle's metaphysical system is similar to Plato's, it is important to see the similarities and differences. Aristotle was apparently the first philosopher to conceive of metaphysics as a separate study.[18] Plato, you will recall, distributes metaphysical positions throughout his dialogues. But in his *Metaphysics,* Aristotle builds a complete system in one work. Aristotle defines his major terms and the aim of metaphysics. He then discusses, for the purposes of rejecting them, other metaphysical positions—in particular that of Plato. Indeed, he states his objections in twenty-three separate paragraphs. Only then does he discuss his own metaphysical system, and—apparently to make doubly sure—he again explains and rejects Platonic idealism.

Aristotle accepts the Platonic belief that philosophy ought to inform men of the good life and the nature of the good state. Thus, while Plato builds a metaphysical position in order to answer such questions as "What is the good life? What is justice? What is the good state?," Aristotle need not answer these questions, for he has already been convinced by Plato's answers. Like Plato, Aristotle believes that philosophy exists to discover true knowledge, by which he also means arriving at the essence of reality, the abiding, unchanging truth that lies beyond simple sensory impressions. Like Plato, Aristotle regards contemplation of the best in existence as the proper aim of living. But Aristotle differs considerably with Plato, first as to the nature of an essence, and second, as to the relative importance of contemplation and observation.

For Plato, the essence—the idea of an object—is in some sense[19] removed from that object, or, indeed, from that entire class of objects. Thus the essence or idea of beauty is another reality and not to be confused with any *one* object of beauty or with *all perceived objects of beauty.* The idea, form, or essence of beauty is the pure and perfect ideal of what men refer to as "beautiful."

For Aristotle, this position is wholly untenable. "None of the arguments whereby . . . Platonists attempt to prove the existence of Forms is valid . . ." he states in one of his objections. It is, says Aristotle, "manifestly impossible for that which is the substance of a thing to

---

[18] This is the belief of Sir David Ross in his introduction to Aristotle, *Metaphysics* (London: J. M. Dent and Sons, 1956), p. xxi. All direct quotations in this chapter are taken from this translation.

[19] "In some sense," but it is not at all clear in what sense the idea or form is removed from the thing. It does not appear that Plato means geographically removed, but where the world of forms is, has been something of a philosophical issue for two milennia.

exist apart from it." Finally—and this is the key issue—"How is one to know for certain of what elements things consist?" [20]

It is this last point that is most relevant to Aristotle's metaphysics. For Aristotle was attempting to provide a basis for *certain* knowledge. To do this, he needed to explore the forms of thought, and that was the essential purpose of his work on logic. But to build a theory of the relationship between the forms of thought in men's minds and outside reality, he needed a metaphysical system. Furthermore, he needed one far more convincing than the Platonic forms, which rested on a poetic, metaphysical description of the transmigration of souls.

Therefore Aristotle must build his own metaphysical system. So he posed the questions asked by other Greek philosophers: "Of what is the ultimate structure of the universe?" "What is it that makes up all being?" If we reject atoms as the ultimate substance, or any of the other "elements" or combination of elements,[21] and if Plato's forms are excluded, what does Aristotle see as the ultimate structure of all being?

Form, Matter and Essence   The answer is "Prime matter in substantial form." Everything, says Aristotle, is clearly made up of something, a basic underlying building block. This basic something he calls "matter." Matter is not any particular thing; it is rather a principle which describes that which is to be arranged in a particular shape. Matter is indeterminate in the sense that it is capable of becoming anything—people, trees, water, rocks.

Matter, however, does not exist by itself. All matter is arranged in some particular *form.*[22] Form, however, is not simply "shape." It is rather a shaping principle, that which embodies the different kinds of matter in some particular arrangement.

Everything in the visible universe is arranged in some combination of matter and form. A statue, says Aristotle, is composed of form and matter. "By 'matter' I mean the bronze of which it is made; by 'sensible form' the plan of its essence; and by their 'compound' the concrete thing, i.e., the statue itself." [23] Everything, then, is reducible to matter and form. You and I are composed of matter—bones, brains, blood, nerves, skin, etc.—arranged in the form of a "human being." A

[20] Aristotle, *Metaphysics,* p. 83.
[21] The "elements" of the earlier Greek philosophers included air, earth, fire, and water. Modern chemists, of course, would not classify any of these as elements, but the problem is that the Greek insights outran their vocabulary. Their word for "element" also has the meaning of "lumber."
[22] There is one exception, "the Prime Mover," which we shall discuss in a moment.
[23] For the discussion of being, see *Metaphysics,* pp. 165–207.

home is arranged, likewise, of form and matter. The matter is bricks, steel, plastic, mortar and glass put together in a way whose end product we refer to as a "house."

Since everything is a combination of both matter and form, the two are physically inseparable. But for purposes of analysis we conceptually separate the two and speak of form *and* matter. This is only a logical separation. All things that we can see are composed of matter in a certain form. So also, the only forms that are perceivable are those composed of matter. Therefore, "the matter, the sensible form, and the compound of these two . . ." make up all visible existence.[24]

When we know something, we know the way in which the form and matter are arranged. The term Aristotle uses to describe the union of form and matter is *substance* or *essence*. Even today we speak of the "substance of the problem" or the "essence of the matter." Our language reflects Aristotle's thinking; we mean almost precisely the same thing he did. The "essence" or substance of something is the heart of that thing. When we are through stripping away all the unnecessary elements and all the irrelevant and confusing appearances, we say that we have reached the "essence" or the "substance" of a matter; we have reached to the heart of *the thing itself*. To Aristotle, essence is that which makes something what it is, something unique, not like anything else. The essence of a fish or a house is what describes it in such a way that we cannot confuse it with any other objects in existence.

Every object has an essence. The essence of man, Aristotle says, is that he is a "rational animal." He is like other animals, but he has something not possessed by any other animal—intellect and the capacity to use it. Man can think; he can abstract; he can conceptualize and express himself. To Aristotle, this is man's essence. It is that which makes man qualitatively distinct from everything else in the universe.[25]

At this point there is a clear contradiction in Aristotle. Although in one place he states that essence is primarily a term applied to the *class*, elsewhere he states that the essence is in the *thing* itself. Philosophers have speculated about this inconsistency in Aristotle, and have concluded that it is simply an unsolved philosophical problem: Aristotle is not entirely certain whether the essence is in the thing or in the class. However, for our purposes we will say that essence is to be applied to class. There is a class of things called cathedrals. This class

---

[24] *Ibid.*, p. 171.

[25] Using the same logic, others recently have characterized man as "homo faber," the one who makes things, for man is a unique tool-making animal. Or we can say that man's essence is his ability to use symbols.

is described by certain characteristics which are permanent. Individual members of the class, of course, are not permanent. They will age and eventually disappear. Thus, Notre Dame cathedral is an individual example of the class *cathedral*. While it will some day disappear, the essence of cathedral will exist forever. John Jones is also a member of a class—man—and he possesses the class characteristics. While John Jones will die, the essence of man will last forever.[26] In sum, an essence is a *definition*. When we are able to define something, we know its essence. Says Aristotle, "Therefore there is an essence of those things whose account is a definition." [27]

At this point we see the crucial distinction between Aristotle and Plato. Whereas Plato's essences are located in a world apart from the things, Aristotle's essences are in this world. They are definitions which we can arrive at by observation of individual members. We deduce the existence of an essence. It is not a mysterious formulation of an unknowable world, nor does it create a duplication of things on this earth. In short, Aristotle provided for a world of reality which men can know and understand.[28]

Accident One difficulty of this metaphysical system—which Aristotle would not have admitted—is that of relating the species or genus to the individual member of that class. The problem lies in relating the characteristics of the individual to characteristics of the species, and at this point we must consider what Aristotle means by "accident."

We can see that all desks have something in common. All desks are pieces of furniture, designed for a person to write on, having a quadrangular surface with some kind of support. These characteristics are common to all desks. However, individual desks possess certain unique, specialized characteristics. Some are small and some large. Some have three drawers, some six, and some have none. Some are made of wood, some of steel, and some are combinations of both. It is these individual differences that Aristotle would call "accidents." That one desk is brown, that another is 30 inches high, that another has an ivory trim is not essential to the classification "desk." Since these differences are not of the essence of desk, they are "accidents." It is not essential that the flat surface be made of wood. By the same token, the fact that you have blonde hair, that someone else has black hair,

---

[26] The discussion of "What things have essence?" is to be found in the *Metaphysics*, Book Z, Chapter IV. The other derived and secondary meanings of essence are discussed there, too.

[27] *Ibid.*, p. 182.

[28] *Ibid.*, Book Zeta, Chapters VI and XV.

and that a third person has no hair at all is no obstacle to your all being classified as "human beings." All human beings are, essentially, "rational animals"; rationality is their essence. But not all human beings need have any particular color hair. Hair color is an "accident." [29] An accident, then, "denotes that which belongs to a thing *per se,* though no part of its essence." [30] The important point to understand is that, in arriving at the essence of something, we must not be fooled by confusing the accidents—the variable, individual properties of the thing— with the essence of that thing.

Entelechy In sum, Aristotle has provided what might be called a *developmental* metaphysics. He holds that there is a force within the thing which shapes the destiny of that thing. In other words, there is a pull which makes a thing develop toward a predetermined purpose. An acorn has a destiny, which is to become an oak tree. The child's destiny is to become a man. Under the right conditions this destiny will be realized, the full potential of the thing will be realized. Of course, Aristotle observed, a thing may not develop as it should. The acorn may be eaten, or the child may become a "monster." [31] But the proper destiny of each is to develop according to an innate striving. Acorns are meant to develop into oaks and not maples, fish, or men.

This process is called *entelechy.* The term means something like an "unfolding inner purpose." *En* is Greek for "inside." *Tel* comes from the Greek word "telos," which means "purpose." *Echeia* means "pertaining to." Thus entelechy is a doctrine pertaining to the inner purpose of something. It is the self-realization of the essence in the thing. There is a purpose, then, and this purpose lies within the thing, and as the essence unfolds, the purpose is actualized.

Actuality, Potentiality, and Potency Aristotle recognized that some things are capable of becoming something else—that is, they have the *potentiality* to be something else. The acorn is a potential tree; the pupa is a potential butterfly. If a thing has reached the inner purpose

[29] This is only one meaning of "accident," but it seems to be the most important meaning in Aristotle's metaphysics. His discussion of accidents is found in Chapter XXX.

[30] *Ibid.,* p. 46.

[31] Aristotle noticed examples of "monsters," such as two-headed children or misshapen trees. These he assumed were the result of matter fighting form. Today, of course, we would probably say that the two-headed monster is the result of an intrauterine viral infection or perhaps of a genetic abnormality. Although Aristotle did a good deal of scientific observation and classification, he could know nothing of this.

enveloped within it, Aristotle designated it as an *actuality*. "Actuality," in Aristotle's words, "means the presence of a thing, not potentiality. . . ." [32] Elsewhere he says, "Now the work is the end, and actuality is the work; the very word 'actuality' is derived from 'activity,' and comes to mean much the same as entelechy, or 'complete reality.' " [33]

Therefore, when matter and form are joined in a complete union so that the inner nature is realized, we say that it is an "actually" existing thing. "Since matter exists actually when it is in its form, it follows that substance or form is actuality." [34]

"Potency" means, roughly, that which causes something else to come into being. There are two kinds of potency, internal and external. [35] An example of external potency is the making of a statue. The sculptor who works on the metal, wood, or clay causes a statue to come into being. The statue is, of course, not the result of anything within itself, but of something outside itself.

"Internal" potency is within the object and causes it to come into being. The development of a baby to a man or an acorn to an oak illustrates internal potency. That which propels a thing toward self-actualization is within that thing.

Aristotle anticipated objections to his theory. One might say that a man has a potentiality for sickness, so that if he becomes diseased he is realizing his inner essence. Not so, says Aristotle, for disease is a *privation* of form. By privation, Aristotle means the absence of some characteristic. [36] Privation may be normal, as for instance the blindness of a mole. The mole is naturally deprived of sight. Or privation may be the absence of something which should be present but is not. A man's blindness is such a privation, for men naturally see. Therefore, when one is ill, he is suffering from privation, a corruption of form.

The Prime Mover To avoid what he called "infinite regress," a chain of causes without beginning or end, Aristotle needed something to act as the source of all being. Such a concept he discovered in what he called the "prime mover." The prime mover is the ". . . principle whose essence is actuality." [37] It is never in a potential state, for it is, was, and always will be. It is an unchanging, eternal substance which, Aristotle reasoned, is devoid of matter.

---

[32] *Ibid.*, p. 233.

[33] *Ibid.*, p. 239.

[34] *Ibid.*

[35] *Ibid.*, p. 235.

[36] *Ibid.*, Book Delta, Chapter XXII, p. 37.

[37] *Ibid.*, p. 342. The discussion of the prime mover is found in Book Lambda, Chapters VI and VII.

The prime mover is in unceasing and circular motion.[38] This is not simply deduction, for, said Aristotle, the prime mover "... is no mere theory, but is actually observed to be the case." [39] It is, of course, anything but clear to us 2300 years later how such a thing is *observed*. The prime mover moves everything—that is, it is the cause of all other motion—but is itself unmoved. In an interesting series of deductions, Aristotle proved that the prime mover "... moves by being loved." [40] The prime mover is eternal and experiences not even "minimal change." It is an absolute necessity and, most important, it is the basis of all that is. "On such a principle, then, the whole physical universe depends." [41]

Midway in this discussion of the prime mover, Aristotle suddenly refers to the prime mover as "God." And, what is extremely significant, he concludes that God, "... is a living being, eternal, and most good; to Him belongs—or rather He is—life and duration, continuous and eternal." [42]

The tendency has been to equate Aristotle's prime mover with the Christian concept of God. They are not the same thing, but Christian theologians in the three centuries following the advent of Christianity incorporated some elements of Aristotle's prime mover into their own conception of God.

The Four Causes   Only one more concept is necessary to complete this brief discussion of Aristotle's metaphysics. That is the theory of the four causes, also called the four ends or principles.

The *material* cause is roughly synonymous with matter. It is that of which a thing is composed. If we use the example of a salami, we can say that the material cause of the salami is meat, suet, garlic, spices, and a wrapping.

The *formal* cause would be the idea or concept of the salami. The butcher who creates the salami starts with a definite notion of what it is to look like—that is, he has a picture of a completed product in his mind before he tackles the job. To use another example, the blueprint of an architect is something like a formal cause, for it is the idea of a house, the plan of the completed product.

The *efficient* cause is that which brings about the existence of something. The butcher is the efficient cause of the salami. The butcher assembles the various components, mixes them in the correct proportion, grinds them up, and encases them in a wrapping.

[38] *Ibid.*, p. 345.
[39] *Ibid.*
[40] *Ibid.*
[41] *Ibid.*
[42] *Ibid.*

The *final* cause is the purpose for which the thing exists. The purpose of the salami is, of course, to be eaten. The final cause, or purpose, of a house is to shelter someone. The final cause, or purpose, of this book is to be read.

Aristotelian metaphysics, in sum, is a complete system designed to describe the grounds of all being. It is a painstaking analysis of what makes up all being, the stages of being, the immediate causes of being, and the source or ultimate cause of all being. Nothing seems left out of this account. Partly because of its completeness and partly because it appeared so logical and reasonable, Aristotelian metaphysics became the framework for a great deal of the science, literary and artistic criticism, political thought, logic, and formal argumentation of not only the medieval world but the modern world as well.

Analysis

So complete are Aristotle's metaphysical theories that they are almost infinitely applicable. We can apply such notions as "form," "matter," "essence," and "potentiality" to an unlimited variety of phenomena. Briefly, here is a description of the relationship between Aristotelian terms and a variety of historically important categories.

Art   Aristotle saw art as an imitation of reality. By this he meant not photographic reproduction, but rather the depiction of the true essence of a thing. The artist was to try to find the nature of the thing and then to make that reality visual. In a sense, this formulation has been the aesthetic belief of people to the very present. A trip to an art gallery with an extensive collection of Renaissance portraits will reveal an abundance of pictures of beautiful people. These people, it will be noted, did not have warts, loving-cup ears, or crossed eyes. We need not ask whether the subjects were really so lovely; the artists omitted what they considered accidental, not real. After all, warts and crossed eyes are not of the *essence* of a noble person.

Something similar is true in classical and neo-classical tragedies. Aristotle thought that true tragedy should be about nobility and not about commoners. Hence in the tragedies of the French dramatists Corneille and Racine, all heroes belong to the nobility.

Contemporary artists and dramatists are often hard put to find a sympathetic audience for their innovative works. Most of us are so used to beautiful people in portraits, for instance, that we tend to reject art that does not conform to our preconceived ideas of what "true" art "really is."

Morality   If one is fairly certain that he knows the "true essence" of something, it is possible to deduce a wide range of *do's* and *don'ts*. If, for instance, he knows the true purpose of a given act, then he can say authoritatively what should or should not be done.

The Catholic position on birth control has traditionally been based on the assumption that the essential reason for the sex act is procreation. Aesthetic or emotional aspects of the sex act are secondary to the major value, which is the production of children. What has been deduced is that whatever interferes with the natural end of mating is wrong and a perversion. Birth control, which seeks to prevent children, is opposed to the true aim of sexual relations and is a perversion and a sin.

Education   Many educational practices appear to reflect Aristotle's metaphysical position. Aristotle defined man as a rational animal. His true nature involved knowing, for he has an intellect designed for this purpose. If man's true essence is intellectual, it logically follows that education exists exclusively to develop his intellect. Thus one commentator on education, Arthur Bestor, says:

A simple definition of education, and simple democratic corollary thereof, will suffice: It is the job of a *democratic* school to teach *all* young men and women to think.[43]

Bestor then takes a position that is quite ancient, one based directly on Aristotelian thought.

If this is, in fact, the central purpose of education, the school must recognize, at the very outset, that certain studies are vastly more effective than others in developing the capacity to think clearly, seriously, and sustainedly.[44]

The assumptions underlying Bestor's position are, first, that man's function is to think; second, that schools exist to help him develop this function; and third, that certain subjects are inherently more able than others to develop the capacity for thought. In all three of these assumptions, Bestor is faithfully echoing Aristotle. Many other educational theorists and critics—Robert M. Hutchins, Mortimer Adler, Admiral Hyman Rickover—would agree that certain theoretical sub-

[43] "A Crisis of Purpose," *Vital Speeches of the Day,* 24 (September 15, 1958): 723–728.
[44] *Ibid.,* p. 726.

jects can best actualize man's intellectual capacities and that these subjects are the *only* ones appropriate for study.[45]

Educational Administration   In Aristotle's philosophy is the assumption that reality is arranged hierarchically—that is (and this point will be dealt with later at more length), some things are inherently better, finer, and "higher" than others. Just as contemplation is higher than action, some men are inherently better than others.

School administration is apparently based on this metaphysical assumption. There exists a hierarchy—teacher to supervisor or department head, to principal, to superintendent, and finally to the Board. The assumption is that decision-making begins at the top, with the most able persons. As we descend this hierarchy, decision-making power is accordingly reduced, until we reach the teacher, who is assumed to have only to understand and interpret decisions. Teachers often refer to this as "the chain of command" and, while they may chafe occasionally, generally seem to feel that this is the way things should be.

Thus we seem to have accepted the notion that salary decisions, curriculum, textbook selection, promotions, and other important educational matters *ought* to be made at the top (with perhaps inoffensive advice from the bottom). The problem with this hierarchical interpretation is, first, that it is inconsistent with one criterion of a profession; and second, that it is inconsistent with certain democratic assumptions. A profession is usually thought of as requiring independent decision-making or autonomous choices. Decisions cannot be made both "at the top" and autonomously by the professional practitioner. Further, the democratic assumption is that he who is affected by a decision has a right to take part in that decision.

Curriculum Rigidity   If one knows the essence of something, his knowledge is not of the uncertain, temporary kind. Either one knows or one does not. Further, if the essence is truly known, the temptation is to dismiss or explain away later, contradictory appearances.

Schools apparently have been perceived as institutions designed to transmit valid knowledge. More accurately, schools have passed on the valid knowledge which is the product of previous thought and inquiry. As a consequence, curriculum is thought of as a body of knowl-

[45] This point is elaborated at great length in John P. Wynne, *Theories of Education* (New York: Harper and Row, 1963), Chapter I, "The Formal Discipline Theory." For a technical discussion of Aristotle's educational philosophy, see Robert S. Brumbaugh and Nathaniel M. Lawrence, Jr., "Aristotle's Philosophy of Education," *Educational Theory* 9 (January, 1959): 1–15.

edge already tested and found adequate and reliable. The teacher's function is to transmit this knowledge to the young.

However, one of the distinguishing characteristics of the twentieth century is the phenomenal explosion of knowledge. Indeed, knowledge is being created faster than it can be organized and disseminated, let alone put into the curriculum. This extremely rapid increase in knowledge creates problems. In the first place, the sheer quantity makes it impossible to understand it in totality—even for experts within a particular field. Second, and this is even more significant, the products of present inquiry replace the products of past inquiry. Thus when the author was taking high-school biology 15 years ago, he learned as fact that there were 48 chromosomes for human beings, 24 provided by the male and 24 by the female. Recent staining techniques developed in Japan have revealed that apparently there are only 46 chromosomes.

The problem, then, is that the *attitude* toward knowledge is not consistent with the production of knowledge. If facts change, positions are modified, and theories are replaced by better theories. Knowledge is not the essentially unchanging thing that Aristotle held it to be. The fact that knowledge is held to be unchanging is precisely what has made it extremely difficult to modify curriculum.

The Nature of Reality

Most persons divide the world into two kinds of reality. One is taken to be a world of objective fact. This world is asserted to exist independent of any knower. A fact simply *is* and is in no way affected by being known. Razor blades are sharp, cement is hard, fire burns, and water freezes at 32° Fahrenheit. These phenomena are the way they are, regardless of who does or does not know them.

Quite apart from the world of fact existing independently of man is another world, in which reality is internal. This world usually encompasses artistic values, preference in music, taste, and other phenomena called "personal" or "subjective." This world is seen as having no relationship with the world of facts and belonging exclusively to one's private judgment. The description of this world lies in the ancient Latin saying "There is no disputing tastes." In this world, what is good is good for *me*. If I like Hoagy Carmichael and you like Chopin, you have no right to attempt to change my taste in music—or in anything else—for my taste is simply and finally mine.

Although most persons would agree with the above description of the two attitudes, such compartmentalization of facts and values has, in fact, little to do with the way people actually behave. One constantly finds people attempting, on the one hand, to objectify values, and on the other hand, to bring to facts a personal, subjective interpretation.

To illustrate the contradiction between what people *verbalize* about facts and values and what they actually *do* with the two supposedly different realms of reality, consider the plight of a home economics teacher. She assigns students to make a dress as part of a unit on textiles. The assignment involves correct techniques of creating a garment—neat pattern cutting, well-spaced stitching, accurate fitting, and so forth. In addition, part of the unit involves something called design. Now assume that a student hands in a dress which is well constructed but whose design consists of purple polka dots alternating with orange stripes. Assume, further, that our hypothetical teacher must give a grade to this student.

A grade is supposed to be an objective evaluation of achievement in which there is an already existing standard against which the work is compared. "Design" obviously involves values and artistic taste. If taste is a purely subjective, private, personal affair, by what logic can it be "graded"? Taste is not supposed to be based on an external and objective ground and a grade, by definition, is an objective, external measure.

The teacher can follow one of two courses of action. She can say that there is, in fact, an external standard of good taste and that purple polka dots with orange stripes constitute a violation of this standard. To do this is obviously to say that there is an external criterion of taste, and that taste is *not* simply personal and subjective. Or she can use her own taste as *the* standard of good taste, which places her in the unpleasant position of imposing her private values on the student.

The point is that, despite assertions to the contrary, teachers constantly attempt to objectify matters of value. The literature teacher and the anthology writer both operate on the assumption that some poems and prose selections are indeed better than others. The music teacher is likely to hold that Beethoven is superior to the latest emanation from the juke box. And art teachers dispense grades.

On the other hand, it seems equally clear that supposedly objective evaluations are less objective than is usually held—if by objective we mean external, uniform, existing apart from perception or evaluation. The best illustration of this is the historical "fact" that Columbus discovered America. This is clearly not an issue, and almost all would agree that it is a certain and clear fact that in 1492 Columbus did discover a new world which was eventually named America. If it is

asked, "What did Columbus find when he got there?" the answer is
"Indians." Why, then, do we not say that the Indians discovered
America? At this point, doubt intrudes for a moment, but the next
answer is quickly forthcoming. It is that the Indians did not make their
discovery known to Europe.

Apparently, then, "discovery" in this case means to make something known to Europeans. It is not sufficient to make it known to
non-Europeans. If this is the conclusion—and it appears to be so in
light of the logic—the term "discovery" contains an inherent value
judgment: it is not sufficient to be the first ones to find a new land
mass; one must make it known to Europeans. Thus the statement
"Columbus discovered America" is anything but an objective fact. It
is an historical judgment with implicit—though not explicit—value
judgments.

Analysis reveals that many supposedly objective facts are much
less clearly factual than appears at first sight. As we have seen, it is
now a "fact" that human beings have 46 chromosomes, and the new
"fact" is the result of a new set of staining techniques. One can say
that a new and better theory, improved instruments, more sophisticated scientific techniques reveal new information. While it was for-
merly believed that each person contributed 24 chromosomes, we now
know better, for more accurate information has been turned up through
a better set of operations which replaced a less adequate set. But
"better" happens to be a value judgment. And value judgments are not
supposed to have anything to do with the world of objective, scientific fact. (As this book goes to press, biologists have renewed the debate about the number of chromosomes. Some insist on 46, and others
lean toward 48.)

Apparently the tidy compartmentalization of facts and values is
based on confusion about the meaning of such terms as "internal,"
"external," "reality," "perception" and "judgment." What is needed
is an examination and critical analysis of two ontologies, one stressing
reality as internal perception and the other emphasizing reality as
objective fact.

Subjective Idealism from Protagoras to the Present

As was indicated earlier, Protagoras, the Athenian philosopher and
representative of the Sophists' position, devised what might be called
the first theory of subjective reality. Protagoras decided that, because
human perception varies widely, it is impossible to say anything
about objective reality. That which is, is that which appears to be. Although Protagoras admitted that there are objects of perception,

"... everyone knows things not as they are, but as they are in the moment of perception for him, and for him only." [46] Since the object of perception is unknowable, the only logical position is scepticism— that is, denial that we can have truly reliable knowledge of reality. The position is summed up in the famous saying "Man is the measure of all things, of things that are, that they are, and of things that are not, that they are not." It follows from this position that values can be only subjective; what is good is only what is perceived by someone as good. Objective standards of goodness are impossible because unknowable.

From this early assertion that reality is only perceived reality, we turn to the English enlightenment and Bishop George Berkeley (pronounced Barclay). In 1710 Berkeley wrote his *Principles of Human Knowledge,* in which he set forth the position usually known as "subjective idealism." At the outset he frankly admits that most men believe that things are what they are, independent of their being known.

It is indeed an opinion strangely prevailing amongst men, that houses, mountains, rivers, and in a word all sensible objects, have an existence, natural or real, distinct from their being perceived by the understanding.[47]

But, says Berkeley, such an opinion is false. It rests on ignorance of the process of perception and abstraction. Reality is not external to the perceiver. Ultimately all reality is reducible to a perceiver.

Light and colours, heat and cold, extension and figures—in a word the things we see and feel—what are they but so many sensations, notions, ideas, or impressions on the sense? [48]

And then, to emphasize the point and leave no doubt in the reader's mind:

... that all the choir of heaven and furniture of the earth, in a word all those bodies which compose the mighty frame of the world, have not any subsistence without a mind, that their being is to be perceived or known; that consequently so long as they are not actually perceived by me, or do not exist in my mind or that of any other created spirit, they must either have no existence at all, or else subsist in the mind of some Eternal Spirit . . .[49]

[46] Wilhelm Windelband, *A History of Philosophy* (New York: Harper and Row, 1958), Vol. I, p. 92.
[47] George Berkeley, *Principles of Human Knowledge,* in *Great Books of the Western World,* edited by Robert Hutchins (Chicago: Encyclopaedia Britannica), Vol. 35, p. 413.
[48] *Ibid.*
[49] *Ibid.,* p. 414.

In one succinct and vigorous essay, Berkeley tries to refute the common-sense understanding of the vast majority of mankind. Nothing exists unless it is in some sense, known. Things are, either because they are perceived or because they are the product of reason.[50] "In short, if there were external bodies, it is impossible we should ever come to know it" [51] except by perception.

The doctrine of subjective idealism is summed up in the famous quotation "*Esse est percipi,*" "To be is to be perceived." There is no "... absolute existence of sensible objects in themselves, or without the mind," and to hold that there is, is either to contradict oneself or to say nothing whatsoever." [52]

Most persons are understandably either puzzled or irritated by this position. How can any normal person assert that something exists only as an idea or sensation in the mind? Common sense tells me that this mountain existed before I came along, exists now whether I know of it or not, and will exist after I am gone. However, if one can temporarily lay aside his bias and follow Berkeley's logic, the position is not as untenable as it appears at first sight.

Assume that one asserts that a razor blade is inedible or that an ice cube is cold, and assume that he asserts also that the ice cube is cold whether eaten or not. The upholder of subjective idealism need ask only one question: "How do you know?" The answer is something like, "Just eat a razor blade and see what happens." But that is precisely the point of the subjectivist. The only way to know the characteristics of the razor blade is to come into some relationship with it. The only proof of the razor blade's sharpness is by means of sensory perception. Berkeley would say that we can generalize further and assert that the existence of anything waits on its being perceived.

This position has inspired heated debate since it was first propounded 250 years ago. The famous lexicographer Dr. Samuel Johnson is said to have kicked a large rock and muttered, "Thus do I refute Berkeley." But Berkeley would say that Johnson refuted nothing, for he only demonstrated the subjectivist's position: The rock was hard because it resisted Johnson's toe. What was required was Johnson's toe to establish the rock's reality.

Berkeley's position, far from being only a provocative intellectual puzzle, has had important consequences. It found its way into the mainstream of philosophy, and along with the writings of other philosophers, such as John Locke and David Hume, provided support for

[50] *Ibid.*, p. 416.
[51] *Ibid.*
[52] *Ibid.*, p. 417.

the position known as empiricism. When in the late nineteenth century, psychologists attempted to disassociate themselves from philosophy, Berkeley's position did not—as was averred—disappear into limbo. For psychologists have since disagreed as to the precise relationship among perception, external reality, and knowledge.

Implications for Education

Several variations of Berkeley's position are still very much alive. At times discussions about matters of both morality and aesthetics are abruptly ended with some such statement as, "If I like it, it's good" or "What's right or good is right and good for me." Thus, without being aware of Berkeley or his philosophical position, many tend to confine judgments about values to the world of the subjective and personal. Some may go farther and say that *all* reality is subjective—and find convincing support from psychologists.

The ontology of subjective idealism is important particularly in the areas of psychology and psychiatry. A number of schools of psychiatry and psychology have taken the position that, whatever may exist externally, the only significant reality is the individual's *perceived* reality. Thus some theorists in the area of counseling psychology would say that if someone asserts that people hate him, the question of whether this is *really* so is beside the point. The only significant reality is that someone *believes* he is hated. The emphasis is on the internal experiences, beliefs, wishes, hopes, and insights of the person involved. It is not on whatever really exists "out there."

Carl R. Rogers, an influential counseling psychologist and theoretician, says, "Being real involves the difficult task of being acquainted with the flow of experiencing going on within oneself . . ." [53] Suppose, says Rogers, that he feels bored by a particular student. He may wish to communicate this feeling to the student.

But here again I will want to be constantly in touch with what is going on in me. If I am, I will recognize that it is my feeling of being bored which I am expressing and not some supposed fact about him as a boring person.[54]

In other words, what I say about an external object reveals nothing objectively true about that object, only about me and my perceptions of it.

[53] "The Interpersonal Relationship: The Core of Guidance," *Harvard Educational Review*, 32 (Fall, 1962): 418.
[54] *Ibid.*

What this should imply for counseling is abandonment of diagnosis, objective testing, and "guidance"—that is, telling someone what is good for him. "In psychological terms, it is the counselor's aim to perceive as sensitively and accurately as possible all of the perceptual field as it is being experienced by the client . . ." [55] Thus, says Rogers,

". . . if we can provide understanding of the way the client seems to himself at this moment, he can do the rest." [56]

The point of view expressed by Rogers may also be found in prescriptions about education, especially education of very young children. It is standard practice to encourage the daubing and smearing of kindergarteners without either criticism or correction. "Show and Tell" time is an opportunity for children to describe anything of interest to them. At a somewhat later age, creative dramatics is another opportunity for young people to "express" themselves. What these teaching practices have in common is the point of view that significant reality is personal and subjective and that, somehow, expression of such reality is extremely desirable.

However, despite the frequently expressed belief—stated so often as to be almost official educational theory—that teachers must pay some attention to the child's private world of meaning, the opposite point of view is also believed. It is held that there is an external world of knowledge and facts, and that the function of teachers is to acquaint children with this world. Unfortunately, it is rarely made clear to teachers just when to pay attention to the internal reality of children and when to acquaint them with external reality.

Reality as Something Out There

The metaphysical position that has been historically opposed to the belief that ultimate reality is internal is known as philosophical realism.

The word "realism" derives from the Latin *re,* meaning "thing." The core of any realistic position is that reality is a "something" that exists external to mind, thought, observation, or belief. In contrast with Plato, who held that ultimate reality consists of ideas or forms, realists usually maintain that ultimate reality is a thing whose structure or function is independent of any knower. In contrast with Berkeley, who located ultimate reality as a sensation or impression in the mind, realists assert that the thing exists first and that knowledge of reality

---

[55] Rogers, *Client-Centered Therapy* (Boston: Houghton Mifflin, 1951), p. 34.
[56] *Ibid.,* p. 30.

is simply a mental picture of the thing out there. To hold otherwise—
to assert that reality is created in the act of perception—is, from the
realist's viewpoint, to confuse knowing with existing.

The central core of realism is called the Theory of Independence.
This theory is a simple and unqualified assertion that ultimate reality
is independent of any knower. What is, is in no way dependent for its
existence on being known. *Esse* is most certainly not *percipi*. *Esse*,
or being, simply is whatever it happens to be. And whatever it happens to be, while it may be knowable, is in no way affected by or
dependent upon knowledge. In the words of Frederick Breed, a
twentieth-century realist, "For the realist, becoming known is an event
that happens to things assumed to *exist prior to and independently of
the act of knowing.*" [57]

The position that reality is a thing which has external being can
be traced to the Greeks. The pre-Socratic Greeks talked about "elements," but whether they meant a "thing" or a "principle" is often
unclear, probably because of the metaphorical and poetic way in
which they expressed philosophical positions.

Leucippus and Democritus, however, provided a philosophy
which is clearly unambiguously based on an assertion that ultimate
reality consists of things. Leucippus, in a manner which is an almost
uncanny prefiguring of twentieth-century atomic theory, talks about
"atoms" which fill a void. To his student, Democritus, however, fell the
task of developing Leucippus' atomic theory. All that exists, we are
told

... are atoms and the void. That is, the objects of senses are supposed to
be real and it is customary to regard them as such, but in truth they are not.
Only the atoms and the void are real. . . . Further, the atoms are unlimited
in size and number, and they are borne along in the whole universe in a
vortex, and thereby generate all composite things—fire, water, air, earth;
for even these are conglomerations of given atoms.[58]

As we have seen, Aristotle devised an extremely elaborate and
systematic metaphysical position. In effect, he was the first philosoph-

[57] "The Realistic Outlook," in Nelson Henry (ed.), *The Forty-First Yearbook
of the National Society for the Study of Education*, Part I, Philosophies of Education (Chicago: U. of Chicago Press, 1941), p. 93.

[58] Diogenes Laertius, in Loeb Classical Library, Series II, pp. 439–443. Legend
has it that Democritus was a prolific writer, but apparently none of his writings
have survived. What we know of Leucippus and Democritus has been gleaned
from latter critics and writers, such as Diogenes and Aristotle. See Diogenes
Laertius on the doctrine of atoms in the Loeb Classical Library, Series II, 453–55;
and Aristotle, *De Generatione et Corruptione* and *Metaphysics*, Book I, Chapter
IX.

ical realist, for the essential meaning of his theory of essences was that
ultimate reality consists of an essence, a thing which exists in a certain
way. Essence is understood only by an act of intellect in which one
apprehends what the thing is. The act of intellect, the knowing of the
essence, depends, however, on careful observation of many members of
a given class of things.

Until Berkeley's *Principles of Human Knowledge,* with its clear
and forceful statement of subjective idealism, however, most philosophers accepted some kind of realistic metaphysics.[59] Since the
eighteenth century, philosophical realists have been forced to provide
a more detailed defense of their position.

Present-Day Realism

Present-day realism is a complex highly refined position, usually
grounded in some theoretical description of the method of the physical
and natural sciences. With the exception of Neo-Thomism, which is
technically classified as a realistic philosophy but which is based on an
Aristotelian ontology modified by certain Christian beliefs, realistic
ontology prefers to adhere closely to what might be called a "hard"
scientific position.

The Theory of Independence carries with it certain corollaries. In
general, present-day realism is characterized by a disposition to act
in accordance with how things really are. What this has come to mean
is that first we must assume that things have an existence independent
of their being known. Then we must discover how things really are.

Realism today is based on the assumption that, however difficult
it is to pierce through the fog of inaccurate observation, preconceived
ideas, and variable perceptions, reality can be known and, what is
most important, *reality can be known on its own terms.* Of course,
what we say about reality, and what reality is, may or may not be the
same thing. It is when what we say about reality corresponds precisely
to what is that we are speaking truth.

Truth, then, is a perfect copy of what exists. This theory of truth,
called the Correspondence Theory, is the test for true, reliable, and
accurate knowledge. If I say that it is 75° in this room, and it is, in fact,
75°, I am telling the truth. What I have said about reality *corresponds*
precisely to what is. Of course, if I say that it is 75° and it is not, in

---

[59] This is not to say that there was no metaphysical controversy in the Middle
Ages. There was a good deal of heated debate between Nominalists and Realists,
for example. See Friedrich Heer, *The Medieval World* (Cleveland: World Publish-
ing, 1962), Chapter 10, "Intellectual Warfare in Paris," for an excellent description
of the Nominalist-Realist dispute.

fact, 75°, I am simply and unequivocally wrong. Whatever true judgment I make about the degree of heat must be shown to bear an accurate correspondence to the actual degree of heat.

Reality is not invented; it is discovered. When we discover or find out something, we have taken the cover—the meaning of the word *dis-cover*—from reality. We have seen what the thing is actually like. We know what it is, in and of itself. Certain forms of reality—for instance, the fact that the ocean is salty—are not especially difficult to discover. Other kinds of reality—for example, the precise structure of the atom—involve years of painstaking research with complicated instruments before they are finally discovered. Still other forms of reality, such as a psychological description of precisely how people learn and remember, are—at the present stage of knowledge—impossible to discover and formulate in clear and unmistakable terms. However, people clearly do learn, atoms do have a definite structure, and ocean water is obviously salty. What is involved is a determination of precisely what exists in each case.

Reality is, therefore, discoverable by observation. In some cases the observation need not be careful or lengthy, for it does not take much observation to determine that elephants are larger than mice or that, on sufficient provocation, wasps sting. But in other cases reality is discovered by careful, systematic, controlled observation. This involves performing certain operations in a precise manner. Recognizing the weakness inherent in casual and unaided observation, man employs mechanical devices to assist observation. The telescope, microscope, spectroscope, encephelograph, centrifuge, and other devices enlarge external observation by giving it more detail and precision.

The realist's position has given rise to a term known as the "spectator theory." One is a spectator—although a highly intelligent and well-trained one—and one "spectates"—observes—what is taking place in a world that is not of his creation. This last point is important, for it must be kept in mind that man is, in a very real sense, apart from the reality he views. The world is not within us. To hold otherwise is to fall into the subjective idealist's fallacy of confusing knowledge of reality with creation of reality. To become confused in this way is to substitute our wishes, dreams, and perhaps unconscious hopes for the way things really are.

Some Implications for Education

It is not easy to deduce a set of educational practices from a given metaphysical position. Since teachers tend to switch metaphysical positions without being aware of doing so, it is somewhat risky to label a particular practice "realistic" or "idealistic." But some generalizations may be made—if we are aware that they are subject to the limitations of all generalizations.

Curriculum   If there is a world external to any knower and if this world must be known on its own terms, certain educational practices logically follow. First, this world can be observed and described as faithfully as possible. The knowledge gathered can then be organized in logical subject-matter divisions: biology, history, physics, psychology, and so on. The organization can then be simplified according to the level of sophistication of those to whom it is to be presented. For instance, the materials of American history in college history classes contain a certain number of principles, facts, concepts, generalizations, and conclusions. The same materials are used in high school classes, but with somewhat fewer principles and facts—in short, the same general subject matter simplified for that age group. An elementary textbook in American history is like a high school text with fewer facts and more simplified presentation. Textbooks, therefore, tend to reflect a realistic ontological position in that they organize subject matter as subject-matter experts would organize it; the difference among grade levels is largely a difference in the amount of material included in the textbook.

The aim of realistic educational practices is to present this material to students on *its* terms—that is, students become acquainted with the subject matter as a pre-established block of material. Successful learning consists of understanding that material.

Methods   Teaching techniques, from a strictly realistic position, consist of any approach that most effectively acquaints students with what they are to know. A lecture is an oral presentation of the material, correctly organized, with adequate illustrations and appropriate generalizations and conclusions. Lectures and textbooks are both designed to give a systematic and well-organized *description* of subject matter.

If audio-visual techniques are superior to lectures in presenting material, they are used. Filmstrips, movies, maps, charts, and educational television may be useful in "putting over" content effectively. They appeal to a number of "sense modalities" rather than just one. One can see, hear, and touch certain audio-visual materials, and doing so may make learning more efficient than simply hearing or reading the information.

Field trips and demonstrations, because they involve concrete, direct experience, may also be utilized. Of course, one may use a field trip for a number of different purposes. But when the object is to acquaint students with what exists, a field trip or a demonstration may be superior to abstract study.

Evaluation Evaluation should be as objective as possible—that is, an evaluation should represent as accurate a measurement of achievement as possible. Achievement is determined by comparing evidences of what has been learned with what should have been learned. Students who have learned the most material with the fewest errors receive the highest grades. If the evaluating instrument—usually a test—can be quantified, so much the better. A number or a percentile score is usually considered more precise than a simple letter grade. The aim of a realistic grading procedure is an accurate and objective measurement of learned content; the standard of measurement is that which exists as reliable and truthful knowledge.

Analysis

Apparently the same person may hold the ontologies of philosophical realism and subjective idealism at the same time. Apparently, too, there is little awareness, first, that there exist two such positions, and second, that they are oppositional. Nor is there any particular awareness that each ontological position leads to rather different educational practices. It is important that anyone concerned with educational theory and practice be aware of the meaning and consequences of both positions—and of the indiscriminate mixing of the two.

As we have seen, many counseling psychologists operate from the position of subjective idealism when they are interviewing clients or providing therapy. The client's perceptions are taken to be the only significant reality, and it is considered very bad practice by many theoreticians for the counselor to "straighten out" his client by acquainting him with true reality—that is, the *counselor's* perception of reality. But the same counselor may decide to use a standardized test, such as a psychological inventory, or an achievement, intelligence, or aptitude test. Standardized tests are based on the assumption of an externally existing standard of reality against which an individual is compared—hence such tests reflect philosophical realism. In effect, this practice would seem to divide diagnosis from treatment. Diagnosis is based on one set of assumptions and treatment on another. This is strange in the light of the usual assumption that treatment *proceeds* from diagnosis, that the two are related. Another consequence of this metaphysical muddling is, first, that counselors who believe they are not intruding their values on their clients often do so unconsciously, and second, many counselors seem to share a pervasive distrust of all standardized tests and diagnostic tools.

While the dominant ontological position underlying educational theory about certain subjects in the primary grades appears to be subjective idealism, there is a rather abrupt change in both theory and practice in the middle primary grades, sometime about the fourth or fifth grade. At that time the emphasis shifts from the child's world of meaning, from expression, from self-development—in short, from attention to the child's perception of reality—to acquisition of external reality. Teachers now correct the children's art—"Johnny, let's not paint the sky green. It is blue," or *"This* is the way we show distance." Other subjects—arithmetic, spelling, geography, social studies—are intro- duced, not primarily as a means of enhancing self-expression, but as subject matters to be learned in their own right.

Although it is not immediately obvious, different ontologies tend to support different curricula. For instance, the sciences are usually taught from the standpoint of philosophical realism. The assumption is that there is a body of subject matter based on tested observation of externally existing reality. The function of the teacher is to acquaint students with that body of subject matter. It is not usually the method by which the knowledge was acquired—the scientific method of knowing—that is seen as significant. Rather it is the subject matter in and for itself.

Analysis reveals a somewhat confused picture with regard to the ontologies supporting the fine arts. From the point of view of the artistic creator—the painter, composer, poet, or novelist—the emphasis is on internal feelings and experiences. Most artistic creators would probably accept the point of view expressed by Benedetto Croce, the Italian philosopher of aesthetics, that the important factor is the *intuition* of beauty; the way the intuition is realized on canvass or in words is secondary and consists of mere technique.[60] This is a modifica- tion of the position that reality is ultimately internal. But the teaching of the fine arts is often a strange blend of the two ontologies. Although lip service is paid to the ultimacy of the private, subjective value judg- ment and to the personal nature of values, the actual teaching of art, music, and literature is apt to be another matter. Typically students

[60] See Benedetto Croce, *Aesthetics* (London: Macmillan, 1909), Chapters I and III.

are confronted by lists of poems, musical compositions, or "great" paintings and *told* (1) what it is they *should* see, (2) how they *should* interpret it, (3) what the music or poem *means,* and (4) the correct *evaluation* of the production. The assumption behind the teaching is that there is an externally existing standard of knowledge and values which students must know and learn to accept as good.

Thus in high schools and colleges, students are told, for instance, that Sidney Lanier was a minor poet and Walt Whitman a major one; that Beethoven's *Eroica* symphony is one of the great musical master-pieces of all times; that the painter George Bellows "captured the spirit of the city"; that Toulouse Lautrec was an excellent draftsman; that Renoir was interested in light and shadows. These assertions, which are essentially informed opinions masquerading as revealed truth, are usually transmitted to students in lectures. At appropriate times such "facts" are written down in test booklets and graded by teachers, who use as criteria the opinions of other teachers and professors. At the end of the course, students may recall that Beethoven is considered a great master, but they may feel—perhaps with some uneasiness—that George Gershwin's *Rhapsody in Blue* is a lot more fun to hear.

Something similar appears to be true in the area of the social sciences. Especially in the public schools, the typical practice is to treat the subject matter of history, civics, sociology and, of late, comparative government, not as someone's interpretation of facts and events but as externally existing, proven fact. Students learn that democracy and/or capitalism are superior to all other "systems."[61] They learn as fact that a group of patriots fought the tyranny of King and Parliament in 1776 to lead their country to freedom. Students exhibit considerable shock when they are exposed to an interpretation of history by British historians. The perception of the American revolution by British historians—that it was a minor skirmish having more to do with the ineptness of the English government at that time than the sterling qualities of Washington, Adams, and company—leaves students somewhat dazed.

Whatever else may be true of such teaching, it reflects considerable philosophical inconsistency. It also reveals that teachers are by no means as clear as they say they are about what is "out there" and what is a matter of internal, subjective reality. It is possible that much

[61] For reasons that are not entirely clear, most Americans do not make a distinction between an economic and a political system. Thus democracy and capitalism are seen as the "same thing." That a democratic political system may be accompanied by a modified socialist economic system seems incomprehensible—even though it happens to be verifiably true, as witness Great Britain today.

of the ineffectiveness of the teaching of the arts and sciences may be attributable to the fact that the teachers of both science and the humanities do not yet know how to relate an externally existing body of knowledge and values to the personal and private perceptions of students.

4

Metaphysics
(CONTINUED)

Reality as Law

One way of describing reality is to classify all phenomena—artistic, scientific, psychological, moral—as coming under the control of absolute, unchangeable law. In the same sense that magnetism and gravity obey certain scientific laws, the activities of human beings obey certain undeviating laws, just as real and as scientifically demonstrable as the Law of Gravity. This position is known as the doctrine of Natural Law. It is an extremely ancient philosophical position, and it has influenced thinking in fields as diverse as constitutional law, sociology, religion, economics, education, psychology, and physics.

One can trace the origins of Natural Law to tenth-century-B.C. Greece. The Greeks seemed to believe that there was some kind of controlling power in the universe which ". . . ordains both what *must* be and what *ought* to be." [1] Since the Greeks did not make a clear-cut distinction between physical events and moral or psychological phenomena, they believed that "the power which presides over the physical order is moral." [2] This power, which the Greeks called "Moira," was beyond the gods to change; indeed, it was a sort of primal force, from which the gods themselves received their power.

Genesis describes a supreme being who established the heavens and the earth. In much the same way, Moira established divisions in the universe. Moira, often translated as "fate" or "destiny," is a blind, automatic force which set up the physical world of stars, rivers, trees,

---

[1] Francis M. Cornford, *From Religion to Philosophy* (New York: Harper and Row, 1957), p. 11.
[2] *Ibid.*

and animals, and also ordered the world of Justice. This last refers to the world of values, that which tells men what they *ought* to do, a realm regulating the "domains, privileges, and honours" of human beings.[3]

The early philosophers, who were attempting to get away from Moira as an explanation, tried to describe the world in what appeared to them to be scientific terminology—the elements. It is by no means clear, as we have seen, what these "elements" are. However, if they are interpreted as *principles* of reality, they are similar to Natural Law.

Although Socrates and Aristotle did not have a Natural Law philosophy, there are some concepts in their philosophies which became important to later development of the doctrine of Natural Law. Natural Law became closely associated with Christian theology, and Christianity, as we have seen, incorporated a good many positions from various Greek philosophies. Thus in the doctrine of Natural Law one may find echoes and traces of "Moira," Plato's forms, Aristotle's prime mover, Neo-Platonism, Stoicism, and other schools of Greek philosophy.

The most complete formulation of the theory of Natural Law was the work of St. Thomas Aquinas, a Dominican priest of the thirteenth century. Why and how did Thomas formulate his position? The intellectual Christian world—in particular the newly created University of Paris—was engaged in constant and heated controversy over the conflict between faith and reason. Those who asserted that faith and God's revealed wisdom were sufficient and primary in Christianity were opposed by those who felt that reason should be paramount. The conflict was brought to a head in the century preceding Thomas by Pierre Abélard and Peter Lombard, whose scholarly research revealed many contradictory statements in the Bible and other official Church writings.[4]

Thomas, who possessed one of the great synthesizing minds in history, tried to reconcile the apparently irreconcilable dispute between faith and reason. If, reasoned Thomas, we can talk about two different realms of existence, each with its proper method of knowing, then all supposed conflict vanishes. What is real, said Thomas,[5] is a Divine World which contains all that exists. This world is God's creation. But one can divide God's creation into a natural and a super-

---

[3] *Ibid.*, p. 28.

[4] The faith-reason controversy actually began with the founding of Christianity, but was particularly heated in the early Renaissance.

[5] In many writings, for Thomas was a prolific writer who was active throughout much of his comparatively short life. The *Summa Contra Gentiles* and *Summa Theologica* contain many important elements of Thomas' thought.

natural world. The natural world Thomas likened to the world of natural events, which included what we would today call scientific phenomena. In Thomas' metaphysics this world is quite close to Aristotle's world of form, matter, and essence. The supernatural world —from *super* meaning above, and *natura* meaning nature—is the special world of God's law. It is the world of angels, which conforms not to Aristotle's *being*, but to God's *existence*. Properly understood, there is no conflict between the two kinds of reality.

There is an order—that is, a kind of law—and a method of knowing which is appropriate to each world. For the Natural World there is Natural Law, and for the Supernatural World, Supernatural Law. There is no inherent conflict or contradiction between these two worlds, and both are part of Divine creation.

We come to know the Natural World by reason; and revelation, based on faith in God, informs us of what we can know of God's existence.[6] Faith and reason cannot conflict, for both have the same end. "[A]lthough philosophy ascends to the knowledge of God through creatures while sacred doctrine grounded in faith descends from God to man by the divine revelation, *the way up and the way down are the same.*"[7] Thus reason, which is an element of philosophy, is grounded in observation of God's creation; and sacred doctrine is based on faith and is God's revealed word.

In time, a distinction was made between the Law which controls human values and relations and that which is applicable to scientific phenomena. Natural Law appropriate to human behavior came to be known as the Moral Law. The Moral Law, having its basis in God's will, is a kind of force embedded in human reason which establishes what is good and what is evil. Moral Law, in its positive aspect, tells us such things as to honor our parents, and in its negative aspect, forbids us to steal, murder, commit adultery, and so on.

Moral Law is not, it must be strongly emphasized, a matter of time, custom, or condition. It is obligatory upon all individuals, regardless of their particular time, place, or circumstances. With the exception, of course, of infants and the mentally incompetent, the Moral Law is binding on all. Moral Law underlies *all* judgments about good or evil.

The rule, then, which God has prescribed for our conduct, is found in our nature itself. Those actions which conform with its tendencies, lead to

---

[6] Keeping in mind that man, who is *finite*, cannot be expected to have anything like complete knowledge of God, who is *infinite*.

[7] Etienne Gilson, *The Spirit of Thomism* (New York: P. J. Kenedy, 1964), p. 39.

our destined end, and are thereby constituted right and morally good; those at variance with our nature are wrong and immoral.[8]

Not only is there a law directing and underlying human relations, but there is also one that establishes the fundamental rules of nature. God not only established those laws which set the orbits of the stars or the orbits of electrons, but controlled the behavior of whatever is. Whatever is, is by virtue of being governed by law.

Positivism: Law for Everything

In the late eighteenth and much of the nineteenth centuries, intellectual activity began to turn from the Moral Law to what, in retrospect, we may call scientific natural law. There arose a school of thought which became extremely important throughout Europe and North and South America known as Positivism, or Logical Positivism. The position of Positivism, reduced to its essence, is that scientific laws control all phenomena, physical and human, and only science can yield true knowledge. There are not only laws governing the physical world, but laws controlling human behavior, human associations, learning, emotions, human history—in short, laws for everything.

If one performed certain operations, he could discover those laws which underlie the behavior of all physical things. With knowledge of these laws one could construct machines that could perform hitherto undreamed of labors and produce in hours what man's unaided hands could not do in days. The steam engine of Sir James Watts or the marvels of electricity in the nineteenth century—the telegraph, the telephone, the incandescent light bulb, and the electric generator—all testified to the wonders that could be produced if one but knew the laws governing nature.

For these marvels to have been discovered and invented, a certain special knowledge must obviously have been employed. Such special knowledge was derived from the scientific method. And, as it appeared to men—both laymen and scientists—in the eighteenth and nineteenth centuries, scientific knowledge was knowledge of nature's immutable laws. There were laws which governed everything—the erosion of rocks, electricity, magnetism, genetics—and these laws were simply unalterable, absolute, immutable forces which determined the structure and behavior of all things. Such laws, while difficult to understand, could be discovered. Once discovered, they yielded both insight

[8] See "Natural Law" in *The Catholic Encyclopedia* (New York: Encyclopedia Press, 1913), Vol. IX, pp. 75–79.

into ultimate reality and power—the power to make nature do what man wanted it to do.

It was a rather small step to applying the concept of Natural Law to the scientific study of human beings. What was true of chemistry and physics should be equally true of the behavior of man. There exists, it was held, laws which govern the behavior of man, whose operations man could discover. We could apply the scientific method to the study of human behavior and discover truly reliable knowledge.

A number of historians believed that they had been able to discover "laws of history." The events of human history move in a certain, definite pattern. To know these patterns is to know the laws of history. Ernest Renan, a French historian, formulated a set of such laws, as did Hegel, Marx, Spengler and, more recently, Toynbee.

Soon sociologists, such as Auguste Comte, declared that they had discovered the laws controlling the behavior of people in groups. Psychologists followed with what they took to be the laws of the behavior of single animals and persons. Significantly, E. L. Thorndike's psychological theory of learning is known as the Four *Laws* of Learning.

Eventually almost every area of human endeavor was seen as coming under the control of some kind of law. There were laws of jurisprudence, which purported to describe the legal arrangements that must regulate human associations. Of particular importance were economic laws, which were seen as beyond the powers of man to modify. Even today one still hears a great deal of the Law of Supply and Demand. Such a law is sometimes seen as regulating all economic activity, determining how much of any given commodity is produced, how much it will cost, and how many persons will make it.[9]

Thus Natural Law was seen as applicable not only to the scientific, physical domain but to the values which people hold and to human behavior in all its forms. It is no exaggeration to say, as Alfred North Whitehead has, that by the end of the nineteenth century most scientists believed that everything really important had been discovered and that what remained was simply to tidy things up a bit and clear up a few facts not yet thoroughly understood.[10] By extrapolating a little, it seemed also true that, through the application of science, a great day of humanity lay ahead. No human wants would remain

[9] In fairness, we should note that very few professional economists hold this belief today. It is more often found among older businessmen whose early education stressed economic laws.

[10] This attitude is described in Lucien Price's *The Dialogues of Alfred North Whitehead* (Boston: Little, Brown, 1954), p. 345.

unsatisfied, knowledge would be universally disseminated, wars would come to an end, and Nature would be forced to obey the will of man.

Implications for Education

If we assume the existence of laws which control physical events, values, and human behavior, what implications exist for education? Obviously, education will consist primarily in acquiring knowledge of such laws. Teachers will first gain knowledge of the laws in their field and then transmit the content of the laws to students.

Apparently without much awareness, some variant of Natural Law has seeped into the teaching of history. At any rate, many secondary and college students acquire the feeling that the history of the world is an evolutionary process in which events move through a predestined order. One stage of history is succeeded by another, more refined and advanced stage.[11] A common feeling is that democracy represents a kind of pinnacle of historical evolution. Our country, it is held, came into being so that a democracy could develop. Since democracy represents the summit of human evolution, it exists as a kind of ideal for other countries to attain. Americans, as many foreign observers have pointed out, tend to judge the worth of other social institutions by the degree to which they approach our own. Thus while we are a *real* democracy, England is less so because it has a monarch.

Language rules are also frequently seen as having their basis in law. Until the rise of structural linguistics in this century, a dictionary was almost universally regarded as the authoritative source for the spelling and meaning of words. A grammar textbook was—and is— regarded by many as a source of laws governing tense, syntax, idioms, and so on. Popular usage had nothing to do with "correctness." There are certain laws of correct usage, and these laws are as eternal as the Law of Gravity and as binding as a Supreme Court decision.

A variation of Natural Law has been applied, strangely enough, in the areas of growth and development and educational psychology. Here there is a concept that may be called "natural evolutionary growth." Children are seen as developing from one stage to another, each stage characterized by certain kinds of behavior. A child creeps before he walks and cries before he laughs. These stages are sequential and represent natural development. In the words of Arnold Gesell, the late psychologist and investigator of growth patterns, "such sequences are part of the order of Nature... Every child has a

---

[11] Students are often shocked to discover that this position is quite similar to the historical interpretation of Marxists.

unique pattern of growth, but that pattern is a variant of a basic ground plan." [12] In other words, the growth and development of children is governed by a natural law of growth and development.

Natural law still forms the basis of certain theories of value. Some values, it is held, are built into human beings, and may be discovered by analysis of "human nature." This position is seen as placing values on as firm an ontological footing as facts. Frederick Breed, a prominent realist, states that moral values may indeed be placed on such a basis: "The basis of discipline in life is nothing more than the requirements implicit *in rerum natura,* the demands of the laws of nature." [13] John Wild, another realist, takes the same stance: "What is good is the fulfillment of being. We strive to complete our existence." [14] In other words, there is a built-in natural tendency in all of us, and to fulfill this natural tendency means to do what we ought to do. Of course, man must use his rational powers to determine what the tendency means, and how it must be realized. Here we see a justification of moral values based on Natural Law and relying rather heavily on certain Aristotelian concepts.

The implications of Natural Law may be summarized by stating that there are laws, either inherent in human nature or in the universe, which must be found out and obeyed. Schools are, or should be, devoted to the job of discovering whatever is discoverable in these laws and transmitting this content to students. In Wild's words,

The student is confronted with a range of existence for which he is in no sense responsible. His duty is to learn those arduous *operations* by which here and there it may be revealed to him as it really is.[15]

[12] *Studies in Child Development* (New York: Harper, 1948), p. 8. Gesell's relationship to this position is described in the chapter, "What is the Nature of Psychological Development," by Morris Bigge and Maurice Hunt, *Psychological Foundations of Education* (New York: Harper, 1962).

[13] "Education and the Realistic Outlook," in Nelson Henry (ed.), *Philosophies of Education. Forty-first Yearbook of the National Society for the Study of Education, Part I* (Chicago: U. of Chicago Press, 1941), p. 102.

[14] "Natural Law and Modern Ethical Theory," *Ethics,* 63 (October, 1952): 5. Wild clearly indicates the Natural Law origins of his position when he states, "When such a tendency is fulfilled in accordance with natural law, the entity is said to be in a stable, healthy, or sound condition—adjectives of value. When it is obstructed or distorted, the entity is said to be in an unstable, diseased, or unsound condition—adjectives of disvalue." (p. 4.)

[15] "A Realistic View of Education," in Nelson Henry (ed.), *Modern Philosophies and Education. The Fifty-fourth Yearbook of the National Society for the Study of Education, Part I* (Chicago: U. of Chicago Press, 1955), p. 52. Note that this quotation uses the term *operations,* a word perhaps equivalent to *laws.* Although Wild designates himself a realist, he tends to shift his ontological position, stressing different emphases within realistic metaphysics.

Reality as Absolute

Whether reality is perceived as ultimately external, as ultimately internal, or as ultimately controlled by law, the three different metaphysical positions share one trait: they are expressions of an absolute ontology. An absolute is either a value or a truth that is asserted to be complete, immutable, and perfect as it stands. The term derives from two latin words: *ab,* apart from; and *soli,* of and by itself. Thus an absolute exists of and by itself, apart from human awareness or understanding. An absolute may be clearly known or it may be dimly sensed. In either case, it exists for all times and all places—is not modified in any way by changes in time, place, or circumstance.

Absolutes are coercive in nature—that is, there is something about an absolute that requires strict obedience. For some, a religious commandment is an absolute. Murder, lying, blasphemy, and adultery are unacceptable and wrong, and they are wrong whether one does or does not know the nature of God's commandment. One must *not* murder, lie, swear, or break the marriage vow. There are scientific absolutes, too, and they may exist apart from knowledge of them. Such absolutes, too, are coercive: gravity acts in a certain, particular manner, and you must know how gravity acts or you will make the fatal mistake of stepping out of a tenth-story window. There are absolutes in other fields as well. In the area of art or education, for instance, one will find statements that strongly suggest that *this* is true or good, and one must always *do* this. Hence absolutes, of whatever species, are such that one must live and behave in conformity with them.

Absolutes are without context: they do not depend on any particular set of relations to be valid. They are out of time, not dependent on location, and unaffected by conditions. Thus if one holds that a given act is evil, the fact that some other culture or some preliterate tribe is unaware of it does not affect the absolute value. That the Carthaginians sacrificed babies in fiery furnaces or that a Bedouin tribe makes its living by robbing its neighbors does not change the validity of the absolutes concerning murder or robbery. Whether known or obeyed, absolutes exist. The holder of the scientific absolute takes much the same position: the absolute exists, has existed, and will exist in whatever form it happens to take. Although man may change his mind about the absolute as he gains more knowledge of it, the absolute itself does not change.

Such a position is for many rather stark and forbidding. Therefore, in recent years absolutists have tended to soften the position somewhat. The scientific absolutist may say something like, "While absolutes do exist in some form, it is of course extremely difficult to know how they exist and what they mean. I am not now certain *how* atomic particles behave, but they *do* behave in a *certain* way, probably obeying antecedent laws. My research consists in finding out *how* they behave, and when this process is complete, if it ever is, I will have discovered the nature of the law." This statement, while somewhat softer than the eighteenth- or nineteenth-century position, is not actually a substantial modification. The absolute is seen as extremely difficult to know, but its existence is not questioned.

An absolute may be defended with highly sophisticated and subtle arguments, or it may be held in a naive way and designated "common sense" or "self evident." On the one hand, the absolutes of the Judeo-Christian religion are defended with complex arguments that are the result of more than three thousand years of thought. On the other hand, many hold absolutes because they appear to be simple, unqualified statements of what is obviously true.

Consider such a statement as "The book is on the table." If we understand the meaning of the terms used and if on observation we see that the book is on the table, what is wrong with a simple assertion that the book *is* on the table? Without doubt and dispute, without qualification, the book *is* on the table. From such a commonsense position, a host of other absolutes are derivable. Cows give milk, not *appear* to give milk. Human beings are *all* mortal. Abandoning one's children and spending one's salary on drinking and gambling *are* sinful and immoral. To quibble about the meaning of such statements, or to doubt that they are absolute, is either to fly in the face of what is obvious or to be addicted to splitting hairs.

To be absolutely certain, then, is not to entertain doubt, for there is no reason to doubt. What could be more certain, as Theodore Reik puts it, than that in the foreseeable future grass will be growing over all of us? There is, further, no doubt that fish swim, that Caesar crossed the Rubicon, or that ice cream is sweet. Absolutists do not, of course, assert that one must *not* express doubt. They do say that about *some* phenomena there is not doubt.

Absolutists make use of such terms as "self evident," "eternally true," "never," "ever," "none," "all," "forever," "clearly undeniable," "ultimate," and other terms descriptive of statements that are simply and finally true. No one, of course, holds that all statements are absolutely true. But most people, at one time or another, express a position that something, some value, or some event is absolutely the way it is said to be.

Subjective idealism, while it differs from realism, is an absolutist position. Reality is perceived reality, and perceived reality is ultimate

reality: one can *never* get beyond perception. The Theory of Independence is also an absolute. Things have an existence independent
of their being known—that is, things exist absolutely apart from
knowers, and whatever we may perceive them to be, they are what
they are. Natural Law, whether Moral Law or some variant of scientific law, is also an absolutist position. Absolutely immutable laws govern the universe. Whatever our knowledge of them may be, these
laws exist *outside of* knowledge and perception. Indeed, according to
one school of thought, there are even laws which govern perception.
Aristotelian essences have an independent existence, and once an
essence is known and defined, it does not change. Platonic forms—
"knowledge absolute in existence absolute," as Plato himself put it—
also constitute absolute reality.

Indeed, it has been said that, until the late nineteenth century
when pragmatism (also known as instrumentalism, experimentalism, or
relativism) appeared, the only philosophical positions which existed
were some variation of an absolute.

Application to Education

There is abundant historical evidence to indicate what kinds of
educational practices are derived from absolutes. If the reader will
bear in mind that the following description is, of necessity, oversimplified, he will gain some idea of the relationship between an absolute ontology and curriculum, methods, administration, testing, and
other educational practices.

Selection of Curriculum

The entire nature of curriculum, from an absolutist's viewpoint,
is conditioned by its relationship to the presumed absolute. If there is
a certain reality and if this reality is known, such reality functions
as subject matter. A variation of this position is referred to as the
"Basic Subjects" theory by Wynne.[16]

The "Basic Subjects" theory states that certain subjects are absolutely indispensable for human society, absolutely essential for human survival. Assume that (1) a substance known as "poison" exists,
(2) the nature of poisons is known, and (3) survival depends on our
knowledge of poisons. Assume, too, that in our culture we designate a
poison by placing a skull or crossbones on any jar or can that contains it. To avoid accidental death, then, it is plainly obvious that (1)

[16] John P. Wynne, *Theories of Education* (New York: Harper and Row,
1963). See Chapter 12.

we must know something about the operations of poisons, (2) we must know something about the cultural symbol, the skull and cross-bones, and (3) we must avoid drinking or eating any poison.

From the standpoint of such an absolute position, it is not difficult to decide what should be taught. The schools should teach that which is clearly essential for understanding life as it actually is. For only by understanding life as it actually is, is survival possible. Schools, then, should identify knowledge of things as they are, and should make certain that *all* children master such knowledge.

Since language is essential for communication and since communication is that indispensable element which keeps human beings intact, schools should teach language. This means that teaching students to read with understanding, to speak clearly, and to write effectively is the responsibility of all schools.

Since, as it has been said often, he who does not study the past is doomed to repeat it, the study of history is essential. Citizens must come to understand how the present situation came to be. Only by studying the past can we understand the present. Only by understanding the present can we anticipate the future.

Because the world is a world of *quantity*, people must learn to deal with quantity. Mathematics gives one absolutely essential information about the world of quantity. Too, since we live in a scientific and industrial age, one cannot function effectively unless he knows something about the principles of science and technology. Hence physics, chemistry, biology, and perhaps other scientific disciplines must be taught.

Since such an approach reflects the belief that reality is external, it is only part of one way of formulating an absolute position. One can also say that the absolute fact of God's existence makes certain subjects essential. We may take the position that man is naturally destined to become more like God. If we assert this, what follows is a curriculum designed to make us more like God. Such a curriculum may resemble the one described above, with the addition of emphasis on God and his creation. Thus history would be studied so that we might learn of God's plan for man. Certain religious absolutes would be inculcated carefully. Parochial schools take this position, and in some public schools, released time for religious training is designed to inculcate the presumed absolute.

If one believes that art is essential for the highest development of personality, then art is an essential study. Usually, however, art is seen as rather more ornamental than essential and is therefore not regarded as of first importance by most lay or professional educational theorists.

Democracy is frequently taken to be an absolute, and many educational theorists have advocated that all children be carefully indoctrinated in democratic beliefs—although the number, variety, and types of democratic beliefs vary with the theorist. Social studies classes are, therefore, a vehicle by which democratic absolutes are indoctrinated. Student government and other extracurricular activities are seen as means by which youngsters can learn democratic attitudes and gain skills seen as crucially important for our democracy.

Literature is also perceived by some as existing to provide insights into the drama and conflicts of human life. Literary masterpieces give opportunities for studying eternal verities. We study Shakespeare's *Hamlet* to learn something about man's eternal conflict between two supremely important values. Great literature thus is seen as embodying an ideal, a truth whose knowledge is absolutely essential for becoming truly human.

In short, whatever is regarded as an absolute is seen as absolutely important to know. The perceived absolute becomes curriculum, in some sense, and the function of schools is to transmit such curriculum —whether facts, values, laws, skills, or concepts—to the young. The end is to ensure that children acquire what is demonstrably of supreme importance.

Methods Certain teaching methods are implied in the position that absolute knowledge exists. One does not allow the immature to take part in choosing what they should learn. Nor does one allow them much latitude in interpretation: they may choose the wrong thing, or their interpretation may be incorrect. Therefore, indoctrination—committing students to a body of facts and values without critical examination—is logically implied. Indoctrination, whether of the subtle or "heavy" kind, is the most frequently utilized teaching technique.

"Covering the material" is another characteristic of an absolute ontological position. The subject matter is divided into logically arranged parts and is "covered" in a thorough, systematic fashion. Nothing must be skipped or gone over too rapidly, for the material is too important to omit. The author recalls one teacher who was extremely disturbed because there were thirty-two teaching weeks in the year and the textbook contained only thirty-one chapters. Such reverence given to textbooks, while extreme, is not rare. Quite frequently, the textbook *is* the curriculum; and the teacher's handbook or syllabus contains *the* teaching method to be employed.

The lecture followed by recitation, a frequently used technique, reflects an absolute ontology. Lectures are seen as a well-organized and systematic embodiment of subject matter. The teacher delivers the lecture and the student takes it down, attempts to learn what was said, and is then tested on the accuracy of his interpretation and memory. In this sense the lecture and the textbook are essentially identical. Recitation or a highly structured discussion may follow a lecture. This is ordinarily not a critical examination of the material, but a follow-up to see that the students have learned what they should have.

Evaluation Certain evaluation techniques reflect an absolutist position. Perhaps the most frequently used is the objective test.

Multiple choice, true-false, completion, and other objective examinations are predicated on the assumption that there is but one right answer. The right answer is the one that corresponds precisely to what is given by the teacher or text. Presumably, of course, it is one that corresponds to what is really true.

Essay questions may be given, but frequently they are not very different in spirit from the objective questions. While students may be asked to "criticize," "contrast," or "evaluate," the most frequent essay test direction is "discuss." Discussion is usually taken to be a logical and systematic organization of the given body of subject matter. The criterion of "correctness" is usually the one described above: agreement with the information given by the instructor or found in the text.

Discipline Although discipline has a rather wide range of meanings, the one most often used stresses the *conditions* under which students may best learn. Such a condition is usually taken to be one in which maximum quiet and order prevail. A discipline problem exists when a student upsets the order. Discipline problems must be dealt with decisively, for transmission of knowledge is too important to be disturbed by unruly students. The erring student is exhorted to pay attention, punished by a low grade, placed in a special class, or, as a final resort, shipped to the school psychologist. It is not usually assumed that the nature of the subject matter should be changed, but rather that the student must be made to conform to the subject matter on *its* terms.

Administration Administration, as we have seen, is usually organized on the assumption of a hierarchy.[17] This hierarchical arrangement reflects the belief that the correct order is *fixed;* hence it appears to be absolutistic.

[17] The best explanation of the cultural habit of ordering things in hierarchical form is in the great philosophical classic, *The Great Chain of Being*, by Arthur O. Lovejoy (New York: Harper and Row, 1960).

In other senses, school administration is also absolutistic. According to a theory now popular, the sole purpose of administration is to facilitate the learning process. In practice, however, we may see enormous numbers of rules, regulations, ordinances, directions, and administrative "requests" emanating from the superintendent or principal's office. A good many of these rules have nothing whatever to do with facilitating learning. They are designed to accommodate the administrator. For instance, field trips may be discouraged, not because they are not educative, but because they interrupt the regular school schedule. The school day with fixed class intervals has nothing to do with learning; such an arrangement simply makes it easier to run things with order and efficiency. The only conclusion is that administration is not really a means designed to enhance learning. It exists as the end. If this judgment sounds a bit extreme, discuss it with those who have tried and failed to innovate in schools. Probably the single most important deterrent to innovation is the belief that innovations disrupt traditional administrative practices.

Relativism: A Construct Theory of Reality

In the twentieth century a metaphysical position often called "relativism" or "objective relativism" has grown out of the philosophy of John Dewey. Relativism appears to be the only contemporary philosophy that explicitly and carefully avoids all forms of absolutes. In developing this position, Dewey and others have attempted to harmonize conflicting positions of many other philosophical schools— realism, idealism, rationalism, and empiricism, to name a few. Because relativism is a non-absolutistic philosophy and because it represents a radical departure from previous metaphysical systems, it is often misunderstood, exaggerated to the point of distortion, or rejected out of hand.

Dewey and his immediate predecessor, Charles S. Peirce, rejected traditional metaphysics but did not attempt to build their own metaphysical system. Dewey, James, Schiller, Mead, and others who shared the same philosophical interests analyzed existing metaphysical systems and in the process of rejecting them developed a position of their own, but one which is implicit rather than explicit. Their rejection of other positions is essentially a rejection of absolutes, and their rejection of absolutes is based on considerations of science, psychology, anthropology, and history.[18] Here are the principal grounds of their rejection:

[18] See John Dewey, *Reconstruction in Philosophy* (New York: Henry Holt, 1920).

First, absolutes are both scientifically unprovable and morally indefensible. What is taken to be an absolute is rather a particular custom which, through the years, has hardened into a fixed way of looking at the world. A particular institution, belief, or value is seen, not in the context of history, but as "natural" or indispensable.

Second, absolutes are often used by an entrenched and powerful institution to defend its privileges and power. A belief in the "natural inferiority" of certain races was revived by Southern slaveowners to protect a way of life. This belief turned into an absolute. To this day there are many Americans who believe quite strongly that racial inferiority is simply an inescapable fact of life. The concept originated with Aristotle and was revived to defend a particular social institution!

Third, absolutes tend to breed arrogance and authoritarianism. The individual who thinks himself in possession of absolute truth tends to feel a compulsion to convince others of this truth and, if others are not convinced, to impute to them either stupidity or wickedness. In the sixteenth and seventeenth centuries, the religious wars between Protestants and Catholics produced atrocities almost unparalleled in the history of the world. Both Protestants and Catholics thought the other under the control of Satan. The theological differences between them centered around differences in the interpretation of absolute doctrines. Similarly, orthodox communists tend to persecute deviants who do not accept the absolutes of Karl Marx.

Fourth, absolutes are one-sided, rigid, and out of touch with reality. Most absolutes are framed in such a way that there is *no* alternative. Either one holds to the absolute or one does not. This, Dewey points out, tends to restrict considerably the range of ideas and knowledge. Thus absolute formulations tend to retard intellectual growth.

Absolutes, said Dewey, whatever their nature, arose originally out of a psychologically understandable desire to possess certainty.[19] In a world in which change, uncertainty, and accident rendered man always at the mercy of the unknown, it is understandable that man wanted to cling to some kind of reality that would withstand change, a reality that was fixed, certain, immutable, and that would forever serve as an object of desire and knowledge.

At first, such a reality was in the realm of the magical and trans-empirical—that is, in a world beyond that which man could see with his sense organs. This realm belonged either to the gods or to God. By reposing faith and complete confidence in such a world, man could

[19] See *The Quest for Certainty* (New York: Putnam's, 1960).

have something that would yield comfort, no matter how unbearable the conditions in everyday existence. Another philosopher, Max Otto, concurs with Dewey and suggests that man has always expressed a desire for cosmological support. There is a fact, asserts Otto, that has endured even changes of civilization:

What is this stubborn fact? It is the fact that human beings refuse to be physically alone in the universe; the fact that they demand that somehow there shall be a Power at the heart of things which will not let them suffer ultimate defeat, let appearances be what they may.[20]

Absolutes, then, have their root in an emotional longing for a harbor that is forever safe from storm and strife. The absolute which would not let us "suffer ultimate defeat" is the same absolute which guarantees that, if man seeks and believes, he can find certainty. Even the scientific metaphysics of the Age of Enlightenment reflected this desire for certainty: Dewey sees Newtonian scientific realism as simply a more sophisticated absolute. Quoting from Isaac Newton, Dewey says:

"All changes are to be placed in only the separations and new associations of permanent particles." In this statement there is contained a professedly scientific restatement of the old human desire for something fixed as the warrant and object of absolute certainty. Without this fixity knowledge was impossible.[21]

Thus, whether conceived as absolute scientific law, unchanging particles, Aristotelian essences, or the revelations of a Supreme Being, absolutes reveal more about man than they do about the asserted truth.

Another basis for rejecting absolutes is scientific epistemology. An absolute is, from the relativist's point of view, incapable of being verified. To the relativist, the only reliable method of knowing is the scientific method. The scientific method operates within a certain time, place, and set of circumstances. Since an absolute is, by definition, not confined in time, place, or circumstance, absolutes are logically incapable of being either confirmed or denied. Thus any scientific absolute, such as "Gravity *always* operates in such and such a manner" is, from the relativist's standpoint, incapable of being proven or disproven—a scientific experiment cannot deal with *always*. Relativists talk only about truths that are *relatively* true, or those characterized by a high degree of probability.

[20] *Science and the Moral Life* (New York: Mentor Books, 1958), p. 134.
[21] *Quest for Certainty*, p. 118.

Further, many positions asserted to be absolute have been demonstrated to be either false or inaccurate. Very often some scientific law or fact has had to be modified because of new data, better theories, or more accurate interpretation. Even very basic scientific knowledge established through many years of observation and experimentation has later been disproved. Since this has happened frequently—particularly in the present era of knowledge "explosion"—relativists have become extremely reluctant to label any position certain, undeniable, or absolutely true.

Relativists do not accept value judgments phrased as absolutes. "Thou shalt not kill" is often taken as an absolute, and as such it means that one must never, under any circumstance, take a human life. But there are circumstances in which taking a human life is considered not only permissible but desirable—for example, killing someone in self-defense. The relativist believes that values are related to other values. An absolute value is, by definition, *not* related to other values. It is valid and binding upon all at all times, in all places, and under all circumstances. It is this position which the relativist, by virtue of his ontological position, rejects.

In brief, relativistic metaphysics originated in the voluminous philosophical writings of John Dewey, but has only recently been systematized or refined. This "refining" process has been helped by considerable borrowing from other fields, especially psychology, biology, and physics. Indeed, it would be no exaggeration to say that relativists perceive their ontological position to consist of the implications of twentieth-century science.

Relativistic Ontology

Relativistic metaphysics combines the ontological positions of both subjective idealism and classical realism. The emphasis of idealism is incorporated in the relativistic position that *one* kind of reality is indeed perceived reality. The term used by Ernest E. Bayles, a relativistic philosopher, is "the world of insight." [22] The world of insight is that reality which one *takes* as reality. It is a private world of one's own perceptions, feelings, understanding, and beliefs. The world of insight is one's interpretation of what comes to him.

Relativism means that psychological reality is defined, not in "objective" physical terms, but in psychological, perceptual terms. So defined, reality

[22] Bayles, *Democratic Educational Theory* (New York: Harper, 1960), Chapters 4 and 6.

consists of what one makes of that which comes to him through his senses or otherwise.[23]

The phrase "what one makes of what comes to him" is equivalent to "what one interprets of the light waves, sounds, smells, and other data coming to us from our environment." This kind of reality is the only reality that we can *deal* with—that is, we do not seem to be able to get beyond our perceptions to some absolute, independently existing reality. That there *is* or *may be* an objective reality is not denied by relativists: nor is it asserted. Whatever may be objectively real, reality is, for the relativist, what one takes it to be.

If I perceive an object as a dangerous bear, I will act on this perception—that is, I will try to escape, to defend myself, or to call for help. The bear may actually be harmless, it may be in a cage, or it may not even exist. But if I *perceive* a dangerous animal, then whatever I see functions as reality for me, at that time, in that place, and under those conditions. Even early in his career, Dewey expressed this same idea: "[R]eal things as well as imaginary things, whatever their absolute existence may involve, exist for us only through becoming involved in what we mentally experience in the course of our self-conscious lives." [24]

However, the world of insight, the world of one's beliefs, feelings, perceptions, and understandings is not the only component of relativistic metaphysics. Relativists talk about a real, external world—but they do not treat external reality as do philosophical realists. The external world is *assumed* but not *asserted* to exist. Bayles refers to the "world of effect," that reality which exerts an *effect* on us, whether we know of it or not. There is, says Bayles, an " 'order' independent of human influence" which "is neither asserted nor denied. But, as a working principle, it is assumed." [25] What does Bayles mean by "assumed as a working principle"?

In order to design behavior, in order to act, individuals must make some assumptions about the things and events they are dealing with. If I am thirsty, I assume that water will slake my thirst. We assume that the sun will come up tomorrow, that razor blades are sharp, that sugar is sweet, that fire burns, that Mrs. Smith is touchy and oversensitive and needs to be treated with kid gloves. Whether or not these constructs we make about reality are really, *ultimately* true, the

[23] Maurice Hunt and Morris Bigge, *Psychological Foundations of Education* (New York: Harper, 1962), pp. 345–347.
[24] "The New Psychology," *Andover Review*, 2 (September, 1884):2, in S. Samuel Shermis, "A Brief History of John Dewey's Interactive Concept," *The University of Kansas Bulletin of Education*, 15 (February, 1961):71.
[25] Bayles, pp. 96–98.

relativist does not know. Nor does he *need* to know whether they are *ultimately* true. They give a convincing appearance of being real enough —real enough to afford a stable design for behavior. And this is all the reality the relativist wants or believes he can have.

> We ... interrogate the world, we ... ask nature what we are permitted to do. We ask by acting in a particular way, then seeing if we have been successful—if, in short, nature has agreed to what we have asked—we are shown that our reality is truthful, that is, that we can accurately predict similar future events. This is an interactive process, one in which mind and matter—ideas and events—act and react upon one another.[26]

If, for example, I am camping in a forest and wish to light a campfire, I break up wood which appears to me to be sufficiently dry to burn. I attempt to light the wood. If the wood lights, I assume that it was dry. Nature has cooperated with me by saying in effect, "I have permitted you to do what you wished." Such "permission" is taken to be indicative of an accurate insight into reality. But note that it is "taken to be," and not "asserted to be." Even after observation and experimentation indicate that his interrogation of the world is in agreement with the world, a relativist is not ready to assert that his statements about the world are absolutely true. They are taken to be "relatively" true, or they "seem" to be accurate, or they "appear" to be true. The relativist does not wish to go beyond probability.

The relativist's reality, therefore, is of two kinds: an internal world of subjective perceptions and an external world independent of us and exerting an effect on us whether we are aware of it or not. However, since relativism is non-absolute, the world of insight—one's understanding of external reality—is not to be taken as final or complete in any sense. Nor is the external world *asserted* to be what it is, whether known or not, for we cannot know what a thing is in and of itself.

The relationship of these two worlds of reality is, to use Dewey's terms, *interactive* or *transactive*. One's knowledge of reality is gained from interacting with reality—one submits one's world of insight to the world of effect to see if it is consonant with that world.

An important constituent of this ontological position is Dewey's theory of experience.[27] An experience takes place when one *under-*

[26] Shermis, p. 76.

[27] Many of Dewey's books have the word "experience" in the title; for instance, *Experience and Nature* and *Art as Experience*. The term "experience" has come to be a fairly stock word in educational writing and in the vocabulary of teachers. However, as often as the term is used, few can define it meaningfully or are aware of the specific meaning Dewey attributed to the term.

goes an event and then *realizes* what the event *means*. An experience, therefore, is characterized by a passive and an active element. The actual undergoing of certain actions may be passive—that is, one simply does certain things. The active realization occurs when one understands what the actions mean. We can illustrate the two aspects of experience by describing a person taking an automobile trip from one town to another. If the person is in the passenger seat and is not particularly concerned with the route taken, if he is simply sitting there casually watching the scenery, his is essentially a passive situation. He is unlikely to be able to answer questions about how far away the destination was, what roads were taken, where one turned left or right, and so on. But if this same person drives between the two towns, he is likely to get a map, ask other people relevant information, note significant road signs and landmarks and, in general, be aware of what is involved. Such a situation requires an active realization, a conscious awareness of what the trip means—as far as directions are concerned.

Dewey applied this concept of experience to almost every phase of education. Eventually, experience became a key element in his philosophy. Indeed, the goal of Dewey's education is the constant reconstruction of experience. One is to spend a lifetime constantly deepening and widening his experiences, gaining more appreciation of what human existence means. Dewey's criticism of formal educational procedures was that very little in the way of teaching and learning had much effect on a person's experiences. Much schooling, he felt, was merely a passive undergoing of situations which meant little and which had the barest relation to the student's purposes or intents.

For Dewey, an experience did not represent ultimate reality. What one understands of what happens may or may not be accurate. One's *insights* into a situation may be more or less adequate and accurate. But what one makes, interprets, or understands of an experience apparently marks the limits of what he can say about reality.

Relativistic ontology differs in another important way from the realistic position. A corollary of the realist's Theory of Independence is that it is, in some way, possible to know the thing in and of itself. The philosophical term for this is *Ding-an-sich*, German for "the thing in itself." The very word "relativism" means that reality is relational— that is, things exist in relation to other things. How a thing—or value —exists is dependent on its relationship to what is around it. This particular emphasis in relativistic ontology was borrowed from psychology and physics. Whether an object is taken to be heavy depends to a considerable extent on what "heavy" is related to. A book is not heavy in relation to a boulder but is heavy in relation to a feather. Paper is inflammable, but relatively inflammable: magnesium is much more inflammable.

Reality is relational in another sense. Whatever is taken to exist is dependent also on *who* is perceiving the reality and how he is seeing it. "That is, a thing is perceived as a figure against a background, experienced from a given angle or direction of envisionment." The author, who stands barely above five feet, recently asked a friend, whom we shall call Bill, if he had seen Joe. The reply was that Bill didn't know Joe—what did he look like? Joe was described as tall and blond, wearing a dark suit. Further discussion revealed that a man with blond hair and a dark suit was there, but he certainly wasn't tall. In fact, Joe was something like 5'9" tall. To Bill, who is well over six feet, 5'9" is not tall. To the author, 5'9" is tall. Joe was "perceived from a given angle or direction of envisionment," and from this angle of envisionment, was taken to be tall.

Implications for Education

Relativists reject the theoretical positions and the teaching methods of both idealists and realists. The latter place too much emphasis on acquainting students with pre-existing bodies of knowledge, whether the knowledge has any relationship to students' purposes or not. The former elevate the student's world of meaning to an absolute. Relativists believe that teaching is a matter equally of knowledge and of attention to the conditions of the learner and the learning process.

In brief, relativistic metaphysics implies emphasis on *inquiry*. The aim is to develop the capacity to inquire, to learn how to ask questions. In Dewey's words, "What can be done . . . is to cultivate those *attitudes* that are favorable to the use of the best methods of inquiry.[28] This educational aim follows quite logically from the ontological position. If absolutes and ultimates are rejected, and if reality is an affair of both knower and what is known, then the teaching is a *both-and* matter: an emphasis on *both* students *and* knowledge.

Method and Content In general, relativists reject the separation of curriculum and teaching method. Such a separation, they con-

[28] *John Dewey on Education, Selected Writings,* edited by Reginald Archambault (New York: Modern Library, 1964), p. 224. This is an excellent collection of some of Dewey's most important writings on education. The original is John Dewey, *How We Think* (Boston: Heath, 1933), an analysis of the thought process as it relates to education.

tend, reflects the realist's tendency to divide a body of knowledge from how it is taught and learned. Dewey and his followers have been in general agreement that what is taught and how it is taught form a unity. The problem of teaching method, says Dewey, is one of forming habits and attitudes:

... The problem of method in forming habits of reflective thought is the problem of establishing conditions that will arouse and guide *curiosity;* of setting up the connections in things experienced that will on later occasions promote the flow of suggestions, create problems and purpose that will favor *consecutiveness* in the succession of ideas.[29]

What is the relativist's definition of content? The traditional view, which in American schools is usually based on realistic premises, is that content is largely a collection of facts, principles, skills, and values, divided along lines established by subject-matter experts. Such an approach to content is seen by two relativistic theorists as "sometimes artificial and a handicap to vital research." [30] Instead, "the content of learning may be regarded as the data of acts of reflective thought." [31] Valid content is "everything a thinker brings to bear on a problem."

Thus content and method are not separate but two elements of an interactive process. Both content and method flow from the relativistic ontological assumption of interaction. In the same sense that a person interacts with his environment to arrive at insights into reality, teaching is an interactive process in which students learn to inquire— that is, to solve problems.

Thus the teacher is not an ideal person whom students are to emulate in order to arrive at ultimate reality; nor is he an objective provider of pre-established subject matter. He is rather a more experienced person who attempts to guide the reflective thinking of students. Although most relativists would say that *any* technique that effectively raises a genuine problem and leads toward answers which "satisfy the inherent conditions of the problem" is acceptable, the relativist tends to rely heavily on free-flowing but structured discussion.

Discussion—give-and-take exchange between teacher and students—is designed to raise problems, clarify positions, introduce and explore relative data, and induce critical thinking on the part of both students and teacher. If this is a valid description of relativistic method, it is, presumably, appropriate to all subjects and all age levels. Such

[29] Archambault, p. 230.
[30] Maurice Hunt and Lawrence Metcalf, *Teaching High School Social Studies* (New York: Harper, 1955), p. 193.
[31] *Ibid.,* p. 214. The authors are discussing the teaching of social studies, but their comments are also appropriate to curriculum in general.

a position does not rule out lectures, field trips, drill, demonstration—
or any other technique. As long as the teaching is based on the prob-
lem-solving method, any appropriate technique is acceptable.

Evaluation The relativist's position on evaluation follows from
his assumption that one's judgments are essentially *inventions*. What
one says about reality is a construct, not to be taken as absolute, objective description, but as human interpretation. A grade or any other
evaluation is one's own interpretation.

A teacher was heard to assert that he is in no way responsible
for a student's grade. A student, he maintained, either answers a question correctly or he does not. A student makes a mark of 50 or he makes
one of 90. In any case, the grade is simply a report of what the student
did. This is not the relativist's position. The relativist remembers that
the evaluation (which is *not* a measurement in the strict sense) is of
the teacher's devising. The questions employed are the teacher's. The
grading reflects the teacher's interpretation of how well the student
did. It is hoped that the teacher's interpretation is a good one—that is,
fair and defensible. But this is only a hope and not an unqualified
assertion.

The relativist's evaluation reflects the influence of the scientific
method, for it is concerned with adequacy in the light of obtainable
data. An answer is good to the extent to which it (1) is in harmony
with obtainable data, and (2) is adequate—that is, reflects as much of
the obtainable data as is reasonable to expect. If this strikes one as
vague and much less precise than, say, the realist's criterion, the relativist would reply that it appears to be as precise as one can humanly
make it.

In a real sense, a teacher's evaluation is also an evaluation of how
well he has taught. This belief arises from relativistic value theory (to
be considered in the next chapter), which states that a value judgment
goes two ways: it judges an object and also the one who makes the
judgment. An examination, therefore, should be scrutinized carefully
by the teacher. Probably it will result in a change in future teaching,
for the relativistic teacher gains insight into what he did not teach
or what he did not sufficiently emphasize, what he taught that was
not perceived clearly. That is, an evaluation is also a device for bringing about change in teaching.

The Value of Metaphysics for Teachers

It should be clear that the particular ontological position one
adopts has considerable bearing on the teaching process. People do

not simply perceive *all* that exists. Rather, there is a selective process in which whatever exists is filtered through one's rather variable perceptions. One selects from an infinity of things, events, situations, and values what he wishes to accept as reality.

Obviously, too, one can be heavily predisposed to accept one *kind* of reality over another. And one is predisposed to accept one method of *knowing* reality over another. Differences of opinion, differences in interest, and differences in values seem to reflect differences in what one takes to be reality. C. P. Snow's observation that there are actually two cultures—the world of science and the world of aesthetics—suggests that some people consider art, literature, and music as somehow more or less *real* than physics, biology, and chemistry.

If one's ontological position, even if unconsciously held, influences choices, preferences, values and behavior, then teachers ought to be aware of what a given ontological position means. That teachers, by and large, do not possess such awareness is evidenced in the recurring and extremely vexing problems they have when confronted by ambiguous and unclear situations.

The matter of grading is a case in point. Teachers are constantly made unhappy every grading period. What does one do with the bright student who does not "work up to capacity" and still achieves at a high level, relatively speaking? How does one grade the student who does well in assignments but is uncooperative, obnoxious, and disturbing in every classroom? What kind of grade should go to the child who tries hard and is cooperative, sincere, and pleasant—but still does failing work? The truth of the matter is that teachers generally do not know what a grade should mean. The usual definition of a grade is that it is or ought to be an accurate measurement of achievement, one that objectively indicates how well a student is doing. Such a definition reflects a realistic ontological position. But such a definition—although an official one which conforms closely to much educational thinking— is simply too troublesome to live with. In practice, teachers are constantly "bootlegging" a variety of desirable character traits that, presumably, ought to have nothing to do with an objective grade. The result is that grading theory reflects one ontological position and grading desires reflect a variety of theories.

The problem of student interpretation is equally disturbing. To what extent should students be allowed to "interpret" material? In what classes is student interpretation appropriate? What is "guidance," and when does guidance become "indoctrination"? This problem is, at base, also a metaphysical one, for it reflects confusion about the ontological status of values. Interpretation—or appraisal and evaluation—are essentially matters of value judgment. But what is the onto-logical status of a value?

One of the knottiest problems in education today—though it is not usually recognized as a problem—is what to do with controversial issues. One cultural pattern in our democracy calls for the fullest, widest, and freest discussion of all controversial issues. Another cultural pattern reflects the belief that schools should hand down an official position. When schools are viewed as transmitters of an official position, there are no controversial issues; the teacher decides for students what position they *ought* to hold. But if schools are seen as places where students learn to make their own decisions, controversial issues must be discussed in the classroom. When there is no official, orthodox position, the assumption is that there is no ultimate reality; that reality is something to be decided again and again. Such a position is relativistic, and although it lies at the basis of democratic theorizing, a teacher can find himself without a job for having allowed students to discuss sex, communism, racial problems—or any other problem deemed "controversial."

In short, selection of curriculum, choice of teaching methods and techniques, grading, and administration practices are educational matters whose understanding requires, first of all, knowledge of different metaphysical theories.

Metaphysical Conflict

One thing seems fairly clear: there is no "perfect" metaphysical system, for any metaphysical position is capable of being criticized—even devastated. Depending on one's metaphysical position, any other metaphysical system can be shown to be weak, faulty, inconsistent, or downright ridiculous.

From the standpoint of any absolute metaphysical system, the theory and practice of relativism are extremely vulnerable to attack. Realists criticize relativists for not acknowledging the existence of independent reality. Idealists criticize them for restricting their metaphysics to the implications of the scientific method. Neo-Thomists cannot accept the relativist's disinclination to accept a divinity who is absolute. Relativists cannot answer these criticisms on the critics' own terms. Ultimately, the relativist says, I accept a theory of reality that is non-absolute and based on the scientific method because *this is the way reality appears to me.*

The relativist's distinction between an assumption and an assertion also is found wanting by other philosophers. If something is real, why not go all the way and assert it? Why assume it? The relativist's answer is scarcely designed to soothe a realist. The distinction, says the relativist, between an "assumption" and an "assertion" is critical. To assume is to act *as if* something *were* true. The relativist does indeed act as if there were an independent existence but, for the reasons given above, he does not wish to go all the way and assert it. The relativist feels that his knowledge does not warrant asserting that reality is indeed precisely as he says it is.

Educational philosophers differ considerably as to the kinds of practices that are supposed to flow from the different positions. Breed, for instance, criticizes the relativist's emphasis on change,[32] and asserts that a construct theory of reality simply does not allow for an inescapable fact: that certain things and relations are stable. The relativist's emphasis on change, it is charged, leads to a curriculum in which permanency—and hence continuity—is all but impossible. Relativists, it is further asserted, emphasize inquiry, but at the expense of the *objects* of inquiry—true knowledge.

Nor are idealists any happier with relativistic metaphysics. Without "ideals"—that is, absolute ideals—there are no true standards. While, to be sure, standards do change, there are still eternal truths and values, and to forsake them because they are, in a narrow sense, unprovable, is to forsake all standards. Without absolutes, it is charged, everything goes. Nothing is right or wrong. To this relativists answer that people's definitions of values and standards change, modify, and shift to such an extent that absolutes do not appear to be warrantable in human experience. Instead of functioning as ideals, as supremely important goals, absolutes tend simply to hide one's motivations from himself: one talks about an absolute, but does what appears to be expedient.

As far as content and method are concerned, there is still no agreement at the level of either theory or practice. Realistic philosophers may state that human experience clearly proves that certain reliable and truthful knowledge exists. What, then, is wrong with teaching it as such? This is not to say that *all* knowledge is truthful and reliable. But certainly some knowledge is. True education is the transmission of knowledge, with appropriate designations as to what is doubtful, what is probable, and what is certain.

But philosophers of a relativistic orientation simply fall back on their ontological position: probability is about as far as man can go. Knowledge may be extremely probable, but nothing has yet turned up to convince them that certainty is possible or even desirable. Thus

[32] "Education and the Realistic Outlook," p. 132.

the focus on teaching ought not be on the transmission of some body of knowledge presumed to be certain but rather on developing habits of mind which lead to better modes of inquiry.

These disagreements and conflicts are not likely to be settled in this century. They are not likely to be resolved even in the golden future, when more adequate knowledge is available. For the disagreements are based not on the amount or kind of evidence that can be turned up but, in the final analysis, on what one takes as his reality.

QUESTIONS FOR DISCUSSION

1. Explain briefly why it is important for teachers to be aware of their metaphysical assumptions.

2. What are the metaphysical presuppositions behind a statement such as "California has some lovely scenery"? What about the statement "John is in authority around here; so do as he tells you"?

3. What is an ideal boy friend or girl friend? What is an ideal student? Are you likely to encounter either? Is there any value in knowing in what an ideal consists?

4. Compile a list of some common dualisms. Is there any difficulty in dividing reality into two, usually opposite, elements?

5. How does Aristotle's notion of causes differ from the current scientific concept of causality?

6. Ask a scientist the following question: "To what extent does science today depart from Newtonian assumptions?" What is his answer?

7. Berkeley's theory of reality is usually regarded as preposterous by those who hear it for the first time. If it is so absurd, why have so many philosophers felt it necessary to counter it?

8. What metaphysical assumptions underlie the system of letter or number grades? Offering art and drama to young students? Including science in the curriculum? The usual organization of school administration?

9. Can you find traces of Natural Law theory in the thinking of those who assert that ethics today are at a new low, that the world is becoming more immoral?

10. Does man *need* absolutes? Why or why not?

11. What practical objections would you have to relativistic ontology in education? What theoretical objections?

12. What evidence is there that current educational practices are supported by a number of different metaphysical positions?

SUGGESTED READINGS

BERKELEY, GEORGE. *Principles of Human Knowledge.* The Irish bishop George Berkeley had a readable literary style, unlike most metaphysicians. This essay is a brief treatment of a topic that is ultimately the most controversial issue in human thought.

COPLESTON, FREDERICK. *A History of Philosophy,* Volume I, Part II. New York: Doubleday, 1962. In this work there is a lengthy but clear discussion of the structure and meaning of Aristotle and Plato. The author's opinions are not shared by all philosophers.

DEWEY, JOHN. *Reconstruction in Philosophy.* New York: Henry Holt, 1920. This is an analysis of traditional metaphysical systems in the light of the insights of history, anthropology, and sociology. Dewey attempts to relate philosophy to the social, economic, and political currents in Western civilization.

GILSON, ETIENNE. *The Spirit of Thomism.* New York: P. J. Kenedy, 1964. This is a fairly simplified version of neo-Thomism by one of the better known interpreters of Catholic philosophy.

LOCKE, JOHN. *Essay Concerning Human Understanding.* In this summary of the principles of scientific realism, written at the end of the seventeenth century, there is an incisive treatment of the empiricist's position regarding our understanding of the external world.

LOVEJOY, ARTHUR O. *The Great Chain of Being.* New York: Harper and Row, 1960. This work, one of the first attempts to treat intellectual history, is a discussion of the influence of *hierarchy* in Western thinking. The author traces the concept from Greek civilization to the twentieth century.

PLATO. *The Republic.* This dialogue, along with the *Theatatus,* the *Phaedrus,* and the *Symposium,* contains Plato's attempt to construct a metaphysical position. Contrast it with the heavy and precise treatment of Aristotle's *Metaphysics.* Read both works with the assistance of Copleston's history.

5

Education as a Value Enterprise

Conflicting Value Systems

A culture transmits more than knowledge and skills. All cultures pass on attitudes, beliefs, wishes, desires, and other modes of thought synonymous with values. Our culture, which is a blend of values from many cultural traditions, often confronts an individual with the problem of which one of the many values he should choose. Ordinarily his choice is not a deliberate one. Since he learns his cultural heritage, usually, without being aware that he is doing so, he tends to be unaware also that he is facing a conflict of values and that he must choose. Typically, also, individuals swing from one value orientation to another without being aware that there are differences in values and that they have made a switch.

In one town, the written philosophy of the school board stated that all extracurricular activities must be justified as having educational value. But a board member was quoted in the local newspaper as saying that the community high school needed a new gym "if we are to make a good showing in league competition." [1] When the school-board philosophy was written, doubtless the writers were sincere in their statement that educational values should be the chief considera-

[1] S. Samuel Shermis and Donald C. Orlich, "Educational Philosophy as Mythology: A Critical Analysis of School Philosophies," *Administrator's Notebook*, 14 (December, 1965).

tion in any extracurricular activity. Doubtless, too, the board member was sincere when he urged the townspeople to vote for a new gym for reasons that had nothing to do with education. It seems unlikely that anyone was aware of the switch in orientation. The effect of the contradiction is to make the school board appear hypocritical, but it is doubtful that hypocrisy was involved.

Another board philosophy stated that the educational system was based on the belief that all children, regardless of race, religion, or creed, should receive equal educational opportunities; but his school system was required to integrate its schools by the federal government with the aid of armed troops! [2]

These two incidents illustrate the consequences of value conflict in our culture. Since we often find it difficult to decide what is truly valuable, large sections of our culture work at cross purposes with one another. The problem is similar to that of the individual: he is sometimes at cross purposes with himself, for whatever he chooses, he may be tormented by the feeling that he should have made another choice. Let us consider the nature of differing value systems within our culture and then explore the implications for education.

Dualistic Value Systems

One important value system in our culture comes from the ancient Judeo-Christian tradition, a tradition marked by belief that true goodness lies in renunciation of the pleasures of the world and denial of one's selfish desires. This value orientation, essentially an ascetic one, is based on the metaphysical assumption that a higher and purer reality is found in the spiritual. In practice the system has emphasized the denial of sexual pleasure, of rich food, of play, and of other experiences most people have found gratifying. In this country, these beliefs were modified to include other kinds of values. The early American Protestant ethic—the socioeconomic value system associated with the seventeenth- and eighteenth-century New England Puritans—included emphasis on thrift, hard work, sobriety, and strict religious morality.

Another value orientation in our society derives from an ancient classical tradition called *hedonism*. As originally formulated, hedonism was a belief that man should seek satisfaction of his desires. Eventually the concept became corrupted to mean that the highest value lay in satisfaction of fleshly desires. In our culture there are many evidences of hedonism, from the almost total emphasis in television on entertainment to the buy-now-pay-later economic pattern. Adver-

[2] *Ibid.*

tising constantly urges people to satisfy their desires, and super-
markets are filled with exotic foods so arranged as to create "impulse"
buying. The sexual motif is so strong and pervasive that it seems almost a national compulsion. The fundamental assumption behind all
these cultural manifestations is that it is not incompatible with man's
best existence for him to satisfy his normal fleshly desires. Indeed,
our economy is geared not simply to meet existing demands but to
create new and ever-widening desires. Hedonistic philosophy, which
states that desires exist to be satisfied, and the ascetic belief that self-
denial is always to be preferred have tended to create a culture that
at the same time smiles and frowns on pleasure. For the individual
it is almost never clear whether certain of his desires are valid, whether
he is being unnaturally materialistic and self-indulgent or simply
normal.

Another dualistic value orientation is the individual-social conflict. Our culture has a long history of exalting something called the
"individual." From James Fennimore Cooper's Leatherstocking and
Deerslayer to Mickey Spillane's private eye, there has been a persistent
belief that the lone, independent, self-reliant person is the finest creation of nature. Many value traditions have grown up around this
image, as illustrated by the belief that the government ought not to
interfere with the individual's economic activities, and by the many
Supreme Court decisions which acknowledge that unpopular, eccentric, perhaps even potentially destructive individuals have a right to
live free from official restraint.

In recent years, however, there has developed another value
orientation treated in such books as *The Man in the Gray Flannel
Suit* and *The Organization Man*.[3] The core of this value orientation
is that the organization is more important than the individual; that
when individual desire and corporate interest conflict, the corporation
should dominate; that one ought to work enthusiastically and coopera-
tively on a "team"; that by submerging oneself in the group, one will
receive the benefits of economic security and prestige. Although the
former orientation is dying, it is still celebrated formally, and although
the latter is pervasive and powerful, it is not recognized for what it
actually is.

Examples such as these can be multiplied. Some kind of sanction
can be found for almost every conceivable value. As a consequence,
what is desirable, what is good and evil, what one should do, what

[3] Sloan Wilson, *The Man in the Gray Flannel Suit* (New York: Pocket Books,
1956) and William H. Whyte, *The Organization Man* (New York: Simon and
Schuster, 1956).

ought to be preferred, are very often in doubt. If values were not a controversial subject, there would be no need for this chapter. But since values are in dispute, it is of central importance for teachers—who are constantly occupied with the transmission of values—to study the origin, nature, and validation of values. Only to the extent to which teachers are aware of what is to be preferred can they effect changes in behavior that will have relevance in the world as it exists.

Education and Value Conflict

The inability of our culture to provide a clear and consistent system of values is, in part, responsible for the conflicts in educational theory described in the last chapter. Value conflicts in education are of concern to more than the philosopher or psychologist; they have had rather serious effects on almost every activity in our public schools.

First and perhaps most serious is the tendency to divorce educational values from educational practice. Many people within school systems talk at length about democracy, respect for individuality, and the significance and importance of knowledge. The values practiced, however, tend to be the reverse of those verbalized. There is no particular evidence that administrative procedures are democratic, and much evidence to suggest that they are undemocratic and authoritarian. Instead of the verbalized respect for individuality, both students and teachers find themselves enmeshed in webs of rules and regulations which have little to do with individuality but which typify enforced and thoughtless conformity. The verbalized respect for knowledge sounds hollow in the light of the starved budgets for school libraries, as contrasted with what is spent on athletic exhibitions. Value conflict here is reflected in a clear separation between verbalized values and practiced values.[4]

Second, the cultural conflict involving values makes any educational judgment unclear. For instance, to pronounce a child "lazy" may elicit the reply that he is not lazy but only "relaxed." Since a relaxed nature is supposedly valuable in a tense world, what is wrong with being relaxed? Another disputed judgment concerns the exact role of the parent with regard to a child's schoolwork. Is the mother who expresses concern for her child's grades overprotective and overconcerned, or ought she to be praised for taking an intelligent interest? Another judgment that could be readily contested concerns the teacher

---

[4] This point is elaborated by Van Cleve Morris in "Axiology: The Question of Value," *Philosophy and the American School* (Boston: Houghton Mifflin, 1961), where a distinction is made between "conceived" and "operative" values. The former are values which people believe in and openly profess, but do not necessarily practice. The latter values are those actually practiced.

who covers a subject thoroughly and carefully. This may be commendable in the eyes of many but damned as an evasion of the teacher's obligation to provide for individual differences by appealing to preferences and curiosities not touched on in the careful coverage of subject matter. The point is that the lack of agreement about most cultural values renders any educational judgment a matter of dispute.

Third, the lack of cultural consensus reduces considerably the meaning of goals, aims, or ideals. A goal or aim is a summary of the most important value associated with a given activity. When goals are in conflict, what is to be desired is in doubt. Within our culture even the supreme goal of human life is unclear. In the Middle Ages the good person was one who had emancipated himself from the frantic desire for material possessions and had learned to cultivate inner serenity. His thoughts were fixed on God, almost to the exclusion of concern with life on this earth. Today the good person may also be considered one who has accomplished something tangible and important, someone who labored mightily to found an industrial empire, or to organize an important business, or to invent a labor-saving device.[5] The question, then, is: Who is the good person, the one who develops serenity and peace of mind and disregards fame, praise, material objects, power, and wealth; or the one who has expended great energy to accomplish something socially useful? We may say both, but we probably never mean both.

Similarly, educational goals are not particularly clear. There are a number of questions about supremely important educational values. What knowledge is of the most worth? To what end should knowledge be used? Are there any really permanent artistic values, and if so, how does one know them? Which personality traits are important and which only superficial? It is precisely these questions that each teacher must sooner or later decide for himself. It is also precisely these questions which constitute *axiology,* the philosophical term for the study of values.

Axiology

Axiology—as is true of many other technical terms in philosophy— is derived from two Greek words meaning *values* and *study of.* Axiology takes as its subject matter the origin, meaning, nature, and

---

[5] Two books discuss the conflict between the older religious ethic and the modern one which has been influenced by industrialism and capitalism. See Roger H. Tawney, *Religion and the Rise of Capitalism* (New York: New American Library, 1958) and Marquis W. Childs and Douglas S. Cater, *Ethics in a Business Society* (New York: New American Library, 1959).

structure of values. Philosophers concerned with axiological problems ask such questions as: What is a value? Where do values come from? How do we justify our values? How do we know what is valuable? What is the relationship between values and knowledge? What kinds of values exist? Can it be demonstrated that one value is better than another?

Let us turn to the question "What is a value?" Philosophers see the apparently simple act of defining the term as anything but simple. The term *value* may be defined in two ways: as "valuable" or as "valued." It makes considerable difference which definition is used, for although the two appear to be the same, there is a difference between what is valued and what is valuable.

Something that is valued is an object of desire. To be valued means to be wanted, esteemed, or prized. If the term *value* is equated with *valued*, then a value is anything that is desired by anyone. If one wants, wishes, esteems, or prizes oysters, power, or money, then these are objects of desire. One may desire them in different ways or in different degrees of intensity, but they function as values.

On the other hand, *valuable* connotes, not specific desire but desirability. The sentence "X is valuable" means not that I actually desire X but that I *should* desire X. To assert that X is desirable is to assert that it *should* function as an object of desire.

The problem raised by these two ways of defining *value* is that what one does value is not always what one should value. In effect, then, the desired and the desirable are not the same. One may wish to rob a bank but most of us would say that stealing is not desirable, that no one should *want* to steal. The distinction between what is desired and what is desirable is not only a difference of definition but a distinction between two different ways of philosophizing about values. Whether one defines a value as the desired or as the desirable is a clue to one's entire philosophy. Generally, philosophers and philosophical schools choose one or the other of the two definitions, but one philosophical position employs both definitions. We shall be considering a representative sampling of different axiological positions.

Ethics and Aesthetics

So long and extensive has been philosophical inquiry into value problems that there has arisen a formal, systematic approach to the subject. Axiology is usually divided into two areas, *ethics* and *aesthetics*. Values or statements about values can usually fit under one or the other of these two categories, though there is a tendency for some twentieth-century philosophers to ignore the categories. In general, *ethics* refers to values in the context of human behavior or conduct. An ethical act is one which has reference to good or desirable behavior. The term *moral* is often used synonymously with *ethical,* but there are a number of distinctions between them. One difference, discussed by Aristotle, is that while *ethics* refers to the *theory* of behavior, *moral* refers to the *practice.* In another sense, the term *moral* refers to any judgment of good or bad arising from a social matrix. *Ethics* may also have the meaning of a particular, specialized code of behavior, such as medical ethics or the ethics of the teaching profession. In its most general sense, an ethical judgment is any evaluative statement about human behavior.

Aesthetics is concerned with value judgments about what is beautiful or what is judged to be art. While related to it, a theory of art is conceptually different from a judgment of beauty. Something may be considered art without eliciting the judgment that it is also beautiful, and vice versa. Aesthetics is directly relevant to teaching, for, as we have seen, teachers often make appraisals that fall within the area of aesthetics. Not only are literature and music within the purview of aesthetics, but the teacher who insists on neatness in written work or who requests that Susy pin her hair back and that Junior use his handkerchief is making aesthetic prescriptions.

The Value Theory of Aristotle

The value theory of Aristotle, which is organically linked to his metaphysics, has been extremely influential in the intellectual history of Western civilization for two milennia. Without being particularly aware of it, most of us subscribe to some portion of Aristotle's thinking about values.

Aristotle distinguishes between two types of values.[6] One is that which is good for something and the other, that which is good in and of itself. The first type of value is called a *means.* A means is a good whereby some other good is to be realized. This distinction is still made: we commonly say, for instance, that eating a balanced diet is good *because* it helps one maintain good health. Eating the right food is a means, a good, whereby health, the higher good, is realized. Of course, health may be a means to some other, even higher good.

Aristotle also distinguishes between ends and *the* end. "Since there are evidently more than one end, and we choose some of these

[6] Aristotle, *Nicomachean Ethics,* Book I in *Great Books of the Western World* (Chicago: Encyclopaedia Britannica, 1952), Vol. 9, p. 339.

for the sake of something else, clearly not all ends are final ends." [7] There is a chief good "which is evidently something final. Therefore, if there is only one final end, this will be what we are seeking." For Aristotle, the final end is that which is worth pursuing for its own sake, that which is ultimately and finally good in and of itself. What is this final good? "Happiness, then, is something final and self-sufficient, and is the end of action." [8]

Aristotle is quite aware that *happiness* is a vague term and that simply to state that happiness is the final end of man is to utter a platitude. One must specify what happiness consists in. At this point his axiology is linked with his metaphysics. To discover the true meaning of happiness of any given thing, we must discover the function of that thing. If the true function of a piano tuner is to tune pianos, the function is realized when the piano tuner tunes pianos well. The good piano tuner—like anything else we call "good"—is the one who best realizes his function. The belief that (1) there is a true function of anything and, (2) goodness consists in realizing that true function, is the core of Aristotelian axiology. Stated another way, Aristotle asserts that a particular class of things has a purpose assigned to it in the very nature of reality and that goodness consists in best realizing this purpose. [9]

What is the highest function of man? If we know this, we can discover man's true happiness. We must first discover what is unique about man. His uniqueness certainly does not lie in the fact that he takes in nutriment, for all living things do this. Nor is growth unique to man. What is unique in man, says Aristotle, is that he possesses the capacity to be rational. Man alone in this world is capable of reason. Only man can take hold of an idea and see that it is necessarily so. He can deduce the consequences of an idea and, what is most important, he can know that he is doing this. In short, man can self-consciously understand that he is reasoning. It is the capacity to reason that distinguishes man from all other beings. The capacity to reason Aristotle calls the "rational principle." Therefore, happiness, "the best, noblest and most pleasant thing in the world, lies in the most perfect development of man's completely unique function: in the perfection of his rational capacity." [10]

Happiness extends, then, just so far as contemplation does, and those to whom contemplation more fully belongs are more truly happy, not as a

[7] *Ibid.*, p. 342.
[8] *Ibid.*, p. 343.
[9] *Ibid.*
[10] *Ibid.*

mere concomitant but in virtue of the contemplation; for this is in itself precious. Happiness, therefore, must be some form of contemplation.[11]

To recapitulate: There are goods and *the* good. The former are means and the latter ends. The highest good exists when a thing realizes its proper end. The proper end of man is the development of his rational capacity, that which makes him unique among animals. For man, to think, to contemplate, is to reach his highest goal, his truest happiness.

Teleology and Goodness

The reader must have noted the thoroughgoing teleology throughout Aristotle's discussion of values.[12] For Aristotle, some final purpose —the Greek word is *telos*—guides the destiny of everything. Nothing exists without a purpose; there is no "blind" chance, no unordered or purposeless event. Even inanimate objects exist for a purpose. "Nature makes nothing incomplete, and nothing is in vain." [13]

To discover what purpose exists in any given thing is also to discover the way in which its highest good may be realized. To discover the function or purpose of an alarm clock is to see that a good alarm clock is one that lets loose its unwelcome sound surely and thoroughly. To discover man's special function and unique nature is to glimpse his natural tendency: to be rational. To develop this natural tendency —to improve his capacity to reason well—is man's highest goodness, his supreme happiness.

Goodness and value lie in the realization of natural tendency. Conversely, badness, perversion, and evil lie in the frustration or lack of realization of natural tendency.

Canaries show no urge to swim or ducks to sing, for swimming is not natural to canaries or singing to ducks. But man is constantly desiring to do that for which he is not endowed by nature. In pursuing what is unnatural, man falls into evil. This evil may involve an excess —for instance, carrying courage so far that it becomes blind foolhardiness. Evil may also involve the betrayal of man's natural intellectual capacities—for instance, when one drinks so much that his words and actions become irrational.[14]

[11] *Ibid.*, p. 43.
[12] Recall the discussion in chapter 3 of Aristotle's theory of entelechy. Purpose exists within a thing and is realized as the thing develops.
[13] Aristotle, *Politics*, in *Great Books of the Western World*, Book I, p. 446.
[14] See Aristotle's discussion of the various virtues and vices in his *Ethics*, Books III through IX.

Aesthetic Judgments

Aristotle's beliefs about the nature of art and of aesthetic judgments have been as influential as his ethical theory. His theory is often designated "art as imitation," but "imitation" does not carry the meaning of a carbon copy of reality. In his *Poetics* Aristotle explains that imitation is not simple photographic reproduction. Rather, the artist reproduces the *essence* of someone or something.[15] This implies that the artist should avoid irrelevant flaws or imperfections, as not of the essence. Thus the artist is to reproduce the thing as it would be if it were perfectly developed. In his description of the form and function of tragic plays, the dramatist ought to use a "higher type" of person as the hero—that is, a member of the nobility, not an ordinary person.[16] In Aristotle's words,

> Again, since Tragedy is an imitation of persons who are above the common level, the example of good portrait-painters should be followed. They, while reproducing the distinctive form of the original, make a likeness which is true to life and yet more beautiful. So too the poet, in representing men who are irascible or indolent, or have other defects of character, should preserve the type and yet ennoble.[17]

That Aristotle's theories in physics, political science, metaphysics, science, and other disciplines have influenced the course of Western thought in the last two thousand years has been adequately documented. Aristotle's theories of art, music, poetry, and drama were derived from contemporary Greek culture, of course. In formulating compact, systematic, and logically arranged aesthetic theories, Aristotle, in effect, bequeathed a Greek artistic preference to his successors throughout the Western world.

What art as imitation has meant in practice is flawless landscapes depicting unimaginably lovely pastoral scenes, statues of superbly muscled warriors, and poetry celebrating the actions of valiant men and beautiful women. Until the nineteenth century, people were accustomed to a stylized art, marked by balance, symmetry, proportion, predictably arranged and always designed to elevate.

In recent times, of course, artists have moved away from art as imitation or as celebration of noble traits. Contemporary poets and painters celebrate not only the noble or heroic, but the commonplace. Dramatists write tragedies not only about the "higher type" advocated

[15] Aristotle, *Poetics*, in *Great Books of the Western World*, Vol. 9, Chapters I, II and III.
[16] *Ibid.*, Chapter II.
[17] *Ibid.*, Chapter XV.

by Aristotle, but also about disturbed traveling salesmen. Painters and sculptors have moved away from photographic imitation and have tried to express what the subject means to them. In this process the traditional canons and rules of art have been either modified or discarded. Poetry does not have to scan. Music does not have to have melody. Novels need not contain plots. Stage characters may speak all their lines from a garbage can. Picasso may depict a woman, not from one perspective, but from three sides at once.

What has occurred is a radical departure from an Aristotelian theory of art which established fixed rules and regulations, which defined in detail precisely what tragedy, for instance, was and was not, which insisted that the true function of art was to celebrate an idealized and ennobled reality. But most Americans are considerably removed from direct participation in contemporary art and literature and still think in Aristotelian assumptions about art. Thus we are faced with the phenomenon of an artistically creative class operating in a manner which is generally at variance with the aesthetic values and understanding of the public.

The Implications of Aristotelian Axiology for Education

It is a matter of considerable surprise for many to realize that Aristotelian axiology, combined with metaphysics, is still a vital force in education today. Despite the influences of many other intellectual forces and of democracy, industrialism, and science, Aristotelianism— albeit in changed form—is still playing a considerable role in education and educational theory.

The former Chancellor of the University of Chicago, Robert M. Hutchins, assisted by Mortimer Adler, a professor of philosophy, is known for an educational theory stressing the importance of Great Books. The Great Books consist of those enduring works of literature, philosophy, and science which are seen as embodying the most important ideas of the Western world. It has been suggested that the Great Books can constitute the total curriculum for the college years, and such a program has been attempted in a few institutions of higher education. The assumption is that higher education—if not all education—exists solely and exclusively to develop the intellect. The ideas and literary expression to be found in the Great Books are taken to be the most adequate method of developing the intellect.

Obviously both Hutchins and Adler are operating under Aristotelian assumptions concerning the nature of reality and the purpose or end of education. Says Adler,

The *ultimate* ends of education are the same for all men at all times and everywhere. They are absolute and universal principles. This can be proved. If it could not be proved, there would be no philosophy of education at all, for philosophy does not exist unless it is absolute and universal knowledge . . .[18]

Such knowledge, says Adler, is absolute, "not relative to the circumstances of time and place." It is "universal . . . in the sense that it is concerned with essentials and abstracts from every sort of merely accidental variation." [19]

Adler, and those of like mind, know clearly and certainly the ends of education and, knowing them, are able to know also the means by which the ends are to be achieved. Their educational philosophy is based on Aristotle's assumption that the highest educational good comes from realizing the natural and unique function of man: the cultivation of his rational powers.[20]

Although the Great Books idea and the philosophy on which it is based are not particularly influential at the public-school level, they are apparently considerably more important at the level of college and university training. Many professors accept such an Aristotelian position, though in varying degrees. College instructors often believe that the central purpose of a higher education lies in the development of the students' intellectual capacities. A particularly sharp conflict arises when students who are not intellectually oriented and who perceive a college or university education as essentially vocational training study under teachers with quite different goals.

Some of the tag ends of Aristotelian value theory are still found in public education. The Aristotelian division between the fine and the practical arts is often retained in high schools. The fine arts, Aristotle believed, are ends in themselves, as distinguished from the practical arts, which are means to a higher end. Often the curriculum of art education is similarly divided, certain students being assigned to work in painting, drawing and art appreciation—the "fine" arts—and others to leatherwork and metalcraft, the "practical" arts. Needless to say, in such an arrangement the "fine" arts are deemed higher and better than the "practical" ones.

[18] See Mortimer J. Adler, "In Defense of the Philosophy of Education," in *The Forty-first Yearbook of the National Society for the Study of Education, Part I, Philosophies of Education* (Chicago: U. of Chicago Press, 1942), p. 221.

[19] *Ibid.*

[20] This point and other tenets of Hutchins' and Adler's position may be found in an excellent discussion in John P. Wynne, *Theories of Education* (New York: Harper and Row, 1963), Chapter 10.

Similarly, certain subjects are still classified, as was pointed out in the chapter on metaphysics, as inherently more "intellectual" than others. These subjects, usually called "solids," are often viewed as better preparation for college and more appropriate to intelligent children. Therefore, the classification of secondary curriculum into the solids—English, foreign languages, history, mathematics, science—and nonsolids—journalism, home economics, technology, physical education, and so on—reflects, after two thousand years, an Aristotelian dualism.

Mental Discipline

Related to this classification of curriculum is another Aristotelian inheritance known as "formal discipline." Formal discipline, based on a number of Aristotelian theories, is the belief that the mind consists of separate but related faculties, that these faculties can be trained, and that there is an automatic transfer of training. These faculties, often designated memory, will, reason, appreciation, and feeling, were believed to be similar to muscles in that they could be strengthened by exercise. It was further believed that there existed some particular subject or subjects especially useful in developing each faculty. For instance, geometry was deemed useful in training the faculty of reason; history and grammar in developing the faculty of memory; literature, music, and art in developing the faculty of appreciation. Once the faculty was trained—for example, once the memory was trained by the memorization of names and dates of history—then one would be able to exercise it easily in similar situations.

The concept of formal discipline was modified to become the "faculty psychology" of the nineteenth century. Both formal discipline and faculty psychology can be traced to the Aristotelian position that the aim of education consists in the development of man's capacity to be rational. This rational capacity was simply divided into many different subcapacities, and to this was added the notion of subject matter inherently useful in training them. Although twentieth-century psychologists—in particular E. L. Thorndike and his followers—demonstrated the fallacies in the older Aristotelian notion of formal discipline and in the nineteenth-century faculty psychology, the position is by no means extinct. It is still common to read about the need for schools to "train" the mind by requiring mastery of difficult subjects and that certain subjects are inherently unable to provide the necessary training.

One contemporary educational trend, for which Aristotle is only indirectly responsible, is the psychological emphasis on education as habit formation. Aristotle believed that an effective education would

produce persons who were habitually rational and who behaved vir-
tuously out of habit. It is a long step from this notion of habit to Thorndike's theory of stimulus and response, but not as long as it would appear. Seemingly Thorndike's neuromuscular theory, with its emphasis
on the formation of responses, is essentially education conceived as
habit training. Viewed this way, both Aristotle and Thorndike see
education as thinking and behaving in a correct habitual manner.[21]

Finally, one general philosophical stance seems to be derived
from Aristotelian thought. It is widely believed that one purpose of
public education is the improvement of the political life of our country.
Education is seen as proper training for future participation in the
government. Aristotle does not specifically define schools as agents of
social improvement, but the logic of his entire position leads in this
direction. If the function of the state is the creation of virtuous men,
and if education is designed to make men virtuous by developing
their rational capacities, it follows that there is an identity of interests
between education and government. A good education leads directly
to the aim of government—the virtuous or excellent man.

Aristotelianism in Catholic Education

The educational philosophy of the Catholic Church, called neo-
Thomism, is essentially a synthesis of Christian beliefs and Aristotelian
metaphysics and axiology. In the twelfth century St. Thomas Aquinas
crystallized the Church's position with regard to a large number of
theological issues. Although certain Catholic theologians have recently
attempted to emphasize the scriptural basis of the Church, in general
the philosophy of St. Thomas is still regarded as the educational theory
of the Roman Catholic Church. We should note that a number of
Catholic educational practices became accepted by non-Catholic educational systems.

The Origin of Values

Certain values are regarded as absolute, not contingent on the
variations of culture, custom, or purely local practice. These values
were revealed to man by God and are regarded as essential for man's
temporal existence on earth. They are interpreted by God's intermedi-

---

[21] See John P. Wynne, *Theories of Education,* Chapters Four and Five, and also
Robert S. Brumbaugh and Nathaniel M. Lawrence, Jr., "Aristotle's Philosophy of
Education," *Educational Theory,* 9 (January, 1959): 12.

ary on earth, the Church founded by Christ through St. Peter. In the perfect life of Christ there is a model for all ages. By understanding the life of Christ, man has a standard against which he can measure his own life.

Values are arranged hierarchically—that is, in descending order, with the highest, ultimate values on top, and the less important, less binding ones in descending order down the ladder. It is incorrect, therefore, to say that all values are absolute or that all values are equally important. To understand the true nature of values is to see that there is no inherent contradiction among values. For instance, while charity is important, the nurture and protection of one's family is more important. To spend so much time in charitable works that ones family suffers is wrong, for it is more important to care for the family.

There are less important values, of course, including the temporal ones of the culture and those which are reducible to private taste. These values vary according to time and place, but the commandment that one must not commit murder or that one must honor one's parents transcends time and place. While the precise implementation of an absolute value may change as man gains more insight into God's will, the value itself is eternal.

As indicated previously, there is no conflict between the intellect and faith. While man's finite understanding cannot comprehend all of God's plan, his reasoning powers may, in effect, cooperate with and substantiate God's word. By reasoning man can glimpse part of God's meaning, but reason extends only so far. There is a point where faith in the revealed wisdom is essential. Both reason and the findings of the empirical sciences are necessary in their own domain. But certain theological and philosophical questions are not within the domain of science. One cannot empirically demonstrate the necessity of ultimate values or logically prove God's existence. Once this fact is grasped, the seeming contradictions between science and reason and faith are dissolved: science and reason can indeed illuminate certain phases of God's creation.

The Nature of Supreme Values

Supremely important values function in a number of ways. They are, of course, ideals. As one understands these values and practices them in everyday activities, they act as guides, aims, and goals. Because of man's imperfections in both understanding and character, no one achieves the ideal. But the values exist, and at any time one can see what his duty is, what he must do, what he must not do, where he falls short, and how he can improve.

Ultimate values are coercive in that they are binding on all men. One may choose to do or not do certain things, as one may choose certain political candidates or exercise artistic preferences. But the ultimate values are ultimate precisely because they are essential both for man's successful life here and as prerequisites for achieving union with God. They are needed to complete life, to fulfill life on earth in accordance with God's will.

Despite the seemingly infinite variations of individual lives and of individual societies, God's word is binding on all men. That there exist individuals who, knowingly or unknowingly, flout God or that there are Godless societies and wicked governments does not negate either God or his absolutes. Indeed, they may serve to highlight them, for experience has clearly shown that evil individuals and societies create the hell on earth which makes life painful or empty for so many.

While it is always difficult for finite man to understand or interpret precisely what God wishes, it is possible to develop some insight. "When God willed to give existence to creatures, He willed to ordain and direct them to an end." [22] In addition, God willed some direction toward this end. This direction is consonant both with man's free intelligence and with our human nature.

Those actions which conform with its tendencies—i.e., natural tendencies—lead to our destined end. They are thereby constituted right and morally good. Conversely, those actions at variance with our nature are both wrong and immoral. [23]

In this description of Natural Law from an official Catholic viewpoint, the influence of Aristotle is most evident. That the good is discoverable through an understanding of natural tendency is only a slight variation on the Aristotelian position that goodness resides within a thing and is realized as the thing works out its natural destiny.

Educational Practices

Catholic education is both systematic and authoritarian. It is systematic in that it includes a thorough curriculum and educational

[22] See "Natural Law" in *The Catholic Encyclopedia* (New York: Encyclopedia Press, 1913). p. 77.
[23] *Ibid.*

methodology for elementary and secondary schools and colleges and universities.[24] It is authoritarian in that it claims the authority and right to teach certain doctrines and values. Such authority is God-given, and Catholics believe that with the commandment to establish a Church there is included implicitly an ordinance to provide a religious education. Both the authority to transmit values and the content of the values are divinely sanctioned.

The content of the values and beliefs are transmitted first by a catechism, an organized series of questions and answers on certain theological and philosophical topics. Certain dogmas—and only certain ones—are transmitted to older children by textbooks and classes in religion, taught by teaching brothers, nuns, and priests. Although it has become customary to designate certain subjects as secular and certain as religious, the values to be inculcated may be found in textbooks and classes in mathematics, English, and science.[25] This practice is consistent with the belief that religious values should permeate all parts of the curriculum. The preaching performed by priests functions as educational transmission for the mature adult as well as for the child. In a sense, then, a Catholic religious education may be communicated in a wide variety of ways and in diverse settings.

The goal of such training is the creation both of certain habits of virtue and certain intellectual processes. The Catholic response to the Protestant Revolt in the sixteenth century included an increase of and certain changes in educational institutions. One of the changes, as typified in the Port Royal school, was the creation of extremely thorough, systematic, organized teaching procedures. These procedures, many of which survive, are designed to turn out adults who possess the correct beliefs and the correct habits of practice. Belief in the good habits and desirable values, therefore, is not left to chance but is systematically inculcated.

Catholic education as inculcation of values, habits, and practices and modes of thought is not to be separated from the ultimate Catholic goal. This goal is called "beatification" and means union with God. The assumption is that the quality of life on this earth—which includes

[24] For some writings by Catholics on education, see William McGucken, S. J., "The Philosophy of Catholic Education," in *The Forty-first Yearbook of the National Society for the Study of Education*, pp. 251–288; Rachel M. Goodrich, "Neo-Thomism and Education," and Pope Pius XI, "Christian Education of Youth," in Hobert W. Burns and Charles J. Brauner, *Philosophy of Education* (New York: Ronald Press, 1962).

[25] For an interesting discussion of the relationship between Catholic theology and Catholic textbooks, see George LaNoue, "The National Defense Education Act and 'Secular' Subjects," *Phi Delta Kappan*, 43 (June, 1962): 380–387.

faith, knowledge, and acts—is related to eternal salvation. It is of course
not true that any man has certain knowledge about who is to achieve
union with God, for this knowledge is possessed only by God. But
it is reasonable to believe that God's institution on earth has His blessing in educating toward that most important of all goals, eternal salvation. The Church, therefore, can claim both a special mission and God's
sanction in creating religiously directed education toward the Church's
goal on earth, the Christian life.

An Analysis of Aristotelian Axiology in Education

Philosophers from many different schools have criticized the value
theory of Aristotle. It is charged that Aristotelian ethics provides a
deceptive and misleading justification for values. The most seriously
criticized concept is that once one knows the end or purpose of a given
thing or activity, he knows what is good. First, the knowledge of the
final end is gained intuitively. That is, one cannot demonstrate empirically or scientifically that one does indeed know the final purpose
or destiny. Thus one's assertions about destiny or purpose are often
based on nothing more substantial than one's private, unverifiable
hunches.

Second, it is possible for one to be quite mistaken about his estimate of any end. This theory allows one to justify any value as long
as he can claim that it is "natural tendency." One does not have to
defend the value from the standpoint of the consequences of an act.
To have gained private knowledge that the value is natural is defense
enough. This entire position can be called "special pleading," or even
a self-serving argument.

Third, Aristotelian aesthetic categories have served as a retarding
influence on both the creation and public acceptance of art in this
century. If one defines a given art form in precise and rigid terms, as
Aristotle did, there is little room for artistic experimentation. There is
no self-evident reason why literature must "ennoble," why dramatic
heroes must be aristocrats, or why art must be representational. It may
well be that the widespread rejection of twentieth-century art, music,
and literature is due to the gap between the artist's conception of art
and the public's beliefs.

It is a simple matter, as both John Dewey and many anthropologists have pointed out, to confuse observed custom with the "natural."
When one becomes enculturated, the prevalent modes of behavior and
common institutions are taken as natural—that is, the norm for all men
at all times. To defend a value because it is natural or absolute is often

to overlook the fact that supposed absolutes are simply conventions, customs that have become hallowed by time. Slavery, capitalism, and war have been defended as natural; anesthetics, birth control, and democracy have been attacked as unnatural. The argument for and against values based on what is supposed to be natural often amounts to a mechanism which hides one's real motives from himself.

Another criticism of Aristotle's value theory is that it places values beyond critical inquiry. While Aristotle did emphasize the role of the intellect in determining values, his "intellect" is not scientific inquiry based on controlled experience. It is essentially reason defined as a self-enclosed, final process. If either reason or intuition is seen as a complete, final, and infallible guide, and if one's values are believed to be the product of reason, it is not possible either to test values critically or to change them when they are no longer appropriate or serviceable. Finally, when values are placed within the framework of revelation, as they are in Thomism, the combined axiology leads to dogmatism and inflexibility. In effect, either one accepts the dogma or he is lost.

The attribution of a value position to a supernatural source (charged Dewey) is an abdication of human intelligence and invention. The assumption is that, since man is not intelligent enough to determine his own values, he must rely on a higher power for them. This, in effect, places values in the hands of an authority which does not necessarily rule in the best interests of the majority.

Finally, it is charged, the educational practices flowing from an Aristotelian basis tend toward the uncritical acceptance of authority. The systematic indoctrination of certain values, beliefs, dogmas, and goals has been shown to produce persons who passively accept what they are told, who are unable to think independently, and whose thinking tends to be rigid and inflexible.[26]

[26] Dewey's attitude toward this position may be found in a number of his works. See, for instance, *The Quest for Certainty* (New York: Minton, Balch, 1929) and *A Common Faith* (New Haven: Yale U. Press, 1934).

6

Education
as a Value
Enterprise

(CONTINUED)

Subjectivism

A theory of values that stands in sharp contrast to the objective Aristotelian position is *subjectivism*. Subjectivism, briefly stated, is the belief that, in the final analysis, one's values are always a matter of personal preference. The only "desirable" that exists is the desire of the individual. There are many variations of this position, but all of them are reducible to the assertion that any statement of like or dislike is ultimately an expression of someone's feelings and not a statement about anything external.

This position, as we saw in chapters 3 and 4, is not new. The ancient Sophist Protagoras believed that there were objects of perception but that, since perceptions varied widely, ultimate reality could exist only in the perception of some person at some given time and place. "Man," said Protagoras, "is the measure of all things," and since men vary greatly, the value that is used as a measure must necessarily vary. Although the metaphysics of Bishop Berkeley may properly be called subjectivism, it fell to another British philosopher, David Hume, to construct a subjectivist ethical theory.

Hume holds two positions which appear to be contradictory. He asserts that morality is essentially a matter of sentiment or feeling. However, sentiment is not without some kind of objective basis.

The notion of morals implies some sentiment common to all mankind, which recommends the same object to general approbation, and makes every man, or most men, agree in the same opinion or decision concerning it.[1]

In contrast with this statement, which clearly implies a commonly accepted value, Hume is able to reduce moral sentiment to emotion or feeling. Neither blame nor approbation is essentially an activity of rational judgment—though reason does play a part in any judgment. Blame and approval are "of the heart," and as such, are not "a speculative proposition of affirmation, but an active feeling or sentiment." To evaluate something reveals nothing about the object, but only about me and my psychological state.

[W]hen you pronounce any action or character to be vicious, you mean nothing, but that from the constitution of your nature you have a feeling or sentiment of blame from the contemplation of it. Vice and virtue, therefore, may be compared to sounds, colors, heat and cold, which, according to modern philosophy are not qualities in objects, but perceptions in the mind.[2]

Here is Berkeley's assertion that reality is only what is perceived translated by Hume to the realm of ethics.

One receives the distinct impression that some variety of subjectivism has permeated British philosophy from the seventeenth century to the present. In his famous political treatise, *Leviathan,* Thomas Hobbes provides another variation of the belief that value judgments are only expressed preferences:

But whatsoever is the object of any man's appetite or desire, that is it which he for his part calleth good; and the object of his hate and aversion, evil . . . For these words of good, evil and contemptible, are ever used with relation to the person that useth them: there being nothing simply and absolutely so.[3]

In contemporary England, A. J. Ayer has taken the position that, while factual statements may be demonstrated to be either true or false, value judgments cannot be. Ethical statements belong in a limbo of existence, being incapable of objective verification. Morals "are simply expressions of emotion which can be neither true nor false." [4]

Events in the twentieth century have removed subjectivism from the realm of a philosopher's quarrel. Research in other scholarly dis-

[1] David Hume, *An Inquiry Concerning the Principles of Morals,* Section IX, Part 1.

[2] Hume, *A Treatise of Human Nature,* Book III, Section 1.

[3] Quoted in Michael Curtis, *The Great Political Theories* (New York: Avon, no date), Book I, p. 296.

[4] *Language, Truth and Logic* (London: Victor Gollancz, 1946), p. 303.

ciplines, literary works, and more widely disseminated information about peoples and events have tended to create a challenge to the older beliefs about values.

By the opening of the twentieth century, scholarly research in all the social sciences had indicated three facts with uncomfortable clarity. First, it was shown that the values that men employ in their everyday life are not necessarily the ones they talk about. Second, the values that appear to be controlling—that is, the aims, goals, and aspirations advanced by those in authority—may cover up the actual values. Third, values not only vary from culture to culture, but change within a culture.

George Bernard Shaw, the Irish playwright, kept busy exposing the hypocrisy inherent in the gulf between professed value and actual practice. Most of his plays are concerned, indeed, with the hypocrisy of Victorian England. What we call patriotism, he says, is blind nation-worship; sentiment is shallow sentimentality; religion is custom elevated to sanctity. Middle-class morality—probably the chief object of his contempt—is irrational, silly, irrelevant, and essentially a cover for avaricious exploitation and materialism.[5]

Historians and journalists found a great deal of evidence that patriotic language served effectively to obscure the selfish motives of the wealthy. For instance, historian Charles Beard's work on the American founding fathers suggests that they were not the high-minded patriots pictured in the textbooks; rather, they were responding to the social and economic aims of their class, and the Constitution they created was designed to protect their privileges and status.[6] Researchers who looked into the munitions industry after World War I found that a few gigantic industrial cartels had made enormous profits from the War. It appeared to many that noble sentiment about saving the world for democracy or protecting the sovereignty of Belgium was a fraud perpetrated to protect shipping industries and gain profit for munitions makers, and that the millions killed during the war were a cruel sacrifice. Similarly, international treaties were found by historians to be based not on principles of social justice but on expediency and the immoral use of power.[7]

[5] For Shaw's criticisms of social institutions, conventional morality, and the middle class, see especially his *Major Barbara* and *Don Juan in Hell*.

[6] *An Economic Interpretation of the Constitution of the United States* (New York: Macmillan, 1923).

[7] From the standpoint of more recent scholarship, these interpretations are regarded as oversimplified and biased. At the time they appeared, however, they were regarded as revelations which shed light on the immorality of the wealthy and privileged in all countries.

Anthropologists added to the climate of disillusionment. By discovering that what had been asserted to be natural law, innate values, and eternal verities were really customs, they cast doubt on the ultimacy of all values. It was discovered that Alaskans did not respect their old—that they abandoned them, and in doing so were conserving a meager food supply. Malinowski and other ethnologists traced religion to the magical practices of preliterates.[8] Margaret Mead described the pleasant, relaxed life of the Polynesians and New Guineans who, with sexual mores that sanctioned premarital sexual experience, managed to live a life free from the neuroses and anxieties which plague the presumably more enlightened populace of our country.[9] The question raised by the abundance of evidence about cultural values was: "If values vary so widely among different cultures, how can anyone talk about a value that is really good for all?"

If, as it appeared, the eternal values did not exist, if morality was tinged with hypocrisy, and if verbalized values shielded the real ones, what sort of value system was really appropriate? From the writings of reformers, muckrakers, dramatists, and scholars arose a climate in which the seeds of subjectivism could grow into a full-grown philosophical system.

Existentialism: The Person as the Ultimate Source of Value

A philosophical system of growing importance that appears to reflect the subjectivist value theory is existentialism, a twentieth-century philosophy that has had considerable influence on religion and psychiatry, and in the last dozen years has become important in the thinking of educational philosophers.[10]

It is quite difficult to discuss the "axiology of existentialism" because there is no well-defined position shared by all existentialists. If the reader can imagine, not a systematic school such as neo-Thomism, but rather a group of extremely diverse thinkers bound together by a shared outlook, he can more clearly understand what the existentialists are saying.

Perhaps the concept shared by all existentialists is Sartre's[11] po-

[8] Bronislaw Malinowski, *Magic, Science and Religion* (New York: Doubleday Anchor Books, 1954).

[9] See *Growing Up In New Guinea, Sex and Temperament in Three Primitive Societies,* and *Coming of Age in Samoa.*

[10] One can detect the growing importance of existentialism in educational philosophy, but its influence on public education has yet to begin.

[11] Jean-Paul Sartre, the French philosopher and dramatist, represents one emphasis in existentialism, the atheistic wing. There are also Protestant, Catholic, and Jewish existentialists.

sition that existence precedes essence. But what, precisely, does such a statement mean? Recall Aristotle's categories and his emphasis on definition. For Aristotle, all classes of things are characterized by some "essence." The essence of something is what makes the class unique; it is what distinguishes that class from all other classes. After one has observed enough instances of a particular class, he can generalize about it and arrive at its essence. Further, the essence of a class does not change or evolve; once one knows the essence, one knows that which persists, that which survives the extinction of any single member of the class.

Such an approach is rejected by Sartre and other existentialists. One must not begin by defining man's essence, for he has no essence. He does not—like a plant, animal, or machine—come equipped with an essence. Each man defines his own essence—not *a priori*, not before he lives, but only after he acquires an existence, only after he is born. In Sartre's own words,

What is meant here by saying that existence precedes essence? It means, first of all, that man exists, turns up, appears on the scene, and only afterwards defines himself. If man, as the existentialist sees him, is indefinable, it is because at first he is nothing. Only afterwards will he be something and he himself will have made what he will be.[12]

An individual person is given existence by others. Such existence naturally sets limits on what one can do or what one can be. But within the limits we are given, we make ourselves.

If man has no essence prior to birth, how does he acquire one? What is it that makes a person what he becomes? The answer is that man makes himself through choice: man quite literally *chooses* his essence. Nothing irrevocably and coercively makes any person what he is. We are all free to choose our destiny, to choose ourselves.

The freedom to choose, the absolute opportunity to create our own destiny, is denied by most. This is understandable, for the weight of civilizations and institutions deceives most of us into believing that we have no choice and that we must do what has been mapped out for us. But it is only that the force of custom, social mores, and expectations of others tend to obscure the real fact of choice. Indeed, so complete are freedom and choice that the only thing we are not free to do is not to choose.

[12] *Existentialism* (New York: Philosophical Library, 1947), p. 18. See also Sartre, *Existentialism and Human Emotions* (New York: Philosophical Library, 1957), Chapter I.

The existence of such complete freedom is not only denied, but avoided. It is much easier to "pass the buck" to something or someone else, to shift responsibility for ourselves to some other source. The person who says that he foregoes the pleasure of an outing because he *must* attend his grandmother's funeral is really shifting the responsibility for choosing and thereby deceiving himself. He does not have to attend the funeral. If he goes to the funeral, he has chosen to do so. Of course, he may say that his presence is expected or that ordinary decency demands that he attend. But this is simply self-deception and he is acting, as certain existentialists say, in bad faith. The choice to attend the funeral or go on the outing is not *dictated* by decency, social expectations, or anything else. The choice is completely up to the person. To pass the buck to social convention is only evasion.[13]

There are a host of factors which blind us to our freedom. We are endlessly attempting to envelope ourselves in categories—rigid, air-tight labels which fool us into believing that we must or must not do this or that. For instance, if we accept the category of "student" we tend to believe that such a role dictates certain paths of action. If we are students, we *must* study, attend class, make good, buy a class ring, join a fraternity. Actually, neither is the role of student forced on us, nor do we have to follow any of these specific paths. We are students because we choose this role. If we study, it is because we chose to study—and if we do not study, it is because we chose not to. There is nothing which, like the Greek concept of irresistible destiny, coerces us to become students—neither our parents nor the realization that we *must* go to college to become a banker or lawyer or teacher. If you are in school because of your parents' ambitions for you, then you have chosen to accept their ambitions. If you are in college to become a teacher—or engineer, physician, scientist or certified public accountant—then you have chosen the vocation and the means of its realization. Such choice is not willed by God or by nature.

Other factors blind us to our freedom. Many philosophical positions and theological dogmas tend to promote the acceptance of an elaborate, well-defined set of categories. Such-and-such is what one must do according to Natural Law, or is what God prohibits us from doing. To some, it appears that inheritance of life eternal is impossible unless one completely accepts certain modes of action or belief. This again is delusive. We need not accept the goal of eternal life, nor need we accept the alleged means of attaining it. If we believe in God, heaven, and right actions, we do so because of our choice.

[13] See Walter Kaufmann, *Existentialism From Dostoevsky to Sartre* (New York: Meridian Books, 1956), p. 47.

Choice, then, is inescapable. Not to make a decision is really to make one—to choose not to choose. The only relevant question is: how do we choose? Do we thoughtlessly deceive ourselves as to our real reasons? Or do we consciously and with full awareness of what our choice entails, deliberately decide? Choice is inevitable, and only the manner in which we choose is relevant. To choose is one thing. To choose to choose is quite another. The latter implies that we acknowledge our absolute freedom and that we grant that we could, at any time, make another choice. We can legitimately go on the outing and not to the funeral.

Science, the demands of the government, the imperatives of the machine age, and the requirements of our culture—all tend toward conformity and loss of individuality and make the doctrine of absolute freedom appear to be nonsense. When "Science says that . . ." or "The law requires that . . ." it does not occur to us that scientists are human and laws are man-made and that scientific knowledge is limited and laws may be repressive and unfair.

Existentialists are in general agreement that ultimately *all* values are arbitrary. This does not mean that all values are capricious or "merely" matters of taste. It means that there is no final and complete defense of those values that we traditionally call "ultimate." We may provide a defense of some particular choice or value with careful logic and adequate factual data. The value may *appear* to be ultimate or self-evident. But in the final analysis, it is arbitrary. This is illustrated by the comment of one philosopher: "One may try to convince me that I ought to give up chain smoking because it is bad for my health and may shorten my life. But, I can always say, 'So, why is this important?'"

Life or good health—seemingly "core" values or those which we *all* agree are necessary and desirable—are not absolute, not cosmically necessary.[14] We *choose* to believe that life and good health are good. We cannot demonstrate that they are absolutely good, and indeed it is a blessing in disguise that they cannot be "proven." For to create even one value that is self-evident, in which we "must" believe, removes the basis of man's freedom. To *have* to believe means that we have no choice in the matter, and that is what existentialists deny.

Finally, the position that all existentialists seem to accept is that only through conscious choice can we improve the quality of our life on this earth. It is not possible to live an "authentic" life with the de-

---

[14] Refer to quotations on page 131 from Hume, and compare them with the position that, in reality, all values are chosen and that, ultimately, there is no objectivity.

lusions that most of us employ in order to shift the responsibility to others. To the extent that we accept the "dreadful freedom" [15] imposed by life, to the extent to which we live authentic existences and accept the complete responsibility for our lives and choices, we may live in a free and meaningful way.

Implications for Education

The precise implications of existentialism for education are far from clear. Although there are numerous articles and books written from an existentialist point of view, apparently few have attempted to relate systematically existentialist thought to education. One person, George Kneller, has done so, and it is to his writing that we shall look for the relationship between the existentialist philosophy and education. [16]

Most existentialists who have written about education feel that much of what schools are doing is antithetical to the free, self-chosen personality. The lists of required courses, the externally imposed authorities, the rules designed for the convenience of adults, the passivity of children waiting to do as they are told and believe as they are taught—all create the automation, the dependent, unthinking, blindly conforming adult who can never know what it means to be himself.

To understand the meaning of an education that truly teaches a person to live a free, authentic, and yet responsible life, we must understand the character of existence. The emphasis on ontology in existentialism is necessary if we are to understand what kinds of existence are open to human beings.

Both Martin Heidigger and Jean-Paul Sartre, leading European existentialists, distinguish between two kinds of existence. Heidigger talks about *Dasein*, a term not precisely translatable, meaning something like "being there." Sartre's categories are the "être en soi" and the "être pour soi." The *en soi* is that which exists in itself, that which has contingent reality, very much in the same sense as the ontology of realism. Sartre's *pour soi*, the "for itself" reality, is the reality

---

[15] The term is Marjorie Grene's; it refers to the existentialist notion that we are, in a sense, condemned to be free, condemned always to choose. See Marjorie Grene, *Dreadful Freedom* (Chicago: U. of Chicago Press, 1948).

[16] In particular, we shall rely on *Existentialism and Education* (New York: John Wiley, 1958). A recent work is Van Cleve Morris, *Existentialism in Education* (New York: Harper and Row, 1966), which also attempts a systematic account of the relationship between existentialism and education.

of man who lives for himself and is conscious of it. The significance of this ontological classification is that it points to two qualitatively different kinds of reality. One kind of lower-order reality is that which simply takes up space but which has no consciousness of itself. This existence is illustrated by rocks, trees, and animals. Human beings have a qualitatively different kind of existence. We live in a universe which is indifferent to us but in which we must constantly choose and where we alone—among all creatures—know that we will someday cease to exist. The ontological concern is crucial, for, since man does have a special existence, he must understand the conditions of this existence.

Because man must come to grips with himself and his destiny, the entire character of knowledge is transformed. For existentialists of all shades of emphasis, there is no absolutely "objective, systematized knowledge—for "knowledge can only be hypothetical, never decisive." [17] Nor must it ever be assumed that man can know completely and finally, for truth is "multidimensional and influenced by mysterious elements which are an abiding characteristic of life." [18]

The emphasis on the subjectivity and incompleteness of knowledge is in contrast both with philosophical realism, in which the world must be known on its terms, and with relativism, where the emphasis is on knowledge as data to be used in the solution of a problem. Rather, knowledge exists only as it rises from human consciouness and feelings. Whatever the significance of truth and knowledge, the significance is for someone at some time and some place. Such an attitude toward knowledge means that schools ought not require the learning of dehumanized subject matter unrelated to human aspirations, needs, and conditions. Quite typically, students are confronted with mathematics, literature, or science, and in effect told that they must study these subjects because society has deemed it proper to do so. Whether children see the relevance of their studies is beside the point. It is to precisely this that existentialists object. The only meaning of knowledge found in the curriculum is the meaning it has for people.

Even scientific knowledge, properly understood, goes beyond the emphasis on the impersonal, objective collection of data. Science is a personal enterprise. Its significance for students lies in allowing them to see the wonders of discovery and the excitement of a "sudden shaft of insight." This approach, says Kneller, does not deprive scientific knowledge of its objective elements:

Thus, when I teach a scientific law or theory, I explain the circumstances of

[17] Kneller, p. 57.
[18] *Ibid.*, p. 58.

its discovery, the men who discovered it and the theories it superseded. By tracing its genesis in history, my students and I recapture for ourselves the moment of original triumph; we re-experience science as it was experienced by those who made it.[19]

From this viewpoint, the value of studying the discovery of penicillin lies not in a bare mastery of facts but in the attempt to recapture the moment when Sir Alexander Fleming's chance observation of a petri dish resulted in a revolution in medicine. The value of studying the astronomical discoveries of Copernicus, Bruno, and Kepler is the appreciation of the profound human changes resulting from the impact of the new knowledge.[20]

Literature and the whole range of humanities share a similar function. To hear Beethoven's Fourteenth Quartet, says Kneller, makes him "want my students to realize how breathtaking it is that a man should produce such art." [21] Poetry is able to illuminate the "plentitude of being" by revealing the poet's apprehension of existence. Even the familiar and ordinary are transformed into the touching and significant as the teacher strives to see that what the poet feels "should penetrate into the hearts of all our pupils." [22]

Biography, too, can illuminate the human condition. To relate the story of Ruth and Naomi in the Bible is to see them in "a concrete situation, involving choice and commitment, a point of departure that is to shape Ruth's future irrevocably." [23] For existentialists, drama brings to light the "hidden significance of the human situation." [24] The plays of Gabriel Marcel illustrate this dramatic aim. Says Marcel, "The central theme . . . in nearly all my plays is a living relationship seen at work in a particular situation." [25] The impact of Marcel's drama is to "startle us into a new awareness—into a new face-to-face honesty about ourselves." [26]

Existentialists would end the current tendency to teach the social studies in such a way that students are "adjusted" to social institutions. A democracy ought not simply adjust the individual to the masses or subjugate him to the majority will. The tyranny of the majority is

---

[19] "Education, Knowledge and the Problem of Existence," reprinted in *Proceedings of the 17th Annual Meeting of the Philosophy of Education Society,* 1961, p. 138.
[20] *Ibid.,* and *Existentialism and Education,* Chapter V.
[21] "Education, Knowledge, etc.," p. 139.
[22] *Ibid.,* p. 140.
[23] *Ibid.*
[24] *Ibid.,* p. 141.
[25] *Ibid.*
[26] *Ibid.*

still tyranny. Nor should man be engulfed in "the world of abstractions, of bureaus and machines," [27] as Camus puts it. The major value of a democracy is as a means to the end, which is freedom: the freedom to say, as Marcel asserts, that "I am I." [28] Such a freedom exists only in a social order wherein all are equally free. Only then can people find the conditions which allow them to seek their personal fulfillment. Only then can man determine his own existence.

To psychology and counseling, existentialists have contributed a sizable number of theories. An existentialist would warmly approve the findings of Earl Kelley or Carl Rogers, who emphasize the importance of the subjectively felt and known. It is not what may have an independent existence that is significant to any person: it is rather what the person perceives, feels, and appropriates. It is not the counselor's task to advise students as to what they should do or how they should view their world. The counselor does not solve anyone's problem. Rather, he frees the person so that he can make an autonomous, uncoerced choice and decide what he believes is best. This is in sharp contrast with traditional perceptions of the school counselor's role and with the traditional authoritarian role that society has accorded the school. Existentialists acknowledge this, but insist that the traditional role is wrong.[29] They assert that if freedom and individualism are really as important as our society has said, schools should alter their structure to provide the conditions of true freedom.

The design of the existentialist's position is to emphasize the individual, to elevate him above the coercion of social institutions, so that he may become conscious of the freedom that is inescapably his. The end product of an existentialist education is the autonomous person who can actualize the potentialities that lie within him.

Analysis of Existentialism

Despite the widespread acceptance of existentialism on the European continent, it has not been without its critics. It has drawn heavy fire from representatives of all philosophical schools, although each tends to criticize it for different reasons.

---

[27] Albert Camus, *Neither Victims Nor Executioners*, quoted in Maurice Friedman, *The Worlds of Existentialism* (New York: Random House, 1964), p. 216.

[28] Kneller, *Existentialism and Education*, p. 89.

[29] For criticisms of the traditional role of counseling, consult the writings of Carl Rogers. See, for instance, *Client-Centered Therapy* (Boston: Houghton Mifflin, 1951) and *On Becoming a Person: A Therapist's View of Psychotherapy* (Boston: Houghton Mifflin, 1961).

From the standpoint of linguistic analysis—the branch of philosophy that is concerned with precision and meaning in language—existentialism is a hopeless mass of contradictory, vague, incoherent statements. Because of the tendency of existentialists to express themselves through exaggeration or metaphor, their philosophical position frequently can be inferred only with difficulty. For example, Sartre, discussing the psychology of sadism, states:

Thus this explosion of the look of Another in the world of the sadist makes the meaning and end of sadism collapse. At one and the same time sadism discovers that it was that liberty it wanted to enslave and realizes the vanity of its efforts. Here we are once more turned from the being-who-looks to the being-who-is-looked at, we do not leave the circle.[30]

How the look of "another" makes the "meaning and end" of sadism "collapse" raises questions for one who is concerned with clearly expressed meaning.

Of course the existentialist might say that we must not read existentialist writings in the same manner as we read a logically arranged description. The apparent contradictions expressed in poetic form reflect the existentialist's attempt to describe an existence that itself is contradictory. But the question remains: "How ought one go about reading existentialists?"

Existentialists are widely criticized, too, for their emphasis on the irrational. Kierkegaard states frequently that a critical examination of God's word is impious and that our faith ought to be of the complete, unquestioning nature of the Prophets'. By stressing the irrelevance of critical examination, Kierkegaard and his followers have placed existentialism in a philosophical position far removed from the mainstream of Western thought. Such emphasis on the irrational and the emotional provides no means of valid guidance or clues to interpretation.[31]

Similarly, existentialists are criticized for their emphasis on choice without providing a framework for the process of choice. How should one choose? By what criteria? What is the method by which one comes to a decision? What kinds of interpretation should we make of evidence bearing on a choice? How does one relate empirical evidence to a range of personal values? These questions, by and large, are not

[30] *Being and Nothingness* (New York: Philosophical Library, 1956). This passage is typical of the style of much existential writing.

[31] Walter Kaufmann develops this criticism in *From Shakespeare to Existentialism* (New York: Doubleday, 1960), Chapter 10.

considered by existentialists, for their interest is not in those philosophical issues which are epistemological. By virtue of their anti-objectivism, anti-rationalism, and almost total emphasis on the subjective, existentialists, it is held, find themselves in the position of advocating choice without providing necessary guidelines.[32]

Nor is their social philosophy seen by critics as relevant or helpful. Existentialists are the heirs of philosophers who, like Rousseau and Thoreau, saw the individual man eternally pitted against society. To be sure, many European existentialists are writing with the experience of having lived under repressive regimes. But, some philosophers point out, it does not follow that society and government are necessarily and always hostile to individuals. Any philosophical position which places a hypothetical individual in constant antagonism with a hypothetical society does not leave much room for theorizing about any kind of mutually helpful relationship between both.[33]

To some, the existentially oriented counseling theory of Carl Rogers and others is of little help to schools. Rogers believes that the solution of any personal problem is within the individual. Apparently the counselor is not to interpret evidence for his client or in any way direct him toward a solution. The counselee contains within himself all the potential for solving his own problem. This has meant in practice a disinclination to give advice, ask pointed questions, or give and interpret tests. Since much of the school counselor's job consists in doing precisely these things, how, it is asked, is it possible for any counselor to function as Rogers believes he should? School counselors must give advice, provide vocational guidance, and plan class schedules. How relevant is a theory which in actual practice is inapplicable?

A classroom teacher may raise similar questions about the relevance of a position that simply does not provide an adequate basis for dealing with selection of curriculum, discipline, evaluation, or other pertinent activities. Most existentialists writing on education are deficient in suggesting methods of implementations. Granted that we study Beethoven or Jean Anouilh to see their contributions to the human soul, what then? Is it not relevant to study the harmony and musical techniques of Beethoven? If so, what is there in existentialist writing that would provide for an "objective" analysis of Beethoven? Existentialist writers have been remiss in suggesting criteria for choice, apparently because such a topic smacks too much of the objective.

[32] *Ibid.*
[33] See John Dewey, *Individualism Old and New* (New York: Minton, Balch, 1930).

The lack of concern or downright hostility to criteria and objectivity—to what exists outside an individual—makes existentialism difficult to relate to education. The existence of group-based norms or standards of conduct, the belief in cooperation to reach accepted ends, the acceptance of the majority will as a basis for action—all implicit in a democracy—are precisely what seem to be rejected by existentialism. In the existentialist's emphasis on the primacy of the single person there is a corresponding de-emphasis of the social. Existentialism as a polar opposite of absolutely objective value theories proves to be another kind of absolute.

That existentialists have something important to say and that they are discussing serious themes is granted by almost everyone. But what they mean, how one would go about implementing existentialist values, what kinds of criteria are to be employed, and how relevant existentialism is to our culture—these are questions which must be asked of this increasingly influential philosophy.

Relativism

A third position, contrasting with both an Aristotelian objectivist position and subjectivism, is *relativism,* known also as *pragmatism, instrumentalism,* or *experimentalism.* An Aristotelian position, as we have seen, carries with it the belief that ultimate values exist apart from the desires of any person, that what is supremely good and desirable can be intellectually determined by discovering inherent purpose or function. The axiology of subjectivism—from which existentialism has been chosen as an important contemporary example—derives from the assumption that all values are ultimately reducible to the desires of given persons. These positions obviously are polar opposites: on the one hand, the assertion that ultimate values are discovered; on the other, that all values are created. Relativism, which takes an ontological position midway between the belief that reality is discovered and that it is created, also takes a middle position with regard to axiology. While relativists believe that values are of human invention, they also hold that, in some sense, values are also objective.

John Dewey, who developed relativism in the late nineteenth and first half of the twentieth centuries, built his philosophical position, as we have noted, on the foundations provided by Charles S. Peirce. Dewey early concerned himself with the problems of values and evaluation. For a number of reasons, his value theory has frequently been misinterpreted and vulgarized—often by his followers as well as

his critics. It is common to see him accused of being a subjectivist or—
in contrast—charged with basing values solely on the public will.[34] This
is probably to be expected, since his position is an intermediate one and
can be fitted into either of the other two, though to do so is probably
a misreading. A thorough examination of some of Dewey's many essays
and books on value theory, assisted by the interpretation of some careful scholars, reveals a position which appears to be quite different from
the one he is usually said to have held.

Values are Relative

The term *relativism* is frequently taken to mean a belief that no
value has validity, that all values are equally acceptable, and that, ultimately, values are not really important. One may verbalize such a
belief by saying, "Well, what difference does it make; it's all relative."
Such a position is not at all what Dewey intended. By stating that
values are relative, Dewey apparently meant that values are of human
origin; that absolute values of whatever nature do not appear to
exist; and that a value exists only in relation to other values.

From the insights provided by cultural anthropology, Dewey concluded that values are what men prize.[35] It appeared to Dewey that
men prize a good many things, and that, depending on time, place, and
circumstance, men value widely different things. It also seemed obvious
that values change, though the rate of change is often so slow that the
change is not noticed.

Although men have often believed that values reside absolutely in
some natural purpose, Dewey thought such a belief incapable of
demonstration. Dewey admired Aristotle's formulation for its intellectual distinction, but he did not agree that "natural tendency" is an
accurate description of the origin of values. Nor did he accept a theological explanation. Both God and nature are apparently cover-ups,

[34] The former charge is made by Frederick Breed in "Education and the
Realistic Outlook," in Nelson B. Henry (ed.), *National Society for the Study of
Education, Philosophies of Education, Forty-First Yearbook,* Part I. (Chicago: U. of
Chicago Press, 1942), and the latter is made by Van Cleve Morris in *Philosophy
and the American School* (Boston: Dodd, Mead, 1962), Chapter Nine.

[35] Dewey seems to have been the first important twentieth-century philosopher
to be strongly influenced by the findings of social scientists. Not only did he read
much of the late nineteenth- and early twentieth-century social scientists, but he
contributed to their publications and corresponded with some of them. Allusions
to Westermark, Tylor, and other important anthropologists are found in many of
his writings. This point is significant only when it is realized that most philosophers
before this century were oriented to art, literature, history, or mathematics. Because
Dewey was acquainted with sociological and anthropological data, he was not
tempted to make the all-encompassing evaluations one finds in, say, Hegel or Kant.

rationalizations and defenses, for values which are either blessed by custom or which serve the (usually hidden) interests of a certain social class. Therefore, values inhere not in an absolute source nor in an absolute natural tendency, but in the social interaction of men. Man is the originator, conservator, and changer of his values.

The term *relative* has another meaning, one which may be inferred from Dewey's writings. Values do not appear to exist in an absolute sense—that is, in an existence apart from some particular context. A value exists in relationship to some other value. For instance, while one may value honesty in one situation, he may prefer tact in another. Honesty cannot be said to exist as a value always to be preferred to all other values.

Relative may have reference to the particular circumstances of a person or group of persons. Obviously, individuals and societies differ in their preferences. The United States and Great Britain, for example, while both are democracies, tend to emphasize somewhat different cultural values. Great Britain places some rather stringent limitations on newspapers, in the belief that such limitations are necessary to protect the privacy of individuals. In this country such limitations would be seen as unwarranted invasion of the press. Here are two cultural values—privacy and freedom of the press—which are esteemed in different degrees, according to the historical circumstances of the two societies.

Facts and Values: Subjective and Objective

The ancient distinction between facts and values occupied much of Dewey's axiology. It has been customary to create an absolute wall of separation between facts and values. The one is subjective and personal and the other purely a matter of empirical evidence and verification based on sensory data. Values, it is held, belong to the human, and facts to the purely natural. But, says Dewey, the assertion that "there is something in the very nature of conduct which prevents the use of logical methods in the way they are employed in other recognized spheres of scientific inquiry" [36] is a misinterpretation of the true relationship between facts and values. The belief that "scientific judgments depend upon reason" while moral valuation comes from a separate faculty which is "not amendable to intellectual supervision" [37] is wrong. And so is the belief that values are either immediate or intuitive and

[36] *Philosophy of Education* (Ames: Littlefield, Adams, 1956), p. 213. This work is known also as *Problems of Men*.
[37] *Ibid.*, p. 214.

that only facts are the result of methodical inquiry and sustained reflection.

Values, Dewey holds, are natural in the sense that they do not proceed from a supernatural realm. Values arise within human experience, and so they are amenable to the same intellectual procedures that characterize scientific inquiry. Ethical judgments require intellectual processes "which state a connection of relevant conditions in general (or objective) form." [38] That is, the process of *evaluating*, of coming to a conclusion about a value, is an epistemological process which involves very much the same objective techniques that characterize science.

Such an intellectual process is vitally important to human beings. If men are to behave in a considered rather than an impulsive or mechanical manner, human conduct requires thought for guidance. What must be done is to apply the method of science, the process of scientific inquiry, to moral and ethical questions. A critical look at the activities of scientists suggests that the process of inquiry begins with a problem arising out of an indeterminate situation, that human beings begin to think reflectively when they are faced with a problem. The scientific method involves the objective gathering of data. Value judgments also ought to be concerned with the acquisition of data. Scientists employ imagination, foresight, and skill in their procedures. Human beings can deal with ethical or aesthetic questions with such imagination and foresight. The end product of the scientific inquiry is not, as has been thought, the ultimate law, the unchangeable universal. It is rather a conclusion, to be held until new evidence or new interpretations of old evidence require a different conclusion. One's value judgments, by the same token, ought to be flexible, so that they can be modified or replaced when new conditions and new information indicate that a change is appropriate.

Moral issues, said Dewey, are not confined to sexual matters or gambling or any of the other narrow ethical classes. A moral issue is any issue, arising out of a social interaction, that involves judgments of good and bad or right and wrong. Further, it is not correct to see moral issues as merely those in which decisions are between good and bad or right and wrong. Moral judgments are also required when individuals face a choice between good and better or bad and worse.

Occasionally an administrator must decide whether to spend money on a new library or a new shop building. This is not a choice between

[38] *Ibid.,* p. 217.

good or evil. It is a choice between one good and something else which must, on balance, be regarded as better. Too, administrators must occasionally choose between two applicants, one intelligent and well trained but somewhat ill at ease among people and the other less well trained and intelligent but an affable, outgoing, extroverted type. Again, the choice is not between good and evil: it is between one good (intelligence and training) and another (affability and good nature). Would, of course, we could have our cake and eat it too! But that is the point. We cannot, and because we cannot, we have a moral decision.

Becoming aware of the problem is the first stage in the "complete act of thought." The awareness should not stay at the preverbal level, in which one is vaguely conscious of a nagging sense of tension. It should proceed to the point where one can see as clearly as possible the choice (or choices) involved. This requires framing the problem in specific terms. Next comes an inferential process, characterized by the use of data and predictions—that is, an imaginative projection of possible consequences. The person says, "If I do this, then this will or may happen." Or he asks himself, "What may happen if I do this?" Or, "What kinds of facts and data do I need to reach a conclusion?" Such questions, it must be emphasized, require objectivity in both the collection and the analysis of evidence. What is to be avoided is self-deception—refusing to face certain facts and refusing to recognize consequences.

This evaluative process may be relatively short or it may continue for a long period. In reaching a conclusion, values are weighed carefully. What weight ought to be attached to the ability to "get along with others"? How important is this man's training and ability in this position at this time? What consequences would likely flow from not building a shop? What advantages might accrue from having a new library? Do the advantages outweigh the disadvantages? How do the teachers feel about it? How does the Taxpayers' League feel about it? How might the students feel about it?

What is involved, in short, is a dialogue between the personal and private world of the individual and the facts which exist external to him. It is precisely this interaction between self and non-self that characterizes the scientific procedure. Dewey's application of the method of science to moral issues was at the heart of his axiology. To remove evaluation from the intuitive [39] and the supernatural and to

[39] In the sense of a complete and final certainty.

place it in a scientific context was probably Dewey's major contribution to both philosophy and education in the twentieth century.[40]

Implications for Education

The implications of this position were spelled out by Dewey and his followers. Given our divided and fragmented society, the enoromous lag between cultural values and prevailing technological conditions, and the sharp antagonisms between different elements in our society, the function of education is to enable students to learn to think independently about the life of which they are part.[41] This is a frank invitation for students to think critically about the social problems that affect them.

To develop the student's ability to think reflectively is the purpose of all education, at any grade and in all subjects. Stated in this manner, Dewey's educational philosophy is a far cry from the bland, mindless conformity with which he has often been charged. Dewey recognized the essential purpose of schools to transmit the cultural heritage. But in addition, he held, schools ought to try to *improve* the cultural heritage. This can be done only when teachers abandon the traditional indoctrinative techniques of education and teach students how to evaluate for themselves, first, what the culture is, and second, how it can be improved.

In social studies this means that schools will not teach, uncritically, the structure and function of government or require students to memorize patriotic fairy tales called United States history. What must be done is to give students a sense of what our culture is really like. This involves introducing students to the problems inherent in our way of life. This position follows logically from Dewey's analysis of the part values plays in thought. Students can learn the meaning of the complete act of thought by being provoked to thought. Thought is provoked only when there is a problem to think about. Hence the social studies should consist of analyses of the problems inherent in our culture.

Problems occur in our culture in great abundance, said Dewey. Our culture has inherited values and practices from a pre-scientific, pre-technological, pre-industrial past. Attitudes, values, beliefs from

[40] Two works that attempt to develop Dewey's value theory for education are Gordon Hullfish and Philip Smith, *Reflective Thinking, The Method of Education* (New York: Dodd, Mead, 1961), and Maurice Hunt and Lawrence Metcalf, *Teaching High School Social Studies* (New York: Harper, 1955).

[41] This last phrase is that of Ernest E. Bayles. See his *Democratic Educational Theory* (New York: Harper and Row, 1960).

the past invariably conflict with those arising as we continue to transform ourselves into a democratic, scientifically oriented, industrialized nation. Students need to be aware of the value conflicts in our society that have tended to be so disruptive. They should learn not simply the mechanical process by which courts function or by which legislation becomes law; they should learn also how political power is really distributed, what sociological and economic factors influence the making of laws. History ought to be not simply a recitation of facts, but an objective attempt to discover the patterns of human association and event. The findings of all the social sciences should be utilized by teachers not simply as facts-to-be-learned, but as data to be utilized in the solution of social problems. The end of such education is an insightful, reflective person, who has a deep understanding of his culture and who possesses the knowledge to participate in keeping it dynamic.

Dewey and his followers have had much to say about literature, music, art, and other subjects often clasified as aesthetic. A prime target of Dewey's criticism was the persistent tendency in Western civilization to create a dualism between the aesthetic and intellectual and the practical and utilitarian. Traditionally, as we have noted, those subjects designated intellectual and aesthetic—usually history, languages, literature, mathematics, and the fine arts—have been seen as inherently civilizing, genuinely intellectual, and the only proper content of a "liberal" education. Whatever is employed in day-to-day affairs, whatever has direct application to life, has been criticized as inferior. If we remember that the traditional aristocratic education usually consisted of the liberal arts, it is easy to see how and why the "liberal" subjects, the aesthetic and intellectual, were rejected by the common man. In our culture, we have not only tended to reject an aristocracy, but the possessions of an aristocracy—and these included serious music, the arts, literature, ancient languages. The consequence of this is that most persons who are formally "exposed" to these subjects generate indifference or scorn for them.

Dewey advocates abandoning ancient, rigid attitudes about what is "inherently" intellectual and what practical. It is possible to grasp the intellectual significance and social worth of a wide range of subjects. What is called "vocational" in our country need not be simply a mechanical and lifeless drilling of facts. Vocational subjects not only possess intrinsic usefulness, but they can be taught so as to become as broadening and humanizing as any other subjects. This can come about only when the vocational is related to a wider range of human concerns and issues.

By the same token, we ought to revise our attitudes about language, literature, and the fine arts. Usually the teaching of prose and poetry is confined to technical analysis, to paraphrasing content, or to an "appreciation" that is usually indoctrination in what someone considers great or worthwhile. If teachers themselves understand and like literature, they will be able to teach it so that students at one and the same time gain the insights into life provided by writers and poets and cultivate aesthetic pleasure in the experience of literature.

In whatever subject and at whatever age, education ought to leave students with a sense of the interrelatedness of knowledge. The values inherent in knowledge ought to be made so clear that, long after someone has finished his formal education, he will want to continue learning. The essential goal and meaning of an education, Dewey repeats, is that the individual continue to grow in depth and breadth of insights, that he be increasingly capable of becoming more educated. The goal of education is developing the capacity to become more educated.

Criticism of Dewey's Value Theory

Before we consider the criticisms of Dewey, it is necessary to distinguish between Dewey and Progressive Education. This is not always done, and consequently Dewey is blamed for offenses committed by various Progressive educators of the 1920's and 1930's. Dewey's philosophy and the theory and practice of Progressive Education are not one and the same. Hence the following criticisms are those that can be legitimately made of Dewey and have no reference to what was done in his name.

The sharpest criticism of Dewey's theories of values comes from neo-Thomists, though philosophers within other schools have been critical. From the position of a theologically oriented philosophy such as Catholicism, Dewey's naturalistic value theory is foredoomed to failure, for without the wisdom and guidance of the supernatural, man cannot build a stable philosophy. By substituting unaided inquiry into values, man can only lose sight of the divine plan which is essential to his spiritual journey. In effect, Dewey replaces a theory of values with a theory of evaluation—that is, the emphasis is on how one knows what is good, not on the final good. This tends to remove the final good, the ultimate end, from consideration. This can only mean that man has no ultimate standards by which to judge his conduct.

From another point of view, Dewey is criticized for locating the source of values in the culture. Dewey says: "In this sense conduct and hence morals are social: they are not just things which ought to be social. . . . Human interaction and ties are there, are operative in any case." [42]

In the opinion of one critic, George Santayana, an American idealistic philosopher, this position suggests a "tendency to dissolve the individual into his social functions, as well as everything substantial and actual into something relative and transitional." [43] The individual has no ultimate importance, no reality of and by himself; his worth is only in relationship to participation in his social milieu. Since democracy connotes a system of human association in which human beings are assumed to be important *per se*, Dewey's emphasis is plainly untrue to democracy.

From the standpoint of linguistic analysis, Dewey's philosophy suffers from two defects. First, it is insufficiently precise at times. Dewey's tendency toward complexity, his use of synonyms and qualifying phrases, and his occasional flight into difficult abstractions often renders his meaning unclear. Second, Dewey is seen as failing to recognize the fact that values are ultimately reducible to someone's feelings. Epistemology is one thing and axiology another, and to miss the obvious fact that a value is simply someone's completely subjective preference is to try to prove the unprovable.

For others, Dewey errs in his overemphasis on the scientific method. So much faith did Dewey have in man's rationality and capacity to apply empirical facts to his value structure that the irrational in man is simply discounted. Events in the last thirty years—World War II, the arms race, racial violence—have clearly shown that the scientific method cannot provide adequate guidance for man's desires. Dewey's faith in democracy as a way of life, it is held, is also naive, for democracy is not sufficient to provide a sound basis for values. Given the pluralistic nature of our society, what kind of stable guide does one have for deciding just what is and what is not democratic?

The application of Dewey's theory of evaluation to education has also been severely criticized. Dewey's emphasis on the "free play of intelligence" as a basis of deciding what is good and bad is often held not adequate for a number of reasons. Among other things, it discounts what man has learned from his experience and overlooks the obvious fact that men need authority figures.

Other critics would insist that the elimination of absolute standards

[42] *Human Nature and Conduct* (New York: Henry Holt, 1922), p. 278.
[43] Quoted in William S. Sahakian, *Systems of Ethics and Value Theory* (Ames: Littlefield, Adams, 1963), p. 337.

is psychologically unsound and morally undesirable. Although absolutists disagree about the origin and nature of absolute values, they do agree that absolute values exist. Committing murder or waging unprovoked aggression against the defenseless, it is generally agreed, is not right and cannot ever be considered justifiable. There are certain values which are supremely desirable and, by the same token, there are offenses against man or God—or both—which are, according to the overwhelming evidence of man's experiences, morally wrong and unacceptable. What, then, is wrong with admitting this? Human beings, it is held, need the comfort of knowing that, no matter what, there is an ultimate standard by which all must abide. To cast man adrift from these standards is to remove what thousands of years of history has shown essential to his existence. Without abiding standards of right and wrong, what keeps man from committing offenses? History has shown that man has a strong propensity for evil and that without the safeguards of absolute morality, his evil inclinations are unchecked.

Conclusion

In these two chapters we have contrasted three different theories of value and traced their implications for education. The first position, usually called objectivism, is that values have an external ground—that is, good or bad are not merely thought so; there are verifiable reasons for calling things good or bad. The second, called subjectivism, is that, ultimately, all values reduce to a matter of perception. What is good is, in the final analysis, what I call good. The third position, relativism, is that in one sense, values are personal; but in another sense, they are objective. In the process of deciding what is preferable, we act as if values were objective; when our minds are made up, when we have reached a decision, the objective process comes to an end and we are on our own.

Each of these value theories is a live option in school systems within our culture. Usually no one is particularly clear about when each is being used or about what consequences flow from each. On the one hand, artistic preferences are supposed to be essentially personal; on the other hand, students for years have complained that it pays to agree with the teacher's taste in literature. The penalty for the nonconformist who asserts in class his real feelings about Whitman or Longfellow is usually enough to dampen all future personal preferences; it is as if there really were objective standards about what is and is not "good" poetry, and it is as if the teacher knew these standards.

The result of lack of awareness of the meaning of values is particularly noticeable in testing procedures. A true-false question appearing on a social studies test was phrased: "The salary of legislators is inadequate." Such a statement cannot be called either true or false, for it is within the realm of value judgment: inadequate in relation to what or according to whom? Similarly, the designation of an "A" grade is not a simple statement of fact. An "A" reflects someone's estimate of how well a person performed in the light of certain criteria—and both the estimate and the criteria are, in the last analysis, arbitrary and personal.

It is not within our province to conclude that any of the three value-theory positions is best or that one is more appropriate to education than the others. It is precisely the fact that none of the three positions is clearly truer or better that makes axiology the persistent philosophical subject that it is. What does appear obvious, however, is that there are differences in value theories and that, unrecognized as the differences are, many educational practices will continue to be sources of conflict and friction. And nobody will really know why.

QUESTIONS FOR DISCUSSION

1. Assume that someone has just discovered that his employer, a very good friend who has helped him in many ways, has embezzled a large sum of money. Analyze the solution to this problem from the position of a Thomist and then that of a relativist.

2. Can one argue that agriculture could be a highly theoretical course and that metaphysics could be highly practical?

3. Assume that the amount of money one is actually willing to pay for something is a true and accurate index of how much one values that thing. How should we interpret the fact that teachers' salaries are well below the median for professional salaries?

4. Can you detect any values that seem to have been held throughout history without change or alteration?

5. Related to the question above, what is the difference between an anthropological universal and a philosophical absolute?

6. What values do you personally feel can be classified as absolutes? Check with your friends to see whether they would have the same list.

7. What evidence is there that schools are suffering from subjective-objective confusion in value theory and practice?

8. Assume that you are a relativist, and that you have three wishes which will be granted. What three wishes would you make to change American education? Now do the same for two other value-theory positions.

SUGGESTED READINGS

BAYLES, ERNEST E. *Pragmatism in Education.* New York: Harper and Row, 1966. This recent work by a leading pragmatist in education sums up a lifetime of thought on relativism, value theory, and education.

BERKSON, I. B. *The Ideal and The Community.* New York: Harper, 1958. Berkson is a committed idealist in education; this book gives his answer to the pragmatism of Dewey and Kilpatrick.

BREED, FREDERICK S. "Education and the Realistic Outlook," in Nelson B. Henry (ed.), *National Society for the Study of Education, Philosophies of Education, Forty-First Yearbook, Part I.* Chicago: U. of Chicago Press, 1942. This is a clear and forceful statement of the traditional realist's position.

SARTRE, JEAN-PAUL. *Existentialism and Human Emotions.* New York: Philosophical Library, 1957. This is perhaps the shortest and simplest work on existentialism by one of the foremost speakers for the position. It defines existentialism and discusses some important implications.

7

Epistemology: Questions about Truth and Knowledge

The Central Problem in Our Culture

Just as there appears to be a central problem of value in our culture, so there is a central problem of knowledge. This central problem we shall call the "epistemological problem." Epistemology is the name for the study of knowledge. It asks such questions as "What is true?" and "How do we know what is true?" Although it may appear that there is no difference between one kind of knowledge and another —that truth is truth and knowledge is knowledge—actually, there are substantial differences in *how* we know. For instance, assume that someone says, "I know that it is 76° Fahrenheit in this room" and also, "I know that Columbus discovered America in 1492." Both these statements are candidates for knowledge—that is, both assert something regarded as true. But when we ask the question "How do you know this?" we can see immediately that there is a vast difference between knowing that it is 76° and knowing that Columbus discovered America.

In the first case, the degree of temperature may be ascertained by looking at a thermometer. This kind of knowledge is gained by the sense organs and is called empirical knowledge. All empirical knowledge is gained by means of the senses—in this case, sight. But sense knowledge is not involved in the statement about Columbus. We do not know that Columbus discovered this country because we have seen him or are able to see him. Our knowledge of Columbus is based on what someone (or a lot of someones) has told us. This knowledge is called knowledge by authority.

Both the statements about Columbus and the room temperature are preceded by the words "I know," and most of us would consider them about equally acceptable as statements of truth. Indeed, there is little controversial about either statement.

But now let us substitute two other sentences: "I know that Luther tried to reform the Church in the sixteenth century" and "I know that nuclear bomb testing is harmful to health." These are similar to the other two in that one is an historical statement, based on what others have said, and the other is an assertion that, at first glance, seems verifiable by sensory experience—that is, we examine the effects of nuclear testing to see whether it is harmful to bone marrow, or whether nuclear testing adversely affects genetic inheritance. But immediately a problem arises. In the case of Luther it is a matter of considerable controversy whether he did indeed try to *reform* a church or whether what he did would more properly be called a *revolution*. Protestants usually refer to the Protestant *Reformation* and Catholics to the Protestant *Revolt*. Presumably both Catholics and Protestant historians have access to the same box of facts, and presumably they should be able to make a clear-cut, decisive historical judgment similar to "Columbus discovered America." Why, then, the problem?

By the same token, scientists ought to be able to decide whether nuclear testing is harmful. The determination of the degree of harm— like the determination of the degree of temperature—is apparently an empirical matter, to be decided by recourse to sensory experience. But if we read the abundant literature on the subject, it is immediately obvious that scientists are by no means in complete agreement about the alleged harm of nuclear testing.

Apparently, then, there is something more to knowing than appears at first glance. The "something more" will be developed in this chapter. For now, suffice it to say that there are different kinds of knowing, that people know in different ways, and that what and how one knows may be disputable.

The central epistemological problem today is somewhat different than it was in this country half a century ago. At that time the conflict was between scientific knowledge and knowledge based on revelation. The evolutionary theories of Charles Darwin, based on analysis of data from archaeology, biology, comparative anatomy, and other scientific disciplines, came into sharp collision with a literal interpretation of Genesis in the Old Testament. The latter described the complete creation of man by God and had formed one of the fundamental beliefs of Christianity for almost two thousand years. This extremely sharp conflict—which culminated in the famous Scopes trial in 1925—illustrates the epistemological difference between knowledge coming from the method of science and knowledge based on faith, on belief in the revealed word of God.

This particular problem, if not completely solved, is certainly not as keen as it was at the turn of the century. Instead, the central epistemological problem of our culture today appears to arise from the clash between the scientific method and intuition. The battleground is not evolution versus special creation, but the scientific method versus intuition in a wide variety of social, economic, and political problems. The scientific disciplines involved are the social sciences—anthropology, political science, economics, and sociology.

Let us see how the problem operates in a wider scope and then how it relates to education. Scientific knowledge is considered to be, at least most of the time, tentative or probable. What is known is known temporarily and may be discarded when better data or better analysis of data is discovered. In any scientific discipline, knowledge is not considered either absolutely certain or immune from criticism. Knowledge is—to use the scientific term—*hypothetical:* assumed to need testing and, very likely, revision and modification. Intuitive knowledge, on the other hand, is certain. When one knows something intuitively, he has complete confidence that his knowledge is an accurate description of what really is. If I know intuitively that modern art is a fraud or that Soviet Russia is a constant threat to our way of life, then I am quite certain that these two are the case: not that they *appear* to be so, not that I *take* them to be so, or that they *may* be so; but that they are really, actually, substantially the way I say they are.

Even though a sizable body of knowledge, most of it reliable and time-tested, has been accumulated by the social sciences, neither the knowledge nor the process by which it was obtained is commonly employed in thinking about social problems. For instance, although neither psychology nor anthropology has yielded the slightest evidence that one race is inherently inferior to another, such a belief is widely held.[1] Many of those who hold such a belief are in positions to make

[1] One anthropologist argues that the entire concept of race is so misleading that we would do well to omit the word entirely. See Morton H. Fried, "A Four Letter Word that Hurts," *Saturday Review,* 48 (October 2, 1956): 21–35.

crucial decisions about education, law, and vocational opportunities, and their decisions are often predicated on belief in racial inferiority. In other instances, many people know, intuitively, that slum-dwellers are ineducable, lazy, shiftless, immoral, and given to periodic binges of violence. It is held that one need only view slum-dwellers to be convinced that they are the way they are because they are incapable of being any other way.

The data from the social sciences suggests, however, that all human behavior, including that of the slum-dweller, is extremely complex. Social scientists do not hold that anyone behaves in any particular way because "that is the way he is." Rather they talk about the interaction of human beings with social forces, about learned behavior, and about the factors which can influence and change behavior. It seems reasonable to suppose that, since most knowledge of slum-dwellers is of the intuitive kind and not informed by the methods or data of the social sciences, most persons take a rather pessimistic view of the slum-dweller, preferring to do nothing about slums because obviously nothing much can be done.

In another sphere, the intuitively held opinions about international relations are often at variance with the conclusions of social scientists. For instance, it is widely held that there is no real alternative to continual stockpiling of nuclear weapons because "the Communists are out to enslave the world" and it is useless to discuss any problems with them, since "all they understand is force." However, Harvard economist and former ambassador John Kenneth Galbraith points out that while such a belief has been the cornerstone of American foreign policy since the end of World War II, it can be proved that the United States has successfully discussed problems with Communists countries, and that negotiations on a wide variety of issues are presently in progress.[2] Nevertheless, many persons base their thinking about world issues on words such as "deterrent," "retaliation," and "containment."[3] As these words are being written, destructive riots are taking place in the slums of a number of large cities, and racial conflicts are perplexing municipal authorities and horrifying the general public. It seems reasonable to believe that the intuitively held knowledge of slums and racial differences is, to a large degree, responsible for the fact that as a culture we have not been able to solve these two festering social problems. And it also seems reasonable to believe that, until we employ the

---

[2] John Kenneth Galbraith, "Foreign Policy: The Stuck Whistle," *Atlantic,* 215 (February, 1965): 64–68.

[3] A social psychologist with an unusual analysis of this situation is Charles Osgood. See his *An Alternative to War Or Surrender* (Urbana: U. of Illinois, 1962).

trained intelligence of social scientists, these and other problems not only will persist but may well engulf us.[4]

Epistemology and Certain Educational Issues

A wide variety of education issues that have been debated for centuries are not really understandable without epistemological analysis. One such issue is whether or not certain knowledge is possible. The belief that certain knowledge is possible may be traced to the Greeks. Plato, for instance, distinguishes between knowing and not-knowing and provides a middle ground between the two which he calls opinion.[5] Plato seems to be saying that certain knowledge, which is the same as pure reality, lies outside our perception. To apprehend such knowledge involves introspection—that is, we can acquire certainty by a purely interior intellectual process. Observation and empirical evidence are not only unessential and unrealiable, but any knowledge gained through observation is probably irrelevant. One searches within himself to discover the universal truth. The universal is then applied to the particular.[6]

From Greek philosophy has come a tradition which may be summarized as follows: (1) There are higher and lower forms of knowledge. (2) Higher knowledge is an intellectual process obtained by introspection. (3) Lower knowledge is empirical and is deceptive and largely irrelevant.

This tradition manifests itself today in many ways. The hierarchy of subject matter discussed in chapters 1 and 2 is based on it. Further, there is still a tendency to disregard empirical observation when such observation may threaten one's deeply held beliefs. (This is recognized in the current saw: "Don't confuse me with facts, my mind is already made up.") There are many controversial issues whose solutions depend on the gathering of empirical data, but such data is often deliberately withheld or ignored. In brief, then, it appears that many believe that convictions about matters social and artistic can never be more than personal beliefs, completely out of the realm of empirical inquiry.

[4] This is an important theme in John Dewey's social philosophy. See, for instance, *Liberalism and Social Action* (New York: Putnam, 1963), and *Individualism Old and New* (New York: Minton, Putnam, 1962).

[5] This epistemological position may be found in a number of Plato's works, especially in the *Theatetus*. For extensive comment on it, see Copleston's *History of Philosophy*, Vol. I, Part 1, Chapter 19.

[6] *Ibid*, Chapter 20. For an interesting analysis of the social context of this position, see Alban Dewes Winspear, *The Genesis of Plato's Thought* (New York: Russell, 1940).

On the other hand, there is another widely held belief that certain knowledge resides *only* in the empirical. This belief is obviously the opposite of that just discussed. It may be summarized by the statement that problems in the physical and natural sciences can always be reduced to empirical data and, once the data is gathered and treated statistically, the solution is automatically within grasp. Whether fluorine in drinking water is desirable or harmful, for instance, can finally be settled by gathering large amounts of data. If a problem cannot be reduced to a statement that can be confirmed or denied by means of empirical data, then, it is held, it is not a "real" problem, or at least not an important one.

To recapitulate: There is a long-standing belief that certain knowledge is possible. The conflict is between those who feel that certain knowledge is intuitively grasped and those who believe that certainty comes only through the precise use of the scientific method and the collection of abundant data. A minority of persons—both philosophers and laymen—believe that certainty is neither possible nor desirable. The advocates of this philosophical belief, however, are likely to be little regarded by both intuitionists and empiricists.

Certainty and the Curriculum

If certain knowledge is possible—whatever its nature—then it is reasonable to want schools to deal with this sort of knowledge. Hence for many years schools have dealt with the curriculum as if it were a body of certainly known facts and concepts. Most subjects have been treated as if they were unchanging bodies of knowledge, to be transmitted without modification by teachers and accepted uncritically by students. Although there is—and has been for most of this century—much talk about the necessity for flexibility in the curriculum and the need to update the curriculum constantly, the fact is that, once introduced, curriculum has proved to be extremely resistant to change. It is a safe bet that as long as those involved in education believe that certain knowledge is possible, it will always be difficult to update, modify, introduce, or discard curriculum.

Indoctrination Another educational issue needing epistemological analysis is the question of indoctrination. Indoctrination has been defined as teaching a body of knowledge uncritically for the purpose of bringing about acceptance and allegiance. The epistemological belief that supports indoctrination is that the knowledge to be indoctrinated is both certain and completely essential: so essential and certain that students may not criticize or reject any part of it. Students may not exercise choice with regard to this knowledge, for to do so may lead to their holding dangerous beliefs. The knowledge to be indoctrinated must be learned completely, accepted, and cherished.

If this description of indoctrination is accurate—and it is fair to point out that both the meaning and desirability of indoctrination are extremely debatable—then it appears that indoctrination is *the* most frequently employed method of education. From the first grader learning the alphabet to high school students learning the truths of democracy versus communism, teachers appear to be indoctrinating most subject matter.

The conflict here is that indoctrination works against another often-stated value of American democracy: independent, autonomous thought. It is logically impossible both to think independently about an object of knowledge and to accept it uncritically. To think independently usually carries with it the connotation of analysis, probing evaluation, and possible modification or even rejection. To be indoctrinated carries with it the connotation of being committed to a belief *a priori*. One cannot be committed to believing something *a priori* and simultaneously evaluate that belief.

Non-indoctrinative teaching utilizes a different set of assumptions about knowledge. Deliberately to avoid indoctrination is to believe that absolutely certain knowledge—if it actually exists—cannot be attained. That is, whether something is certainly true for all times is not an issue that can be settled by any known human means. The avoidance of indoctrination also implies the assumption that the truth is not given beforehand. What is taken to be true is assumed to be always susceptible of change in the light of different data or interpretations. This is based on the principle of non-certainty—that whatever knowledge is taken to be true is regarded not as a statement of ultimate reality, but as an assumption which is more or less probable.[7]

Knowledge and Curriculum Another serious problem in education arises from the traditional conception of knowledge. Knowledge has usually been conceived as "bundles" of concepts, facts, skills, beliefs, and so on. These bundles are usually called "academic disciplines" and go by the name of history, biology, medicine, art, literature, mathematics, and so on. The assumption is that these bundles are divided into bodies of manageable size, which are then known collectively as the "curriculum." For example, biology is broken down into in-

[7] This point is discussed at some length in Ernest E. Bayles, *Democratic Educational Theory* (New York: Harper and Row, 1960), pp. 178–185.

troductory biology, genetics, ecology, mammalian biology, inverte-
brate biology, and so on. Literature is broken down into the writings of
a particular century, or a particular place, of a particular mode (essay,
poetry, novel), or into a particular style (realistic, naturalistic, romantic).

The high-school curriculum is usually similar to that of the university, except that the concepts are reduced in both number and
complexity. Thus a high-school course in American history has about
the same scope as a college course (for example, the founding of
America to the beginning of the Civil War), but less factual data is
included, and the complexities of interpretation are reduced. The
elementary-school curriculum is often similar to the high-school curriculum, with the material being reduced even further in size and
complexity. For instance, the high-school courses in biology, physiology,
chemistry, and physics are simplified and combined in elementary
school and are called "general science." The general science course
contains bits and dabs from most of the subdivisions of the discipline.

The problems arising from curricular organization based on this
conception of knowledge are these:

1. Clear-cut distinctions between the disciplines have vanished.
There is no sharp division among chemistry, biology, and physics at
the forefront of knowledge in these fields. Nor is there an absolute
dividing line between the content and method of physiology and
certain branches of psychology.

2. The data in each field accumulates so rapidly that it has become impossible for any one discipline to describe its scope and content accurately. For example, how does "biology" describe a subject
whose content is enriched daily by thousands of researchers working
in hundreds of laboratories, writing for scores of specialized journals?

3. It is impossible for any one person, no matter how hard he tries,
to "keep up" with the changes and growth in any one field. The changes,
combinations, additions, and permutations in the various fields of
knowledge have rendered obsolete the idea that there exist disciplines
which consist of stable combinations of immutable facts and concepts.

However, the traditional conception of knowledge persists and
seems to have created problems for teachers and students. For instance,
the idea of ioslated bundles of knowledge means that knowledge is
distinct and separate from individuals. That which is perceived as
separate is often perceived as unrelated to one's needs and interests.
Thus teachers for centuries have encountered students who won't
get interested in what they are supposed to learn.

The perception of knowledge as separate and unrelated bundles also appears to have resulted in the individual's inability to relate ideas. For instance, a friend of the writer who is a professor of pharmacology says that many of his students who take courses in physiology are unable to relate physiological concepts to pharmacology. The author recalls one student who complained bitterly because his paper in a social studies class had been graded on style. Why did he have to use good English? This wasn't an English class!

The practice of separating knowledge into isolated units which theoretically requires "mastery" has also created a situation in which one who finishes a particular class regards himself as having "mastered" the subject. Such "mastery" frequently prevents further interest or involvement in the subject. After all, what point is there in studying what one has already "mastered"?

Another difficulty inherent in a conception that knowledge must be mastered is that, once a subject has been learned and a student feels that he is in possession of the truth, he often has difficulty learning more about that subject. The college undergraduate who is faced by interpretations that conflict with his previous understandings often either does not learn the new material or compartmentalizes it—that is, new and contradictory ideas are kept separate from the old.

It seems apparent—but not realized—that the situation described above cannot be other than what it is unless and until a sharply different conception of knowledge prevails. As long as it is widely believed that knowledge exists external to persons, that it is possible to collect that knowledge and put it in a box, and that teaching consists of the transmission of boxes of knowledge, no significant change in teaching is possible. Talk of "learning to learn," "acquiring structure," or "training in inquiry and creativity" will remain on the level of talk.

Knowledge and Personality An unexplored but extremely important issue in education is the relationship between the possession of knowledge and certain personality characteristics. The use an individual makes of knowledge is influenced by personality characteristics. But what these personality characteristics are and how they are related to knowledge is but dimly understood. One may ask, "How much does one need to know in order to function in some particular capacity?" For example, how much does a teacher of science need to know in order to teach the subject properly? It is assumed that there is a floor under knowledge, and that one *must* possess a large body of information before he can effectively function in a discipline. It is also held, though unconsciously, that possession of sufficient knowledge is the sole requirement for success. But possession of information is obviously not enough to yield an effective professional.

We all know of the very intelligent, well-educated teacher who cannot enforce discipline, the engineer who cannot control his temper, or the cold and unsympathetic physician. Such persons may possess a large amount of subject matter content, but they are obviously ineffective in utilizing it. Thus it would appear that there is no simple answer to the question "How much must one know before he can successfully operate?" The answer may be, "One must know something, but in addition, must also possess certain personality qualities." But this answer raises a host of other questions, such as, "What are these other personality factors?" "How important are they?" "How do they relate to the knowledge possessed?"

Viewing the problem in another perspective, it really it not clear how much knowledge is essential. Before one can teach partial differential equations, he obviously must know the subject. But if the context is changed, the answer becomes less obvious. How much mathematics does an elementary-school teacher need to know before she can teach arithmetic to a seven-year-old child? What kind of background in political science or history is needed by a high-school teacher of civics? How much insect morphology must a high-school biology instructor have? How much musicology must be known by an elementary-school music teacher? Available data sheds very little light on these questions.

Indeed, very little is known about the relationship between intelligence or mastery of knowledge and success in teaching. Neither the grade point average, the intelligence quotient, the number or kinds of courses taken in college, nor other cognitive factors give an infallible index to the quality of teaching.[8] Nor has much really impressive evidence turned up to indicate precisely what kinds of personality factors make for successful teaching—although hundreds of lists of such characteristics are available. Apparently the entire relationship among personality variables, cognitive factors, and successful teaching remains to be explored. It may well be that the amount of knowledge essential for a teacher is less important than the attitude of the teacher

---

[8] Not that the issue has been ignored. Numerous studies on this problem are available, and many researchers have tried to correlate cognitive and personality characteristics with good teaching. But the problems in such research are extraordinary. A good review of the literature on this subject is to be found in N. L. Gage (ed.), *Handbook of Research on Teaching* (Chicago: Rand McNally, 1963). See especially the article by J. W. Getzels and P. W. Jackson, "The Teacher's Personality and Characteristics," the section on "Cognitive Abilities."

toward the nature of knowledge. If this is true, the entire problem is essentially philosophical. The attitude one has toward knowledge is directly influenced by what one takes to be knowledge—that is, his conception of how knowing takes place.

Transfer of Training   Another educational issue of long standing concerns transfer of training. "Transfer of training" is the name for a process in which the knowledge, concepts, skills, or techniques one possesses in one area are related to another, different area. An example of transfer of training is relating one's knowledge of the principles of motivation to the selling of cars or the teaching of a subject.

Transfer of training has been of concern to educators in this century since Thorndike became interested in the problem at the end of the nineteenth century. The older, nineteenth-century notion was that transfer of training was automatic. If one developed his faculty of memory in any area, he would then be able to memorize names, faces, dates, and anything else. For this reason, grammar and poetry were often taught deliberately to improve the faculty of memory, and geometry was taught to improve the faculty of reason.

The problem of transfer of training was related to the question "What knowledge is of the most worth?" The answer was "That knowledge which can most facilitate transfer." The belief that certain subjects—and only certain subjects—were most useful in transferring mental skills led to a fixed curriculum in which these subjects were taught for centuries with little modification. However, in the nineteenth century, when schools were forced to reassess their traditional role, the question "What knowledge is of the most worth?" was raised anew. The answer now was that the most worthwhile subjects were those which had the most practical value—for it was now assumed that schools should teach people how to deal with practical problems. Probably this answer reflects the influence of Herbert Spencer and William James, both of whom emphasized scientific knowledge and believed that education should prepare one to live life as it actually was.[9]

In the first quarter of this century, a powerful movement in educational theory brought into the schools a rather radical approach to transfer of training. Curriculum theorists like Henry Clinton Morrison and Franklin Bobbit thought that the schools should teach what students would actually be doing in later life—but teach them in such a way that they would do it better. It was thought that the curriculum

---

[9] A good discussion of Spencer's and James' position is in Lawrence A. Cremin, *The Transformation of the American School* (New York: Knopf, 1962).

should be based on what people actually did, and what they actually did could be determined by objective observers. In effect, one would learn those spelling words which were used, and not difficult or exotic words; one would learn those arithmetical fractions that were actually used in business and industry and not simply unusual or difficult fractions. The assumption behind this was fairly simple: to facilitate improved practice, teach precisely what was actually being done in life out of school.[10] Because science and technology had become more and more important in this century, what happened was that scientific and practice-centered subjects dominated the curriculum, at the expense of the traditional literary, grammar-oriented courses.

However, the last decade or so has seen the rise of new conditions which have caused many to raise questions about the belief that "practical," or utilitarian, subjects are of the most worth in education. Because of extremely rapid technological advances, many vocational skills have been rendered obsolete at an increasingly rapid rate. It is now expected that the average person will be required to change his vocation perhaps three or four times within his lifetime. The question is now, "What kind of education will most facilitate the expected vocational changes?" The curriculum that has grown up in this century—practice-centered, empirical, fact-oriented—apparently has not provided students with the kind of background they need to shift from one vocation to another. What, then, should replace it?

The answer now being proposed is that schools should not teach a narrow range of practical skills which may be obsolescent within a few years. Rather, they should teach those subjects which will give a person the broadest kind of conceptual background, one that will enable him to transfer his knowledge and training to new vocations and new skills. Such a curriculum is thought of as emphasizing reading skills, the ability to solve mathematical problems, knowledge of scientific procedures—in short, a curriculum that will facilitate transfer of cognitive skills.[11]

Thus we seem to be returning to a conception of knowledge that

[10] For instance, Thorndike's famous wordbook contained the 10,000 most frequently used words in this country. This book became the basis for spelling in schools throughout the country. For a detailed discussion of this educational development, see Ernest E. Bayles and Bruce L. Hood, *Growth of American Thought and Practice* (New York: Harper and Row, 1966).

[11] This problem is a perennial one in educational research. For an introduction to it, see Ole Sand, "Six Basic Issues in Determining What to Teach," *Chicago Schools Journal*, 43 (January, 1962): 170–177. For a more detailed and technical discussion, see the section entitled "Transfer of Training and the Formal Lecture," in William H. Lucio (ed), *Readings in American Education* (Chicago: Scott, Foresman) 1963.

was prevalent more than a century ago. Despite the changes in educational methodology, learning theory, and psychology, the central assumption behind many recent curriculum proposals is about what it was prior to the twentieth century: that knowledge is of most worth which can find the widest possible application through transfer of training.

These epistemological problems have been cited because they seem to support the contention that properly to understand theories of learning, curriculum, motivation, educational methods—really all educational problems—an understanding of theories of knowledge is essential.

The Language of Epistemology

To understand problems of truth and knowledge, one must understand the terminology philosophers have used. Much of the specialized terminology centers around the the modes of knowing: knowledge grained from the senses, knowledge gained from a higher power, and so forth. Following is a discussion of the most commonly used terms, with explanations, examples, and analyses of the difficulties of each mode of knowing.

Empiricism

The term "empiricism" or "empirical," as we have had occasion to see in other contexts, refers to any knowledge gained by the senses —hearing, smell, taste, touch, and sight. To say that something is cold or that it is brown is to base an assertion on knowledge gained through the senses. Empiricism has the additional meaning of knowledge *capable* of being known by sensory experience. For instance, the discussion of the moon at this moment centers around the surface—is it soft, dusty, thin, hard? The discussion is somewhat speculative, for as yet no person has been to the moon. But it is assumed by all that whatever knowledge is gained about the moon will be gained empirically. Thus empiricism may refer not only to knowledge that *is* known by the senses but also to knowledge that *may* be gained through the senses.

It is generally admitted that all scientific knowledge is empirical—in one or the other of the two senses just described. Knowledge about comets, cell structure, atoms, is gained by sensory experience. Even if, as in the case of atomic physics, the knowledge must be inferred, the basis of the inference is still some empirical fact—some event that may be verified empirically. But empirical knowledge is a classification yet more inclusive than this. Most persons prefer to believe that, in some sense, *all* their knowledge has an empirical ground. It is generally hoped that what we say about the world can be shown to have an empirical basis in the world. Even statements for which there is no available empirical evidence—statements about the existence of a supernatural power or an afterlife—are assumed to be grounded in what can be known in some way through the senses.

What are the problems of empiricism? A major problem lies in the thing being sensed. If we are sensing ice cream and say that it is cold, our knowledge is based on the ice cream as it is now. But in a few minutes the ice cream will be drippy and warm. Thus, as Heraclitus observed, the objects of our senses change from moment to moment and render knowledge of objects always susceptible of change—hence always doubtful. Knowledge about ice cream does not usually constitute an epistemological problem, but empirical events that last for an infinitesimally brief time or which extend for millions of years do constitute real problems. The life of an atomic particle, for instance, may be a millionth of a second; knowledge of this particle may be inferred only with difficulty by observing tracks left on photographic plates. Events that take thousands of years are, in another way, equally difficult to understand. In short, empirical knowledge is limited and often highly problematical by reason of the nature of the thing observed.

In addition, empirical knowledge is influenced by the one who does the observing. The position that one occupies in relation to the object affects one's perception of the object. The famous legend of the seven blind men examining an elephant illustrates this fact. From the vantage point of one, the elephant was clearly like a rope; from that of another, it was very much like a wall, and so on. We might generalize and say that observations are affected by the capacity to observe. A better trained observer is likely to obtain more accurate knowledge than a poorly trained one. A more intelligent person is likely to observe more competently than a less intelligent one. Too, empirical observation may be affected subtly by little-understood factors—fatigue, anxiety, emotional illness.

These points may be readily granted. But it must be seen that such terms as "better trained," "less intelligent," and even "emotional illness" are ultimately value judgments. Thus when we are forced to choose between empirically based conclusions of two different observers, we must often rely on some rather subjective judgments about who is the better trained, the more competent, or the more stable. As in the case of a jury weighing conflicting evidence, the determination of what empirical event really occurred is likely to be based on a judgment about which witness appears to be more honest and less biased.[12]

The relevance of all this for teachers is that apparently simple facts are not simple: nor are they necessarily only factual. A fact is enmeshed in a context that clearly involves values and value judgments. A simple historical fact—Columbus discovered America in 1492—depends for its acceptance on one's willingness to accept the definition of "discovery" as meaning discovery by Europeans who made the new information known to other Europeans. Whether one wishes to accept a biological fact depends ultimately on one's confidence in the training and ability of the biologist who enunciates the fact.

Apparently simple categories that appear to be factual may be deceiving. The terms "Revolt" and "Reformation," discussed earlier, illustrate this point. That a given series of events occurred in the sixteenth century is granted by all historians. But whether the events constituted a "revolt," which carries with it the connotation of a rebellion against rightfully constituted authority, or a "reformation," which carries the connotation of a cleansing and purification of a socially diseased situation, is a value judgment. The simple factual category, therefore, depends on the biases, experiences, preconceptions, prejudices, beliefs, and attitudes of the one who is categorizing. Clearly, the person who observes or describes an object or event has much to do with the report of that object or event.

This problem is not confined to the social sciences; it is also of considerable importance to the so-called "hard" or "precise" sciences. The author recently attended a meeting in which a cellular biologist attacked a statement by a biochemist and was vigorously refuted by the biochemist. Both were, presumably, utilizing empirical data. But there was little agreement, first, on what facts existed, and second, on the meaning of certain facts. Both of the disputants—brilliant, experienced and colorful individuals—were apparently doing something very different to what is often called the cold, hard, facts.

Despite the problems inherent in empiricism, teachers must understand and use it. It has been shown that concept formation in young children depends on observation of many individual objects. Thus the concept of "animal" is built up through empirical observation of

---

[12] In a trial in which the author happened to be a member of the jury, some critical decisions were reached because most of the jury members were impressed by the honest naiveté of one witness and repelled by the slickness of another. Even though the latter was a professional and a trained observer, the jury members tended to discount his evidence.

many animals. That animals give birth, take in sustenance, and die is learned, usually slowly and over a period of time, by means of observation of different kinds of animals in different circumstances. If we believe that concept formation is rooted in knowledge gained through the sensory process, many implications follow. For instance, it is now thought that many learning problems, particularly in children who are classified as "deprived" or "underprivileged," may be traced to lack of sensory stimuli.[13] The difficulties in reading may well be traced to inadequate sensory experiences in infancy, a lack which, in ways now only guessed at, interferes with proper concept formation.

Finally, if classroom teachers come to understand the nature and limitations of empiricism, they will probably tend to be less assertive, less insistent on the sacred, unchanging certainty of their data, and more cautious and restrained.

Rationalism

The term *rationalism* describes a philosophical attitude completely opposite to empiricism.[14] Whereas empiricism stresses that truth comes only from the senses, rationalism holds that true knowledge proceeds only from unaided reason—that is, truth is something ultimately reducible to the workings of the intellect.

Of course, rationalists do not ignore the senses. Sensory evidence constitutes the basic building blocks, the raw material of knowledge. But until the raw material is worked on by reason, it has no significance. That which is thought out and intellectualized, and that which reveals consistency and agreement among ideas, is true. All else is either less true or untrue.

One may understand the rationalist's position by examining the thinking of Socrates, one of the first of the rationalist philosophers. Socrates did not trust the knowledge that comes from observation of things. Objects, he felt, are intrinsically illusory. The things we know from our senses change, die out, disappear, and often contradict one another. To place full reliance on observation of things is to depend too much on that which is not sufficiently permanent to yield truth or

---

[13] This observation is supported by evidence that, as of now, is most sketchy. See A. Harry Passow (ed.), *Education in Depressed Areas* (New York: Columbia U. Press, 1965), especially the article by Martin Deutch, "The Disadvantaged Child and the Learning Process." See also Benjamin S. Bloom and others, *Compensatory Education for Cultural Deprivation* (New York: Holt, Rinehart and Winston, 1965).

[14] For a good discussion of rationalism, see Harold H. Titus, *Living Issues in Philosophy*, Fourth Edition (New York: American Book, 1964), pp. 30–31.

sufficiently coherent to be universal. Ultimate truth comes not from observation, but from reflecting, from attempting to discover not the limited and inaccurate generalizations stemming from sensations, but from aiming through thought at the permanent, unchanging principles, concepts, and truths.

Socrates felt that the ultimate truths known by the intellect were either metaphysical or mathematical in nature. Questions about ultimate reality, the ends of existence, and ultimate values were known by a process of introspection. As we have pointed out in the chapter on metaphysics, Socrates believed that ultimate truths were glimpsed in some kind of pre-existence and that only through introspection could one recollect them. Too, Socrates held a belief shared by many rationalists today: that mathematics represents a key to the understanding of reality. Mathematics, with its emphasis on consistency and agreement among concepts, its deductive process, and the assumption that it need have no relationship to the empirical world, has always fascinated rationalists. The most important knowledge is judged to be either mathematical or that which most resembles the mathematical— that is, which shares emphasis on agreement, deduction, coherency, and harmony.

The influence of rationalism has been extremely powerful in education. As we have seen, the very heavy emphasis in the Middle Ages on abstract, non-empirical subjects—logic, mathematics, grammar— appears to be in the mainstream of rationalism. Such subjects are, of course, still taught in universities and still command a considerable amount of prestige. There is today a continuing disagreement between those of a rationalist temperament, who prefer to emphasize the products of thought, and empiricists, who believe that more important truth comes from observation of the tangible world. This disagreement is not simply a matter of personality and style differences, but a disagreement as to what constitutes true knowledge.

Intuition

One of the sources of rationalistic knowledge is intuition. Intuition —in the traditional sense of the term—is direct and immediate knowledge without the intermediary of either sense perception or conscious thought. In a sense, an intuition is a sure and certain feeling that something is true or real. An intuition, which may or may not be verbalized, is often a welling up, a surging knowledge that *this* is the way things are.

The intuitive approach to truth may be found in many intellectual activities. Benedetto Croce posits that an artist experiences an intuition and later translates the intuition into a work of art. The intuition, says Croce, is all important, while the translation into canvass, wood, or marble is merely secondary technique.[15] Intuitions also operate in the context of ethics. One may intuit a particular value—that is, one feels that a given act is evil, or that a given act is absolutely and necessarily good. One can analyze the Biblical prophets' moral pronouncements as essentially intuitive: the phrase "Thus saith the Lord" may not mean literally, "God told me thus and such." It may mean that in the very nature of things, in the very order that God created, oppressing the poor, for example, is evil. If this interpretation is sound, then the prophets' moral code is an example of intuited values.

Mathematicians also make use of a kind of intuited knowledge. Certain mathematical propositions, often called axioms and postulates, are intuited truths. There is no way to demonstrate empirically that one and only one straight line can be drawn through two points or that certain other mathematical propositions are true. These propositions must be accepted as self-evidently true, intuitively known.

Intuition, as we have been discussing the term, may be viewed as both an inestimable boon to mankind and a tragic barrier to knowledge. Creative thinkers, and those who admire creative thought, have come to value intuition as the source of beautiful and useful productions.[16] But in many cases, once the intuition has been felt, the end of the epistemological process occurs: one "knows" or "feels" the truth and hence need not test the intuition to see if it is, in some sense, valid. Thus the thinkers in the nineteenth and twentieth centuries who intuitively realized that some races were inherently inferior, or that some nation was destined by God or history to rule the world, acted on the intuition and wreaked unspeakable horror.[17]

Further, an intellectual system built on intuited premises may be logically harmonious and impressive but have nothing whatsoever to do with the observable world. Many brilliant systems that are internally satisfactory cannot be put into practice. And when they are—as when

---

[15] Croce even equates intuition with the perception of reality. He says, "By intuition is frequently understood *perception*, or the knowledge of actual reality." See his *Aesthetic* (London: Macmillan, 1909); reprinted in Morris Weitz, *Problems in Aesthetics* (New York: Macmillan, 1959), p. 94.

[16] An interesting work on this topic is Harold Rugg, *Imagination* (New York: Harper and Row, 1963).

[17] See S. Samuel Shermis, "The Probable Bases of Racial Prejudice with Emphasis on Concepts of Inferiority," *Educational Theory*, 15 (April, 1965): 143–153.

Pestalozzi attempted to implement Rousseau's educational system—they may fail miserably, as in fact Rousseau's ideas did.[18]

Teachers need to realize that intuition is the source of much of what we call knowledge. It is philosophically desirable, for instance, to realize that Western civilization is built on many intuitions; that St. Paul's or Socrates' vision of the truth reflects the way these two individuals, in certain conditions, at certain historical periods happened to view the world. It is also desirable to realize that certain intuitive knowledge is not universally true, but rather reflects the insights of a particular culture. Beliefs about right and wrong, property values, the necessity of achievement—in short, some core values of Western civilization—are not regarded as necessarily true or self-evident by much of the rest of the world.

Teachers ought also to realize that many students rely on intuition lazily as a thought-saving device. When such students are asked to explain a thought process or defend a point of view, they retreat into "That's the way I feel about it," or "Isn't this obvious to everyone?" To be sure, this may indeed be the way they feel about it, and it may appear that "everyone" should see it this way. But even then, good thinking requires that personal and private thoughts be brought out for logical or empirical examination to see if they are clear and consistent, coherent, valid, or empirically true. Hence teachers need to recognize when students are operating at the intuitive level and to question students' conclusions in order to elicit more awareness.

Logic, Reason, and Deduction

Another epistemological source employed by rationalists is logic, which we shall treat as equivalent to reason and the deductive process. The traditional logical process is embodied in the syllogism. In his discourse on logic, the *Organon*, Aristotle defines the syllogism as follows: "A syllogism is discourse in which, certain things being stated, something other than what is stated follows of necessity from their being so." [19]

The syllogism proceeds in this manner: There is first a generalization, called a *major premise*. The generalization is assumed to cover all cases—that is, to hold true in every instance. The traditional exam-

[18] This judgment, while harsh, is supported by most historians. For a good evaluation of Rousseau and Pestalozzi, see Frederick Eby, *The Development of Modern Education*, second edition (Englewood Cliffs: Prentice-Hall, 1959), Chapter 17.
[19] Prior Analytics, Book I, Part 1.

ple of a major premise is "All men are mortal." This is followed by a *minor premise,* a specific instance of the major premise: "Socrates is a man." From the major and minor premises a conclusion may be deduced—in this case, "Therefore, Socrates is mortal." The assumption is that if the major and minor premises are properly stated, a conclusion or inference may be drawn about the relationship of the generalization to the specific case. There are many qualifications and rules that control the syllogistic process, and these usually require an entire book or a complete course to cover.

The deductive process in general is essentially an intellectual one in which symbols are manipulated according to certain rules. The assumption is that if the major and minor premises of a syllogism are true, and if the manipulation is correct, the conclusion will be a kind of truth. But this truth is not empirical. In the case of our example, that "Socrates is mortal," we see not a typical empirical statement but rather a logical deduction, a conclusion expressing a particular relationship between the general "truth" and the specific "truth."

There are a number of difficulties in the use of deductive logic. First is the assumption that the major premise is true in all cases. Major premises taken to be self-evidently true often are not evident to all individuals. Second, the conclusion may be logically valid but untrue. This means that the inferential process may be *formally* correct but *materially* wrong: even though the process follows the correct rules of deduction, it may still yield a false conclusion. For instance, let us assert that everyone who reads this book has an I.Q. lower than 80. John S. is reading this book. Therefore, John S. has an I.Q. lower than 80. The logic in this instance is impeccable and the conclusion logically valid; but perhaps the conclusion is sufficiently disturbing to enable you to see the fallacy.

For many reasons the logical process often has been taken to be a complete, self-enclosed and perfect mode of knowing. We have noted (Chapter 3) that a group of university students in the seventeenth century debated the origin of well water. In this particular debate, typical of many university debates at that time, the two disputants made considerable use of logic to "prove" their points. It would be a strange person today who would not use observation to decide the facts in such a matter. But in this case, and in many others, extensive and subtle deductive procedures were used, not to accompany, but to substitute for observation or experimentation. Similarly, logic has been used to provide knowledge that is taken to be reliable. But such knowledge, although verbally convincing, may be hollow.

Despite the difficulties inherent in logic, the ability to reason consistently and accurately is essential to good thinking. Most people regard logical errors—for example, over-generalization, hasty conclusions, incorrect deductions—as undesirable. Teachers need to point out to students when and how their logical analysis suffers from these or other weaknesses. Often if a term report is neat, a prepared speech conventionally eloquent, or an examination paper covered with facts, teachers will overlook logical blunders. Too, a student may arrive at a right answer by luck, having committed logical errors in the process. The teacher should attempt to probe the thought process of the student and not simply welcome a correct answer arrived at faultily.

Opportunities exist for teachers in all disciplines—especially in science, mathematics, and the social studies—to teach students the reasoning process. Teachers may ask how students reached a particular conclusion, what steps were involved in arriving at a particular answer. Attempts may be made to examine both the empirical data and the inferential process used in a conclusion. It is sometimes necessary for teachers to point out that a student has made or is headed toward a logical fallacy.

As we have seen, logic and intuition are the preferred methods of rationalists. Both are essentially introspective mental processes, and they have proven extremely absorbing and gratifying to many thinkers. Many intuited and deduced "truths" have later been demonstrated empirically, and others have been first steps in inquiries that ultimately depended for their conclusions on empirical support. If, however, logic or intuition is taken as complete and self-contained, it is likely to lead to dogmatism, rigidity, and contempt for empirical observation and experience.

Authority

Most of what we claim to know is not based on either our own observation or our own analysis. Most of our knowledge has been handed down to us by sources we designate as "authorities." There is a simple reason for this: most knowledge is simply beyond our capacity to verify. We have no way of knowing about Columbus except through the writings of historians—who, of course, relied for much of their information on other authorities.[20] Similarly, most of our knowledge of scientific events is gained from the writings of scientists or, in many instances, from those who are themselves not scientists but write about

[20] Not that historians do not use documents or other kinds of evidence. Indeed, they spend much of their time searching through archives for diaries, letters, orders, newspapers, and other data that bear on their problems. Often a newly unearthed document may force revision of a standard and accepted historical interpretation. However, historians must rely on the interpretation of others for many of their conclusions.

scientific developments. And most of our values are not the result of personal commitment or analysis but are "given" to us by those we accept as authorities. There is nothing inherently wrong with this if we are aware of our reliance and if we pay attention to the nature of the authorities we rely on.

One or more persons may constitute an authority. For communists, Karl Marx and Vladimir Lenin function as authorities. For Roman Catholics, the Pope is an authority. Many persons interested in Italian Renaissance art accept Bernard Berenson as an authority. Groups of persons may function as authority figures. For instance, the phrase "scientists say" reveals that anyone who fills the role of a scientist may claim considerable authority. Once the United States Supreme Court, a group of nine men, has made a legal decision, it has the weight of great authority in the thinking of attorneys and judges throughout the country.

A book may serve as an authority. *Das Kapital,* the Old Testament, Gray's *Anatomy,* the *Encyclopaedia Britannica,* the *Koran,* and *Webster's Unabridged Dictionary* are examples of books looked on as authoritative by many. Institutions may also function as authorities. Congress, the Church, and the Bureau of Standards are cultural institutions which illustrate this kind of authority.

The principal characteristic of knowledge by authority is that it is usually accepted without reservation or criticism. Since, as we have seen, it is impossible to avoid basing our beliefs largely on authority, it is important to recognize the problems involved in accepting authority.

First, authorities may and frequently do conflict. Two scientists may come to very different conclusions, or two historians may disagree about the meaning of the "same" event. There are many instances of this kind of disagreement. At present scientific authorities are in disagreement about the potential danger to health of nuclear testing, the efficacy of certain drugs, the archaeological character of the Pacific Northwest, the statistical significance of data about the relationship of cigarettes and cancer—to name only a few. Too, there may be different authority *systems*—for example, the Catholic Papacy and the Central Committee of the Communist Party.

Another problem regarding knowledge by authority is a basic one of definition: Who is an authority? If we say simply, "Anyone considered an authority by some group," then we run the risk of being thoughtless. However, what is the alternative? How does one identify and appraise an authority? We may appraise the credentials of an authority by the usual criteria of the length of his study, his accuracy in predictions, or his widespread acceptance by competent judges, but these are ultimately extremely subjective criteria, which most of us can hardly apply. How does one decide whether Bernard Berenson and Paul Dudley White are truly knowledgeable authorities about art and heart disease? How many of us know even enough to begin to evaluate authorities?

Finally, it should be recognized that authorities are quite capable of making not only minor errors but serious blunders—that is, the authority is not infallible. Karl Marx was most definitely wrong in his prediction concerning the occurrence of socialism.[21] The great theoretical physicist Albert Einstein admitted that a theory of his, on which he had spent many years, was wrong. Many predictions by experts about the end of the great depression were flatly erroneous. This list could be multiplied almost indefinitely. In the first few pages of each issue of *Scientific American*, a monthly journal of general science, there is a column of excerpts from scientific articles originally printed fifty and a hundred years ago in the same journal. Many of the sage comments made by recognized authorities of those times now elicit only chuckles.

The fallible and contradictory nature of authorities is often not recognized. Many who are dimly aware that they hold beliefs supported by two different, oppositional authority systems compartmentalize the disagreement. One may operate in his business according to the Machiavellian stereotype: shrewd, aggressive, willing to use any means to gain an end, exploitative, engaging in constant duplicity. On Sundays the same person will sincerely assent to the spirit of Scripture and verbalize adherence to the ethic of charity, love, and brotherhood.

Schools have not made a serious attempt to teach students to appraise and examine authorities. Rather, they tend to inculcate acceptance of authority by an exaggerated emphasis on the "rightness" of teachers and textbooks. Indeed, students may incur severe sanctions by questioning acceptance of authority, a fact which works against one of the stated aims of American education: to teach students to think independently. It is not possible to inculcate reverence for authority and also encourage independent thinking.

Since authoritative knowledge is—or certainly appears to be—unavoidable, schools should make students aware of the characteristics of authority. Specifically, students should realize that much of their knowledge is gained by means of authority. Second, students should learn something about the nature and problems of knowledge by

[21] Marx predicted that the most industrialized and technologically advanced country would be the first to adopt a socialistic system. He had in mind Germany. In fact, the first major country to become socialist was Russia, the least advanced technologically and probably the most backward country in Europe.

authority. Third, whenever possible, students themselves should learn to appraise authority; for instance, by placing two contradictory authorities side by side and examining both. It should be realized that blind veneration which we often show to some authority figures is more appropriate to a totalitarian social system than to one in which each person is assumed capable of appraising meanings for himself. Finally, one may learn that there are different ways of behaving toward an authority. One may regard an authority as the repository of ultimate truth and literal fact; or one may view an authority as *one* good source of opinion. The former, although emotionally satisfying, tends to shut off intellectual growth. The second, although extremely difficult—because it involves appraisal and a high degree of sensitivity to different shades of meaning—tends to enhance intellectual growth.

Revelation

Revelation is a method of knowing that is quite similar to intuition.[22] The essential difference between the two is that intuitions are supposed to arise internally, from within the individual, and revelations are supposed to come from an external source. The similarity between the two is that both are assumed to reflect *certain* knowledge and both are difficult to explain by the commonly accepted rational or empirical methods.

The assumption behind revealed knowledge is that there exists a higher power, usually called "God" or the "deity." The higher power, in a fashion not easily understandable, communicates certain kinds of knowledge to man. At this point there are two other assumptions. Usually only certain kinds of people, sometimes called "prophets," are assumed to be capable of receiving and/or interpreting revelations; and the knowledge given by God to man usually (but not always) is moral knowledge which he would not be capable of discovering independently—that is, left to himself, man would flounder in ignorance. To prevent this, the higher power sends his word to some men,[23] who are under obligation to communicate this knowledge to all.

Revelations usually consist of prescriptions or proscriptions about behavior. The higher power tells the recipient that all *must* behave

[22] Van Cleve Morris makes this distinction in *Philosophy and the American School* (Boston: Houghton Mifflin, 1961). See the section on "Varieties of Knowing."

[23] Usually men are the recipients of revelations, but not always. The Old Testament talks about some "prophetesses," and occasionally a woman will appear who claims to have received the word of God. Ann Hutchinson, the American colonial figure, claimed to know God's word through an "inner light."

in a certain manner or that all must *not* behave in a certain manner. The Ten Commandments exemplify this kind of revelation. But the higher power may also communicate advance information about an event that is to take place, as when God told Jeremiah of a future invasion or when He informed Joseph Smith, the Mormon prophet and leader in the early nineteenth century, of the Golden Plates.

The manner in which revelations are known is always difficult to explain. In some cases the revelation proceeds by means of a dream, as the Pharaoh's dreams which Joseph was required to interpret. The revelation may appear by a visible sign, as a figure in the sky or a burning bush. Often the revelations are brought directly by God's emissary, perhaps an angel. The revelations of Hebrew prophets have been interpreted by some as not the literal communications of God, but as a kind of intuitive knowledge which the prophets, especially sensitive "consciences" of the people, were simply called on to publicize.

Because the precise nature of the communication is unclear and because the entire concept of knowledge by revelation rests on a metaphysical assumption that many do not accept—the existence of a higher power—many do not regard revelation as a valid means of knowing.

It is pointed out that revelations are often employed to rationalize some particular value or even defend some line of behavior that is not readily acceptable. It is also pointed out that the data of a revelation is not empirically demonstrable. Finally, it is alleged that the very occurrence of revelation is not open either to inquiry or public examination. We must rely on the person's word that he has experienced revelation, for in the nature of revelation it is not possible to produce empirical data to support any claim of its occurrence.[24]

Whatever the validity of revelation, it is fairly obvious that our moral code is based, to a large extent, on what has been considered revealed wisdom. Insofar as this is so, students should realize that much of what we take to be ethically desirable is not self-evidently good. Our notions of truth, social justice, obedience to external authority, sexual chastity, and many other values—although they may be defended on other grounds—are derived from the Old and New Testa-

[24] There is an important distinction to be made between a scientific prediction and a prophecy in the Biblical sense. A scientific prediction is made prior to the event and there is usually, implicit or explicit, a rational explanation of the event. A prophecy is not characterized by empirical checks, operational definitions, or specifications of time, place, and circumstances. For a good but lengthy and technical discussion of the meaning of prediction, see Richard Lewinsohn, *Science, Prophecy and Prediction* (Greenwich: Fawcett, 1961).

ments. The subsequent interpretations and elaborations, no matter
how they "fit" with the social and economic movements of the time,
are still grounded in the revelations claimed to have been received
by the Hebrew prophets and early Christians.

Despite the fact that any religious concept is extremely sensitive
ground in our pluralistic culture and may provide difficulties in the
classroom, teachers can still deal with revelationally based beliefs. It
is not necessary for teachers either to endorse or refute revelation or
the beliefs derived from revelation. It is necessary, rather, to help
students recognize the character of revelation. This may be accomplished by employing a principle proposed by Professor Wilbur
Murra.[25] Professor Murra claims that public schools can deal only
with temporal knowledge. That is, only events that can be shown to
exist in a particular time and place should be admitted as valid for the
purpose of public school teaching. Teachers, for instance, may not
say that "God sent the Puritans to this country," but rather that "Puritans believed that God had sent them to this country." The first statement is an explicit acceptance of revelation and as such is a creedal
admission. The second is an acknowledgment that revelation played
an important part in the history of our country.[26]

In short, teachers need to be more sensitive to revelation as a
mode of knowing—just as they need to be more sensitive to all other
modes of knowing. Educational philosophers, too, need to investigate
this mode of knowledge, for while its specific inclusion in classrooms
is ruled out by the secular nature of public schools, it has so permeated the thought process of Western civilization that it cannot be
disregarded.

Common Sense

Knowledge by common sense combines some of the elements of
both authority and intuition. Common-sense knowing is usually
thought of as understanding which is available to the untutored awareness of the average person. "I know enough to get in out of the rain"
or "Don't tease barking dogs" are examples of the kind of knowledge
said to be common sense, or "good, old-fashioned horse sense." The
assumption is that "anybody" can observe a situation and immediately
determine for himself the obvious and important elements. From this

[25] "Suggested Theory for Determining the Role of Religion in Public Schools,"
The Proceedings of the 18th Meeting of the Philosophy of Education Society, 1962.
[26] See Joseph Gaer and Ben Siegel, *The Puritan Heritage: America's Roots in
the Bible* (New York: New American Library, 1964).

determination are supposed to come prescriptions. For example, barking dogs can be observed to bite. Therefore, any normal person would want to avoid teasing a barking dog.

When one examines the assumptions underlying the common-sense mode of knowing, problems appear. Who or what is the "normal," "average" person on whom the given common-sense theory depends? How certain is it that there exist, independent of people, certain intrinsic, absolute meanings which can be determined? The assumption that meanings exist independent of all persons but that all persons could or should derive the same meanings from the identical situation is philosophically naive. Finally, the assumption that the meanings are somehow self-evident is replete with philosophical difficulties. In brief, when one applies a vigorous philosophical analysis to common-sense knowledge, it is seen that this mode of knowing depends on a large number of shaky assumptions about the nature of reality and the nature of knowing.

Further, the very content of common-sense knowledge is often contradictory and inconsistent. The sort of maxims to be found in *Poor Richard's Almanac*, for instance, do not provide a coherent framework. We are told that "he who hesitates is lost," meaning presumably that in a crucial situation one must not equivocate but must act swiftly and decisively. But we are also told that "haste makes waste"! Apparently, too, maxims enshrined as common sense reflect the cultural values of a previous historical time and may conflict with cultural values of the present.

One hears the argument that certain kinds of knowledge are truly common in that they arise out of the shared, instinctual drives of the human race. However, employing a theory of instinctual behavior to support common sense is most risky. "Instincts" is a vague label often used to hide the fact that one really does not know much about some puzzling behavior. Whether instincts exist and how they function is a question better left to biologists and psychologists. In any event, as a rationale for supporting common-sense knowledge, the instinct argument will not do. How an inherited biological *tendency* could be responsible for knowledge is far from clear.

Since common-sense knowledge reflects cultural values and traditions so thoroughly, and since most of us have been so completely enculturated, we are likely to label any and all frequently seen phenomena as "natural," "self-evident," or "common sense." In a classroom discussion in which these terms are employed, the teacher ought to stimulate students to inquire into the assumptions underlying their statements. Is it, in fact, common sense for the strong to prey on the weak, or for the oppressed to rise up against the oppressor, as is often stated? Is it really common sense that people are "naturally" selfish? Is it common sense that severe punishment is necessary for criminals because such punishment acts naturally as a deterrent? In these examples the critical terms "selfish" and "deterrent" need definition, and the evidence that is supposed to support the assertions needs closer critical scrutiny.

Teachers should also realize that common-sense knowledge, while it may contain elements of truth, reflects hidden biases. The common-sense assertion that production is controlled by the law of supply and demand—a position which probably made much sense when Adam Smith discussed it in the eighteenth century—reflects not an infallible truth but an economic conviction peculiar to our culture. Thus the law of supply and demand, a common-sense notion widely believed, should be examined to see to what extent it holds and to what extent it does not hold. Indeed, the assertion, discussion, probing, and analysis should reveal both the wisdom and the inconsistencies of common-sense knowledge.

The Scientific Method

The scientific method is a mode of knowing developed and elaborated since the early Renaissance. In the original Latin, *scientia* meant "what is known." Science, then, referred broadly to true and valid knowledge. Today "science" usually refers to systematized knowledge gained through methodical, empirical observation, collection, testing, analysis, or experimentation.

Although there are some important differences among scientists and philosophers of science as to what scientists actually do and how they really operate, there are many points of similarity. It is with these areas of agreement that, for the most part, we shall be concerned.

The reader must remember that the operations of scientists are actually full of surprises and unexpected results, that guess work and inspired hunches, as well as plodding and repetitive drudgery, are the norm; that any description of the scientific method falls far short of what individual scientists do, or at least think they do.[27] With this caution, however, it is still valid to attempt to generalize about the method—if the reader will keep in mind that these are generalizations and subject to the limitations of all generalizations.

[27] See R. Taton, *Reason and Chance in Scientific Discovery* (New York: Science Editions, 1962), and A. B. Arons and A. M. Bork, *Science and Ideas. Selected Readings* (Englewood Cliffs: Prentice-Hall, 1964).

Although it was originally supposed that the scientific method begins with a hypothesis, John Dewey pointed out that hypotheses do not simply spring into existence. They are the result of a troubled state of mind. The troubled state of mind occurs when some thought process is blocked: the hypothesis is an attempt to find a way of getting around the block. A blockage may result from lack of knowledge: something is happening which one does not have sufficient knowledge to explain. Or a blockage may result from conflict of beliefs or feelings: for example, I believe that it is important to obey those in authority, but a person in authority is making a request which my convictions will not let me obey.

Whatever the nature of the blockage, what is involved is lack of clarity. The term "problem" has been coined to describe a situation in which a person (or an animal) does not know what to do or what to think. It is important to realize that a problem *per se* is not necessarily bad or unpleasant—even though common usage identifies problems with something unhappy. Indeed, problems may be so desirable that one may seek them. It has been said that both science and art are essentially artificial problems—that the scientists and artist go out of their way to look for problems because of the pleasure and satisfaction they derive from solving them.

After a problem has been grasped or felt, the next stage in the scientific method usually involves casting around for a hypothesis, a tentative explanation of the puzzling, unclear, or disturbing situation. A person may hit on one hypothesis or he may entertain two or three hypotheses. Hypotheses may be phrased as statements or as questions. The investigator may say, "This is the way it happens," or "Is this the way it happens?" Whether phrased as a question or as a statement, a hypothesis is always regarded as a tentative solution to a problem, not as the necessarily correct answer. By *tentative* is meant a possible, a hoped-for solution, one to be used provisionally.

In the scientific method, one of the hallmarks of a hypothesis is that its truth or falsity may be determined by the use of empirical data. Unless a hypothesis can be tested empirically, it is not considered valid or scientific. It may be extremely interesting, perhaps brilliant and exciting, but unless one can develop a method to submit it to empirical confirmation, it cannot be said to have gone beyond the stage of an inspired hunch or an interesting suggestion. Speculation—in the sense of an imaginative jump or even intellectual play—is extremely important in the scientific process, but scientists distinguish between the speculative solution and the solution which can be tested empirically.

At this stage we need to recall both intuition and empiricism as methods of knowing. Scientists make use of intuition, but not in the traditional sense, as a complete and truthful disclosure of reality. The scientific intuition may be an inspired guess, a sudden or a slow perception of a particular relationship. But the scientific intuition is not regarded as the end product; it is rather the beginning of the process of acquiring knowledge. The scientist must test his hunch, insight, or guess by an empirical procedure to see if it is accurate. A study of the biographies of scientists who have made very important contributions —Archimedes, Newton, Rankine, Pasteur, and many others—reveals that they were often visited by sharp, penetrating insights. But in each case the scientist did not feel his work complete until he had somehow checked his idea out.

The process of "checking out" the original idea involves the use of empirical data. In the scientific method there are a number of important qualifications which govern the use of such data. It must be gathered in a controlled, careful manner. One does not simply observe an empirical event and then arrive at a conclusion. One observes an empirical event in a certain, prescribed manner. And while each scientific discipline has its own tools and its own set of rules and regulations regarding the use of empirical data,[28] some general procedures are shared by all scientific disciplines.

The gathering of empirical data may involve an experimental situation. The word "experiment" usually refers to the creation of two situations which are alike in all but one regard. For instance, two groups of white mice may be alike in age, size, strain, diet, amount of space in the cage, and environmental temperature. But one group— the experimental one—is given a particular chemical which is withheld from the other—the control group. Observation may reveal that the experimental group has a life span shorter by 8 percent than the control group of mice. The *assumption* is that the one variable, the chemical ingredient, was responsible for the difference in the life span.[29]

The gathering of empirical data may involve collating rather than experimentation. For instance, if one wishes to know more about the distribution of a certain species of insect, the procedure may require

[28] For example, while biologists use microtomes and microscopes, astronomers use telescopes. They may both use photographic equipment. While both biologists and astronomers observe physical events, the biologist may require years to complete an observation and the astronomer may be forced to record his observations in a fraction of a second.

[29] Of course, it may happen that other variables, not known to the experimenters, are crucial. Indeed, many well-planned experiments are useless for precisely this reason: the observed results were the function of an unrecognized variable. This is the scientist's nightmare.

the collection of data in a certain geographic area. While the observation, recording of data, and statistical analysis resemble a laboratory experiment, there is no experimental or control group. Much scientific inquiry is of this type.

After the data has been gathered, the scientific inquirer must now submit it to analysis. It is at this point that the crucial distinction between common-sense knowledge or casual observation and the scientific method is most evident. Many of us observe situations and make instant inferences: "I saw this and it can mean only this." The scientist does not permit himself to reach such rapid and facile conclusions. He may have planned his experiment carefully and gathered abundant data, but now he must ask the question, "Does the data really support my hypothesis?"

Analysis of data usually involves mathematical or statistical procedures. For instance, the following questions may be asked: Granted that there is a difference of 8 percent in the lifespan of the two groups of mice, is this difference statistically significant? Could the difference arise from chance alone? Were the samples of adequate size? Was the data recorded accurately? Were there factors not taken into consideration which could have affected the outcome?

Another kind of analysis of data may involve close examination of the logic and assumptions behind the inquiry under way. Being entirely human, the scientist or group of scientists may have built their investigation on certain assumptions of which they were unaware. For instance, early scientific inquiry about the relationship of dietary cholesterol to heart disease was based on the assumption that an excess of this chemical in the body was a causal factor in heart disease. Data gathered from many hundreds of thousands of subjects throughout the world supported such an assumption. However, subsequent data revealed that the first experimental design had not taken into account the following important factors: the varying amount of exercise and physical activity performed by the persons comprising the different samples, and the existence of a regulatory mechanism in the body which affected cholesterol production. The results of the earlier investigation did indeed support the hypothesis; but subsequent investigators in the field of biochemistry forced a re-examination of the assumptions which underlay the investigation.

It is for these reasons that a scientific conclusion—like a scientific hypothesis—is regarded as tentative and is almost always advanced cautiously. Because later experiments, better analysis of data, more rigorous experimental procedures, new inventions, and other factors often force re-evaluation of the conclusions, scientists are given to phrasing their statements with extreme caution. Scientific statements abound with such expressions as "it would appear," "the research would seem to indicate," "our evaluation of the data seems to show," "under these circumstances we may possibly conclude that," "our experiments suggest that," and other expressions which, while perhaps maddening to a layman who wants something more definite, indicate the necessity for being extremely guarded and tentative.

So far we have discussed the scientific method as if it were purely an inductive process, in which one gathers individual data and arrives at a conclusion or generalization. Actually, deductive processes function at several stages. As we have already seen, deduction is the conceptual opposite of induction. Whereas induction reaches a generalization or conclusion from many single instances, deduction is reasoning to a specific instance from a generalization.

Assume, for instance, that we have gathered data about the effects of a particular drug on the human body. We have concluded that x amount of this drug, administered in a certain way, will produce a particular reaction. For this conclusion to be considered valid, the experiment must be repeated in such a way that one can predict the results of the drug on another sample—that is, the conclusion arrived at inductively is now used as a general premise to be re-tested.

This point may be made clear with a simple illustration. Assume that we have gathered data about Siamese cats and have discovered that all such cats have blue eyes. Assume that after we have reached this conclusion, someone says, "My cat, William, is a Siamese." The inductively reached generalization "All Siamese cats have blue eyes" is applied to the statement that "William is a Siamese." The conclusion that William must have blue eyes involves a logical deduction.

The realization—by no means accepted as a valid description by all scientists—that there are deductive procedures in science has resulted in a somewhat modified conception of science as the "hypothetico-deductive" method. The "hypothetico-deductive" method has led to a concern for what has been called "model-building." A model is a description, as complete and as detailed as possible, about what one expects to find. A model predicts what will be found under given circumstances. In some cases the model will include a discussion of *why* a particular situation is as it is. In effect, a model says, "If one does this, under these specified circumstances, this ought to happen." The extent to which what does happen conforms with what is predicted is taken to be confirmation of a particular model.

Because the scientific method is limited and makes no guarantee of certainty, scientific knowledge is often accepted with great reservations or perhaps not accepted at all. Many maintain that the scientific method has no application to human behavior because human beings are too variable (that is, complex) for the precision of this method to yield any valuable results. Others maintain that scientific knowledge is acceptable, provided it does not conflict with intuitively or revelationally gained knowledge. Others who have seen scientists change their mind repeatedly have grown to distrust any scientific conclusion. For many, the provisional character of scientific knowledge does not provide enough psychological security to be acceptable. In short, even though the products of science are welcomed, the method of science as an epistemological source is often doubted, ignored, or rejected.

We must understand that this discussion of the scientific method is itself a kind of model. It is not a complete and finished account. It is necessarily incomplete and oversimplified. For instance, one may develop a hypothesis and make an imaginative jump to the conclusion. In some cases, the major problem is simply to see what the problem is —not to construct a hypothesis. At other times, the major task is to design methods of collecting data. For example, the idea of vaccination against disease was old when Dr. Jonas Salk attempted to devise a polio vaccine. The real problem in this case was to develop methods of refining the vaccine. In other circumstances, the hard core of the problem is to discover what the data means. This is precisely the difficulty in the recent International Geophysical Year inquiry. While most of the data has been gathered from outposts around the world, the problem is to interpret and analyze the vast quantities of data from many different scientific disciplines.

There are other aspects of the scientific method which do not readily lend themselves to neat, formal descriptions. The part that chance plays in scientific discoveries or inventions is difficult to describe. The discoveries of penicillin, the Carbon 14 method of dating, vulcanization of rubber, and X rays were essentially the results of happy combinations of circumstances. To be sure, the inquirer in each instance was in a position to take advantage of a stroke of luck. But very often the only description of a particular discovery is the phrase, "an unexpected and accidental circumstance." [30]

Because of the recent interest in creativity, some thinkers have pointed to the importance of "serendipity" in scientific research. "Serendipity" describes what happens when an investigator, having begun

---

[30] The Carbon 14 method of dating certain prehistoric objects was the result of a chance meeting between a physicist and an archaeologist who were casually chatting in a garden.

a process of inquiry in one direction, notes an interesting phenomenon and veers from his course to pursue a different line of inquiry. Serendipity requires a high degree of sensitivity to new ideas, a background sufficient to grasp new problems, and a mixture of curiosity and persistence. It appears to be an extremely important factor in scientific inquiry, but because of its unpredictable and apparently unquantifiable nature, it is difficult to describe.

8

Epistemology
and the
Classroom

Epistemology, Interest, and Understanding

The realization that we come to know in different ways and that different ways of knowing are related to different subject-matter disciplines can greatly improve teaching. Of course, different epistemological modes may be associated with the same discipline, but this makes an understanding of epistemology more and not less essential.

The difficulty in relating epistemology to classroom teaching is that education has usually proceeded on the assumption that the *content* of education is the most important concern of teaching. This assumption ignores the equally important element of the *process* by which a content is acquired. The result is doubly regrettable: because students do not understand the means by which they acquire a certain kind of knowledge they may be inefficient in studying for the course; and because the emphasis is on objective measurement of content assimilation without consideration of other values, learning often tends to end with the close of a semester. If students truly learned how to learn, they would not say, as they very often do, "I have read nothing about this subject since I took the course, and I have forgotten whatever I learned."

The very important skill of learning how to learn can probably be better developed in students by a teacher who understands the epistemological assumptions underlying a given discipline and the epistemological processes of the learning situation in that discipline. To understand, for instance, that historical facts are gathered empirically should bring an understanding of the limitations of historical knowledge. If empiricism is marked, as we have noted, by the limitations of the observer and the observed, an awareness of these limitations should deepen and sharpen historical judgment. Some of the best history teaching the author has seen took place when an instructor assigned some students to read the traditional interpretation of the Reconstruction period and others to read some of the newer interpretations, by such men as John Hope Franklin. The traditional interpretation, as typified by Claude Bowers' *The Tragic Era*,[1] is that Carpetbaggers and Scalawags, in collusion with an inept newly freed Negro populace, exploited the prostrate South. Franklin's interpretation is, on all points, diametrically opposed: that corruption was not confined to Southern legislatures, that Negroes did not dominate Southern legislatures, and that, in general, much of value occurred during the Reconstruction period.[2] The instructor pointed out the historical facts which each historian employed, the facts which each omitted, and how the value judgments differed. By discussing what factors could have influenced each interpretation, the class reached a somewhat deeper level of historical understanding. The class concluded the analysis with a discussion of the meaning of observation, the methods of recording observation, the kinds of facts that tend to be remembered and the kinds that tend to be forgotten, the difficulty of obtaining necessary data, and the relationship between bias and judgment. This approach undoubtedly deepened their understanding of both history and the epistemological problems of historiography— a most valuable by-product of the direct objectives: a good grasp of the Reconstruction period and a considerable interest in the history of the United States following the Civil War.

The author recalls a class in physics in which the instructor made the comment that a century or so ago, the atom was indivisible, that it later acquired two parts, then three, and that a year ago atomic physicists had discovered dozens of atomic particles. Knowledge of the increase in atomic particles, the instructor asserted, has made it very difficult to theorize about the structure of the atom. The students wanted to know why this was so. The instructor replied that previous theories had proven inadequate to account for the increased data and the resulting complexity. From this, the class spent a profitable hour inquiring into the nature of theory. The students apparently saw that

[1] Cambridge: Houghton Mifflin, 1929.
[2] *Reconstruction: After the Civil War* (Chicago: U. of Chicago Press, 1961).

atomic theory was not simply a description of facts-as-they-are but a model used to describe, explain, and predict behavior. Understanding scientific epistemology seemed to order the data for students, to render it somehow more meaningful and, as the instructor noted, to help them learn the content of twelfth-grade physics.

In another situation—referred to in chapter 1—a discussion of clothing styles by students spilled over from the home economics class to the lunch period. Some of the students had apparently not been content with the teacher's statement that certain colors "go together." The home economics teacher had asserted that there are certain rules or criteria which "govern" style. A few students took the position that taste is a personal judgment, and that rules about style must eventually bow to an individual's likes and dislikes. Said one student, "If I like these two colors together, why isn't that okay for me?" The teacher replied that the two colors violated the usual criteria for harmonious color arrangements. Some students asked questions about the source of the criteria. At this point the discussion moved away from color combinations to what is clearly an epistemological issue—the source of criteria, the relationship between facts and value judgments. The issue was not solved in the class, but it was obvious that the discussion both enhanced understanding of the subject matter and generated enthusiasm.

These three examples seem to indicate that relating questions about the nature of knowledge to a given subject matter leads to insight and interest on the part of both teachers and students. We will now attempt to sketch with somewhat more detail how a more conscious and specific relationship between epistemology and teaching may yield better learning.

Literature

Ordinarily literature courses are built around two often apparently unrelated goals. One is the analysis of literary techniques, usually consisting of discussion of such devices as onomatopoeia and hyperbole or of literary genres, such as plays, poems, short stories. The other is the derivation of the expressed or implied meaning of the literary vehicle —for example, What does this poem by Frost mean? The over-all goal of literature classes has traditionally been something called "appreciation." This appears to mean that, once exposed to a work selected by the teacher as typifying "good" literature, students will then "like" that work. The actual result of much teaching of literature is often the rapid forgetting of technical terminology and a vague dislike of whatever teachers consider "good" or "great" literature. Despite the almost universal exposure of American children to literature, often for as much as seven or eight years, the evidence is that most adults do not continue to read serious literature.

An analysis of the goals of literature classes reveals a very shaky set of assumptions: that technical considerations and meaning are independent entities in a literary work, that each is able to be taught and learned in isolation from the other, that sensitivity to the aesthetics of literature—and pleasure in it—is developed automatically from exposure to aesthetically successful works. It is very probable that these assumptions, carried to their logical conclusion in teaching practice, have resulted in the dessicated and spiritless teaching that has deadened whatever zest students have for literature.

Literature *should* have a significant place in any curriculum. The beautiful rhyme, the well-turned phrase, the absorbing plot, the brilliant descriptions of setting, or the striking insights into character and motivation are some of the elements of literature that can add dimensions to one's life. But perception of these elements cannot be separated from what is called "technical" or "cognitive" considerations, the means by which the elements are communicated. To develop an understanding of the author's full intent, students must be able to formulate conceptions about literature—that is, they must learn something about the reasons for use of a given rhyme scheme, effectiveness of a particular grouping of words, choice of a given way of developing plot, success in delineation of a particular character.

There is an important similarity between attempting to grasp the theme of a literary work and casting a scientific hypothesis. A theme is essentially the philosophical implications of a particular work; it is what a writer is getting at, the point he is making. To formulate a theme requires that one be able to view isolated pieces of evidence, to grasp the overall pattern, and then to generalize. The reader, for his part, must "read between the lines," an important cognitive skill, but one which is usually ignored. He must grasp the intent of an author, and this means a balanced consideration of all aspects of a work—not distorting meaning or overlooking or exaggerating evidence. Understanding a literary theme, like hypothesizing, requires clear and careful thinking.

The development of good taste is generally considered an important outcome of literature classes. The usual practice is to assign only "approved" literary classics and take the position that these are wholly meritorious. This practice does not develop taste. Taste appears to be developed inductively, to be formed when one has an opportunity to compare many different works of varying quality. Learning to distinguish differences and similarities of character, plot, setting, dialogue, and theme will help develop taste. One must compare, say, a Tarzan novel with *Treasure Island* to see how the authors treat character, how they develop plot, how each builds the mood of romanticism or realism. Only when students acquire a standard of comparison by which literary value may be judged can we talk about the development of taste. The development of such a standard implies a great deal more free and independent reading than is now the case. It also implies a much more serious attempt to help students clarify their own feelings about literature.[3]

It may seem iconoclastic to the teacher to recommend that the student read "trash" as a part of forming literary taste. But if we talk with adults who read widely and who possess considerable discrimination, we are likely to find that their early reading was wide and, at first, not discriminating. Literary discrimination came after a period of reading mysteries, Westerns, essays, weak verse and good poetry, detective stories, good and bad novels—and only after a long period of reflection and discussion.

It is also possible to make students aware of the meaning of induction, and inference in a more direct fashion. One may point out when authors are having their characters make inferences. To use a simple illustration, Arthur Conan Doyle constantly contrasts Holmes' masterful use of inference with Dr. Watson's clumsy jumping to conclusions. While Watson blunders from incorrect observation to fallacious conclusion, Holmes notes faint clues and correctly establishes distant relationships.

It is also worthwhile to point out to students how writers develop character. The skilled novelist or short story writer usually avoids the obvious technique of telling the reader that his character is generous, stupid, cruel, or confused. He lets his character act and allows the reader to make inferences from the actions. To an experienced reader this seems obvious and elementary. To a student, there is considerable value in understanding how inference is utilized by a writer.

Literature also affords students an excellent opportunity to understand the nature and use of intuition. To grasp an author's insights or intuitions into human beings is admittedly difficult, but many students are capable of doing so. Oscar Wilde, for instance, tosses off his in-

---

[3] "Project English," a curricular reform in the teaching of English, emphasizes the use of inductive teaching in literature. Through the use of carefully designed "opus-centered units," students are taught to formulate literary generalizations inductively.

sights into human conduct with epigrams. Somerset Maugham, in his masterful novel, *Of Human Bondage,* presents, in quite different fashion, his insight into how one human being reacts to a hideous deformity.[4] Students may also gain an understanding of how insights differ by contrasting Richard Wright's *Black Boy* with William Faulkner's *The Sound and the Fury.* Both works are concerned, at least in part, with the Southern Negro, but one is written by a Southern Negro and the other by one who strives to empathize with Southern Negroes.

A teacher who is sensitive to the relationship between facts and values can transmit some of this sensitivity to students. For instance, a student who is asked to evaluate a literary work is likely to say simply, "I liked it because of the writing." This vague statement should be examined further with the question, "What is there about the writing that you admire?" The answer to this question will probably be in the form of a factual statement: something like, "It seemed believable to me" or, "I think it could have happened." What the student is saying in this case is that realistic writing is somehow good. As teachers help a student clarify a preference by defending it with evidence, they will also teach him to verbalize inchoate feelings and gain skill in conceptualizing. The point is that teaching literature well is not just a matter of asking discerning and probing questions. The teacher's questions become effective as he understands the relationship between values and facts—and this clearly implies philosophical grasp.

Science

Science classes inescapably involve such epistemological modes as empiricism, intuition, logic, authority, and the scientific method. Unfortunately, few textbooks include adequate treatment of the process by which scientific knowledge is gathered. The emphasis in most science teaching—despite many recent excellent innovations—is still on acquisition of facts for their own sake—that is, the various laws in physics, the organization and categories in biology, and the classification of rocks or soil formation in geology.

If we assume that the data of science is changing rapidly and that a major objective of science teaching is to develop the student's ability to think scientifically and to continue to learn more about the scientific

---

[4] There may be some value in comparing elements in this novel with the psychological theory developed by Alfred Adler. Both Maugham and Adler are concerned with the psychology of those who suffer from physical deformities. But the approach of each to the nature of the subject is so different that a comparison may throw some light on the methods and procedures of literature and psychology.

world, then it appears that the traditional approach is self-defeating. What can teachers of science do to generate scientific curiosity, to develop scientific attitudes, as well as to transmit the content of the sciences? How can a knowledge of epistemology be of service here?

First, much more can be done empirically to bring students in contact with the phenomena they are studying. Very often they see only printed descriptions in textbooks, or if they do glimpse actual objects, the teacher will tell them *what* they should see. Their job is often taken to be memorization of the defining characteristics of mammals, the location and names of fins or the formulas of chemical reactions. It might be more effective—though admittedly more time-consuming—to do as the famous nineteenth-century scientist Louis Agassiz did, and have students describe what *they* see. Instead of requiring them to memorize a chart listing the characteristics of insects, it might be more to the point to have them observe insects and themselves decide what characteristics insects possess in common. Even though cockroaches, grasshoppers, flies, and mosquitoes differ, they all possess a three-part body, two pairs of wings, six legs, and other insect attributes. These characteristics may be observed, similarities and differences noted, and generalizations reached inductively. The students, in other words, can derive their own lists.

Discussion might then involve the characteristics of empiricism: What are the difficulties of perceiving? Did everyone see the same thing? What facts were missed and why? Are there any limitations on the generalization reached in class because of the limited sample?

A particularly neglected area in the sciences is the history of science. Yet this is a fruitful field for gaining insight into the methods and approaches of scientists. Discussions centered around inventions and discoveries might include such pertinent questions as: How did the scientist actually arrive at his hypothesis? What part did chance play? How many obstacles stood in his way? How many times did it appear that a particular lead was promising only to have it play out? What part did established authorities have in either discouraging or encouraging a particular innovation? These and many other topics, if applied to a study of the history of science, may actually yield more insight than conventional laboratory experiments. For example, students will learn that vigorous controversy among scientists is the norm, not the exception. They will learn how established scientists and schools of science function as obstacles to new approaches—that, in the history of medicine, such experiments as those of Jenner in the area of inoculation, Lister in antisepsis, and Reed in yellow fever proceeded in the teeth of opposition by established scientific authorities. Students may stop perceiving science as a rigid and predetermined method by which true knowledge is accumulated and begin to understand it as a human enterprise characterized by the failures and strengths of human beings.

Research is now proceeding on the problem of teaching students to inquire. At present much questioning in class is not designed to inquire into a problem, but simply to fix the information in students' minds. Suchman is now probing a technique which requires students to ask only questions that can be answered "yes" or "no." [5] His contention is that this process may teach students to see problems, formulate hypotheses, contruct relevant questions, connect related information, and build up concepts by relating them to data—all skills associated with the scientific method.

For many years students, particularly in elementary and junior high schools, have carried on limited experiments in classrooms. Doubtless much learning has come from observation of plants, animals, and insects. But often teachers do not capitalize on these experiments by integrating them with discussion and analysis of the scientific method. As students make and record observations, or as they write up the results of experiments, there is an excellent opportunity to make them conscious of the procedures they are employing. The characteristics of observation as an empirical process may be explained and discussed: What are you doing when you observe? Why do you keep a detailed and precise record? What conditions of the experiment are recorded and why? What else might account for the observed results? For example, if the rat or guinea pig suffered certain effects, is it possible that a factor other than the assumed variable could have been responsible?

If the animal used in a classroom experiment does not develop the predicted symptoms, the assumption is that the experiment "went wrong." If the seed in the second-grade classroom does not germinate, the teacher is apt to consider the experiment a failure. But there can be much educational benefit from understanding a failure. First, it may be pointed out that the "typical" animal growth rate, or the "expected" rate of germination is only a statistical concept and is not expected to occur in all cases. Variations from an assumed mean also ought to be considered, for when the experiment does not turn out precisely as the textbook says, students may be able to understand that experiments often do not turn out as hoped: that modification of hypotheses is the norm and that there is rarely perfect consonance be-

[5] J. Richard Suchman, "Changing Conditions for the Pursuit of Meaning," a lecture and demonstration at Purdue University, September 21, 1965.

tween prediction and conclusion. Students may also come to realize that they have not been sufficiently precise in carrying out the steps of the experiment. The point is that an experimental failure can be a learning opportunity.

Since there is a vast amount of information on scientific events reported in magazines and journals, much benefit may derive from utilizing them. In particular, the difference between journalistic and scientific reporting ought to be noted. For instance, in one class students read about a new "wonder" drug in a popular weekly magazine. The author described the drug in glowing terms and made unqualified predictions that the drug would revolutionize medicine. The teacher invited a professor of pharmacology from a nearby university to answer questions about the drug. His discussion of the drug, in sharp contrast with the magazine article, emphasized what scientists did not know about it, how limited the experimentation had been, what questions had been raised by researchers, and how much was yet to be discovered before the drug could be marketed. The students emerged with a keen insight into the shortcomings of popular journalism—possibly a very good thing in view of the fact that much of what the lay public knows about science comes from the mass media.

In many cases, scientific journals written for a rather literate readership often print correspondence relating to a controversial scientific article. This correspondence, much of it by well-qualified experts in their fields, is often marked by sharp disagreement. For instance, in the pages of the *Saturday Review* considerable discussion was published some time ago on the issue of fluoridated water as a cavity-prevention method.[6] It is difficult to read this correspondence without becoming aware that experts often disagree about interpretation of data.[7] Awareness of scientific disagreement is very likely to make a layman extremely cautious about accepting all scientific conclusions—a desirable attitude, one inherent in the scientific method itself.

The Social Studies

What has been said of the sciences is equally true of the social sciences or, to use the more common term, the social studies. The social studies, too, are enhanced by epistemological discussion. In-

[6] Articles and correspondence on the subject of fluoridation of water appear in the *Saturday Review*, March 7 and August 1, 1964, and April 3, June 5, October 2, and November 6, 1965.

[7] The problem of disagreement by experts on interpretation of data was summed up by a wag who said, "It's amazing but true that Eastern rats perform much better for Eastern psychologists."

deed, perhaps even more than the physical and natural sciences, the social studies involve clashing attitudes, differing beliefs, oppositional frames of reference—factors that tend to motivate concern and interest.

The uses of epistemology in the social studies may be illustrated with a discussion of a particularly important problem: that of developing attitudes. The avowed intention of teachers of the social studies is to shape attitudes. These attitudes are to be harmonious with our democratic way of life: students are to become tolerant of others and of differing points of view, to value all shades of personality, to learn how to share and cooperate, and to respect the democratic process. Unfortunately, the evidence does not indicate that these undeniably important democratic attitudes are learned in social studies classes.[8] The often-verbalized concern of social studies teachers to create attitudes of respect and tolerance for those of different races has not yet been translated into anything like effective results. Polls indicate that Americans—most of whom, presumably, have attended social studies classes —possess a surprisingly large number of undemocratic, bigoted attitudes.

Analysis indicates that the inability to transmit desirable attitudes is fundamentally an epistemological problem. The student's knowledge appears to be qualitatively different from that of the teacher and/or the textbook.[9] Whereas the teacher and the textbook present scientific evidence that there is no basis in fact for a belief in racial inferiority, the students "know" intuitively that there certainly is. The teacher and the textbook point out that anthropologists and sociologists have not demonstrated that any race is inferior, that differences in behavior may be attributed to culture and not faulty genes, but students "know" on the basis of self-evident truth that all minorities are crime-ridden and/or destitute. The point is that the teacher and the textbook are operating on one epistemological level and the students on quite another. The failure to realize this results in students' memorizing scientific data in the textbook or lecture but not applying this to the hemisphere of their mind that tells them that Negroes are constitutionally lazy, Mexicans naturally delinquent, and Jews innately aggressive or dishonest.

Further, some bias apparently has a basis in an authoritarian, or-

[8] It may be objected that to teach attitudes is to indoctrinate. This is not necessarily true. It is impossible to avoid teaching attitudes, and it therefore makes sense for the learning of certain attitudes to be a legitimate goal of teaching. The problem lies in how attitudes are to be taught.

[9] See S. Samuel Shermis, "The Probable Philosophical Bases of Racial Prejudice with an Emphasis on Concepts of Inferiority," *Educational Theory*, 15 (April, 1965): 143–153.

thodox position. For instance, certain religious sects in this country base their knowledge of racial inferiority on Biblical authority. God, it is believed, condemned some races to inferiority. Often, too, the biased attitude is supported by a distorted conception of evolution: a race is inferior because somewhere along the evolutionary line it missed out. A mixture of evolution and revelation, indoctrinated since early childhood, is an extremely potent epistemological combination, and it is no wonder that an exposure to the "facts" does little to change racial biases.

Often the biased attitude is supported by recourse to what seems a self-evident truth. The individual notes that a particular slum area contains a large number of certain racial or ethnic groups. He also notes considerable criminal activity. Confusing correlation with causation, he assumes that there is some kind of identity. Violence, dope-peddling, poverty and dirt exist in a slum setting because slum inhabitants "naturally" prefer to live this way. Somehow, the deduction is made that inhabitants are "naturally" anti-social.

If it is true that racial and religious biases are supported by such epistemological modes as intuition, authority, incorrectly inferred conclusions, and self-evident truths, then it may be speculated that the reason social studies teachers have not changed racially biased attitudes is that the class is conducted on an epistemological level completely different from that of the students.

If the attitudes of students are to be changed so that they are more harmonious with democracy, close attention must be paid to the method by which students gain their knowledge. Much classroom discussion should center around the validity of knowledge, emphasizing its acquisition, characteristics, and limitations. In other words, in addition to handling the relevant subject matter, attention should be paid to exploring the philosophical assumptions that support the subject matter.

For instance, when students utilize a fact in defense of their position—for example, the fact of the lower measured I.Q's of Negroes—the teacher may ask such question as: What does this mean? How are you interpreting the given facts? What sort of facts are you using? Could you arrive at another interpretation of these same facts? What limitations are there on these facts? Is it possible that important, relevant data is lacking for a clear understanding of the facts?

Students who buttress their position with quotations from an authority, in particular the Bible, may be asked questions about their use of the authority. For instance: What does this Biblical quotation mean? Could it be interpreted in another way? Have others used the

Bible to support opposite conclusions? Is this interpretation your own, or is it others'? How does one go about interpreting a document? What are the difficulties of interpreting a document that has been successively translated into four languages? Similar questions may be asked about any other authority. If he handles the matter tactfully, the teacher may render his students and the community a considerable service by acquainting them with the nature and limitation of authority as a source of knowledge.

Teachers should also realize that the data they utilize—usually facts from the disciplines of the social sciences—may not be the facts that the students possess. Attention should be paid to the nature and characteristics of facts. The teacher may ask questions such as: How do you know this? How did you acquire this knowledge? From what source? How reliable is the source? What kind of evidence are you using? Is your evidence factual—that is, an empirically demonstrable event—or is it a value judgment? If it is a value judgment, what kind is it?

Attention should be given to the relationship between facts and values. Questions may center around such themes as value conflict and value assumptions. For instance, the teacher may ask: You have asserted this to be true, but can you tell me what value you are assuming? You have expressed this belief, but what facts do you have to support it? You have used this adjective to describe something, but is this a factual description or does it reflect your feelings—or is it both? Since students often tend to verbalize two different value positions, it may be valuable to inquire: If you feel this way, how can you assert the opposite?

Another approach is by way of semantic analysis. The teacher may ask: What do you mean by "inferior"? Are you defining a term or identifying it? To what extent are you reacting to a word without considering what the word denotes? Do you have any criteria for your meaning? The emphasis here is on allowing students to recognize the distinction between denotations and connotations, to see how unrecognizable value sets influence one's verbal picture of reality. Students may come to see that emotion-laden connotations often interfere with accurate analysis.

The self-evident truth may similarly be treated in classroom discussion. The student who unconsciously slides from a premise to a conclusion that does not follow may be asked: Is this equally obvious or evident to everyone? If not, why not? What are the steps in your chain of reasoning? What is your premise or assumption? Does this conclusion follow necessarily from your premise? Have you left anything out of your reasoning process?

The point is that, unless students are made conscious of their thinking processes, little can be done in the way of changing attitudes. At best it is quite difficult to alter long-held beliefs and attitudes. But if this is the goal of the social studies, then it would seem desirable to pay attention to the relationship between attitudes and cognitive processes. It has been suggested here that this may best be accomplished by integrating some more or less formal analysis of epistemology with the content of the subject under consideration.

Although the problem of racial attitudes and theories of inferiority and prejudice have been considered in this analysis, the integration of epistemology with subject matter is probably applicable to any other topic in the social studies.

Conclusion

Efforts to relate epistemology to the teaching of subject matter are implicit in many of the newer curricular reforms. The "new" mathematics programs, such as the School Mathematics Study Group (SMSG), are attempting to move away from exclusive emphasis on the algorithmic (step-by-step) approach in mathematics to heuristics (an understanding of the logical process). Thus current thinking in mathematics is directed toward making students aware of the nature and process of deduction and induction and their function in mathematics.[10] Similarly, advocates of the Biological Science Curriculum Study (BSCS) are moving away from memorization of biological categories to teaching the scientific method—including the nature of hypotheses, inference, induction, prediction, and verification. Jerome Bruner and others who emphasize the concept of "structure" are also advocating epistemological analysis.[11]

The trend in educational theory is very clearly that, if teaching is concerned with knowledge, then we must be aware of what knowledge is and how it is acquired. It also seems clear that many educational reformers are moving away from a conception of education as transmission of content to education as the development of tools for ac-

[10] Allen F. Strehler, "What's New About the New Math?" *Saturday Review*, 47 (March 21, 1964): 68–69, 84.

[11] "Structure" is a somewhat elusive concept, but it apparently means something like "those central concepts within a discipline that function as organizers of subject matters in order to render the learning process more efficient." See Jerome Bruner, *The Process of Education* (Cambridge: Harvard U. Press, 1961).

quiring content. Another way of saying this is that the improvement of the teaching-learning process necessarily involves certain philosophical questions. Certainly many of the philosophical questions are epistemological. On the basis of present trends, it seems very possible that teachers of the future will need to be as aware of the meaning of epistemology as they now are of psychology.

QUESTIONS FOR DISCUSSION

1. Do you agree that the most important epistemological problem in this century centers around the conflict between intuition and the scientific method? Why or why not?

2. Note the definition of indoctrination on p. 160. Is it possible to develop allegiance to, say, the democratic process without being indoctrinated? Give reasons for your answer.

3. Assume that transfer of training is a desirable outcome of education. What kinds of transfer can or should arise from taking a course in educational philosophy?

4. Is it a fact that $2 + 2 = 4$? Is it a fact that the Founding Fathers were wise and discerning people who planned well for the future? Is it a fact that life on this planet is evolving? Is it a fact that Bach was one of the great composers of all time? What are these questions getting at?

5. What are the different meanings of *intuition*?

6. Since many problems occur in the use of authority, why don't we simply discard all authorities?

7. Cite some instances where "common sense" has been used to defend or rationalize a judgment.

8. Why have theorists of science come to believe that deductive methods are as important as inductive? Why was science long considered completely inductive?

9. Note footnote 30 in chapter 7. How does this occurrence support the tradition in science that scientists need maximum freedom and interchange of information? Are there any traditions in this nation that tend to obstruct such freedom?

10. How can knowledge of the nature and characteristics of empiricism help in the teaching of agriculture? Of art? Of educational psychology?

11. Submit to an English teacher at the secondary level the proposition that very extensive reading—even of what is considered trash—is essential for the development of taste. What is the reaction? Now submit the same proposition to someone you consider a well-read person with good taste. What is the reaction?

12. Why has there been so much massive federal support for science and mathematics and so little for art, music, and literature? Contrast the

cultural emphasis on science in this century with that on the humanities in the thirteenth century in Italy.

SUGGESTED READINGS

BERLIN, ISAIAH. *The Age of Enlightenment.* New York: New American, 1961. This work, like the one following, contains essays from certain philosophers with reasonably simple explanations. See especially the works of and comments on Locke, Hume, and Berkeley.

ELAM, STANLEY (ed.). *Education and the Structure of Knowledge.* Chicago: Rand, McNally, 1964. This work is a collection of essays, originally talks for the Fifth Annual Phi Delta Kappa Symposium on Educational Research. See especially the essay on the structure of physical knowledge.

HAMPSHIRE, STUART. *The Age of Reason.* New York: New American, 1961. See especially the essays by Bacon, Galileo, Descartes, and Leibniz.

KÖHLER, WOLFGANG. *The Place of Value in a World of Facts.* New York: Liveright, 1938. Köhler was one of the leaders in Gestält psychology who came to this country in the 1930's. This book is an exposition of the relationship between facts and values from a Gestältist's point of view.

RUSSELL, BERTRAND. *Mysticism and Logic.* New York: W. W. Norton, 1929. Russell is one of the outstanding realistic philosophers in this century. See especially his lucid discussion in the first chapter of the two strains of thought: the mystical emotive and intuitive, and the scientific. How do you suppose Russell would define *science?*

WALKER, MARSHALL. *The Nature of Scientific Thought.* Englewood Cliffs: Prentice-Hall, 1963. This is a thorough and well-illustrated discussion of scientific method.

WEBER, CHRISTIAN O. *Basic Philosophies of Education.* New York: Holt, Rinehart and Winston, 1960. The author is particularly interested in Kant's epistemology. See Chapter 7. Kant is considered particularly important in his influence on the philosophy of both idealism and pragmatism.

9

Social
Philosophy

It is widely thought that our country is unique in that we successfully combine maximum freedom with abundant opportunity. It is also believed that, because this is so, our educational institutions are distinctive in that our political, social, and economic institutions in some way direct the course of public education. What is supposed to follow, then, is that public-school teachers in training must grasp the nature of this heritage so that they may perform their duties in the unique way implied.

Unfortunately this is only theoretical description; actually, there is a shocking dearth of insight into the theory and practice of democracy. Most teachers—and others, too—cannot define democracy in such a way as to differentiate it adequately from other systems. Typically such words as *freedom, liberty, right, opportunity,* and *equality*—terms supposed to characterize our way of life—are either confused with one another or are treated as only vague, if admirable, abstractions. The lack of understanding of these terms leaves our educational system without the guidance it really needs. Despite a flow of words about democracy and education, democratic classroom discipline, and democratic school administration, classroom discipline and educational administration continue to be authoritarian and anti-democratic.

If an understanding of our way of life is supposed to have the results that are always anticipated, teachers must comprehend certain concepts that are usually called social philosophy. The subject matter of social philosophy consists of answers to such questions as: How should man govern himself and to what end? How can we reconcile the demands of freedom and order? What is human nature? What is the meaning of freedom? How should an individual relate to society? These questions will be discussed, and certain answers—which seem to be those our culture accepts—will be related to public education.

Human Nature: Four Theories

Most men have believed that there is something called "human nature." The usual conception of human nature is that it is the essence of all men and that, regardless of one's place in history, his social class, his culture, intelligence, or aptitudes, he possesses a nature that is everywhere the same. There are some important deviations from this belief in a universal and static human nature, but human nature is usually seen as a constant that makes all men everywhere what they are.

Perhaps the most persistent theory of human nature, at least in Western civilization, is that man is innately evil. In the Old Testament there is a statement that "the imagination of man's heart is evil from his youth." [1] Similarly, "Behold I was shapen in iniquity; and in sin did my mother conceive me." [2] This belief was re-emphasized in the Protestant Revolt during the seventeenth century. In particular the Puritans, strongly influenced by the theology of John Calvin, stressed the sinfulness and depravity of man. [3] Man in his primal state rebelled against God, and to this day he has an innate propensity to do evil, to disregard God's laws, to choose deliberately the wicked, the unwholesome, the diseased, and the sinful.

Children were thought to be born in sin and destined to become more evil—unless their natural inclinations were sharply curbed. The curbing of their natural inclination to do evil [4] required constant co-

---

[1] Genesis 8:21.

[2] Psalms 51:5.

[3] John Calvin, *On the Christian Faith* (New York: Liberal Arts Press, 1957). The following quotation, reflecting his position, is taken from *The Institutes of the Christian Faith*, Book I, on Knowledge of God the Creator, 1.2, Man's unworthiness in the light of God's perfection: "Because, from our natural proneness to hypocrisy any vain appearance of righteousness abundantly contents us instead of the reality; and, everything within and around us being exceedingly defiled, we are delighted with what is least so, as extremely pure, while we confine our reflections within the limits of human corruption."

[4] The "natural inclination to do evil" is a precise and literal translation of an ancient Hebraic word. The Hebrews believed that within each man are two forces. One, the *yetzer ha tov*, is the inclination to do good. The other, the *yetzer ha ra*, is the inclination to do evil. These two forces are constantly battling to become uppermost in each person.

ercion by family, church, state, and school. Thus laws were frequently harsh and punishments cruel; but such severity was taken to be an absolute necessity if naturally sinning man were to be deterred from evil.

School discipline thus was harsh, and corporal punishment was the rule, for unless children had the devil—literally—beaten out of them, they would become yet more evil and lose their slender chance for salvation.[5] The end result of stringent laws, coercion, verbal exhortations, and constant social control was not an altered human nature, but simply a person whose natural inclinations were deterred enough to keep him to the "straight and narrow." [6]

In the eighteenth century, during the period known as the Enlightenment, another position rapidly developed. This position is that human nature is essentially good, that men are naturally decent and well disposed. The person probably most responsible for this theory of human nature was Jean-Jacques Rousseau, a French writer and philosopher, who elaborated it in many novels and essays. Rousseau's basic theme presents a strange paradox: man is basically good; his instincts are to do right, to be kind and generous to his fellow man; but he is made evil, selfish, and corrupt by organized society. As he lives in society, his original good nature is distorted and warped. This theme was continued and amplified in a hundred variations by subsequent thinkers, educators, novelists, and artists.[7]

A third conception of human nature is the classical, wherein human nature has two essences—one in those who are superior and another in those who are inferior. Plato developed this theme in his *Republic* and Aristotle carried it even further. Aristotle asserts that "Nature" has made a distinction between those who possess an ample amount of rationality and those who do not. The former are "useful for political life in the areas of war and peace," and the latter are fit only for servile labor. Says Aristotle, "It is clear, then, that some men are by nature free and others slaves, and that for these latter, slavery is both expedient and right." [8]

There are numerous variations on this theme. One variation is racial; some races are by nature inferior and some are by nature su-

---

[5] See Maurice Hunt and Morris Bigge, *Psychological Foundations of Education* (New York: Harper, 1962), p. 35.

[6] *Ibid.* This topic is also discussed at length in Joseph Gaer and Ben Siegel, *The Puritan Heritage* (New York: New American Library, 1964).

[7] Among thinkers who reflect this position are the educational theorists Pestalozzi and Froebel, the novelist Leo Tolstoy, and the American educational philosopher William H. Kilpatrick.

[8] *Politics,* Book I, Chapter V.

perior.[9] Another variation is that superiority inheres in intellect: the more intelligent individual, capable of learning and appreciating the finer things of life, is naturally superior. Of course, such persons are few: the crude, stupid, unreflecting "mass" must be ruled by an elite, whom, naturally, it resents and hates.

A fourth and quite recent position is that human nature is neither innately good nor inherently evil, neither naturally superior nor naturally inferior. This twentieth-century theory arises from the findings of social scientists, especially anthropologists and psychologists. The assumption is that "good" and "evil" are value judgments which always depend on a particular culture, that what one culture considers evil may not be so considered in another. This position is summarized by Horney:

> Making further use of anthropological findings we must recognize that some of our conceptions about human nature are rather naive, for example the idea that competitiveness, sibling rivalry, kinship between affection and sexuality, are trends inherent in human nature. Our conception of normality is arrived at by the approval of certain standards of behavior and feeling within a certain group which imposes these standards upon its members. But the standards vary with culture, period, class and sex.[10]

Thus human nature is assumed to be *neutral*—neither good nor bad in any absolute sense—for good and evil are defined by the culture. The assumption is that one *learns* to be good or evil. Human nature is acquired through the process of interacting with other individuals in a particular cultural setting. To be sure, all men are born with certain structural and functional potentialities. These potentialities are developed in a cultural setting and the result we call human nature. But human nature here means *acquired* human nature.

Implications of These Positions

Innate Depravity   Each of these theories of human nature carries certain implications for structuring social relationships and in particular for structuring educational institutions. The position that man is innately evil carries with it the implication that society, especially

[9] The racial motif is analyzed in a most interesting article by Ralph McGill, "The South Has Many Faces," *The Atlantic Monthly*, 211 (April, 1963): 83–98. The history of racial theories is also discussed by Oscar Handlin in *Race and Nationality in American Life* (New York: Doubleday, 1957).

[10] Karen Horney, *The Neurotic Personality of Our Time* (New York: Norton, 1937), p. 18.

through its educational institutions, must redirect, change, or strongly modify man's naturally evil propensities. The Founding Fathers assumed that men were a naturally bad lot and government must take this into consideration. The three-part checks-and-balances system adopted at the Constitutional Convention is based partly on the assumption that people in power tend to abuse power and that unless men are checked and their authority limited, elected or appointed officials tend to degenerate into tyrants and despots.[11]

The famous phrase by Lord Acton, "Power corrupts and absolute power corrupts absolutely," reflects the view that human nature is weak and extremely corruptible. If power does indeed corrupt, then it is essential for a government structure to neutralize this by providing for frequent elections, short terms of office, distributed decision-making, and ample opportunity for recall and referendum. Americans seem to think that our governmental structure has worked out, on the whole, rather well; in fact, we have not suffered under a tyrant since our founding. But there is another side to the picture. The assumption that innately weak human nature needs constant checking to prevent an undue accumulation of power has resulted in a governmental structure in which it is difficult to locate responsibility, and in which there is friction between different branches of government, expense of frequent elections, duplication of power and function (as in the bi-cameral legislature), and general unwieldiness of a fractionated government.[12]

The belief in an innately evil human nature has had an extensive history in education. In our colonial period, church, state, and school worked together to redirect man's wicked nature. If children were actively bad—active in the sense that they would get worse—then schools must redirect their nature, must teach them to be good. "Teaching children to be good" meant, on the one hand, teaching them the commandments and ordinances of God and, on the other, suppressing their natural inclination to do evil. The former meant that most of the

[11] The widespread belief that Hamilton thought that only the rich and well-born were capable of ruling because they were better than the common man and that Jefferson believed that the common man is good enough to rule himself is an oversimplification and a distortion. Both Jefferson and Hamilton believed that human nature is inherently weak and that all people are ruled by passion and self-interest. In *The Federalist*, Numbers 8, 9 and 10, Hamilton and Madison make it fairly clear that the proposed constitution is really a device to check the inherent defects of human nature.

[12] *Ibid.* "Factions" which Hamilton defined as a "number of citizens . . . who are united and actuated by some common impulse of passions, or of interest, adverse to the rights of other citizens . . . are . . . sown in the nature of man." Factions are diseases inherent in republics, the cure for which is a check-and-balance system and a written constitution. See also *The Federalist*, Number 51.

curriculum was what we would call religious, consisting of the Bible, sacred songs, theology, dogma, Church history, and doctrine. The latter meant that the teacher must repress natural activity, and to this end whipping and beating were frequently employed. School discipline—or more correctly, punishment—was, from today's point of view, unduly strict and harsh, but this was essential to the redirection of the child's soul.

In sum, the practical consequences in education of belief in the innate depravity of human nature have been many restrictive regulations, frequent punishment, constant spying on and supervision of behavior, extensive prohibitions on behavior—ranging from frills in dress to unsanctioned sexual activity—and the permeation of education with religious doctrine. The reader is asked to judge whether or not this description still applies. The answer is obviously that many schools today may be so described. Should you ask an administrator why pupils are so tightly controlled, the answer may well be, "Unless we really clamp down on these kids, they'll run wild."

There is one more implication of the ancient belief that human nature is innately bad: the assumption that education must consist of indoctrination in certain ethical and moral beliefs. To be sure, the notion that such indoctrination is necessary for salvation is no longer acceptable in public schools. But it is still widely held that schools should indoctrinate children in a set of moral precepts. What is not realized is that—unlike colonial America in the seventeenth century—we have no official morality: cultural pluralism has rendered obsolete a simple, unqualified notion of goodness. Nevertheless, teachers seem to believe that their job is to make children good—although the teachers themselves do not know very clearly what goodness consists of.

Innate Goodness The theory of human nature associated with Rousseau—that children are naturally good and should become even better—is also part of American educational theory and practice. This position was taken by Johann Heinrich Pestalozzi, the great Swiss educator, who directed a number of schools in the last part of the eighteenth and first part of the nineteenth centuries. Pestalozzian theory and practice were transmitted to this country and formed the basis for what later became known as Progressive Education. The educational theory of a German philosopher, Friedrich Froebel, was also brought to this country, and it too was basic in the thinking of many Progressives.

Both Pestalozzi and Froebel believed that children are basically good, that adults should interfere with their natural, spontaneous activities as little as possible. Froebel likened children to plants: just as a plant will blossom into a lovely thing, children, too, should develop into something beautiful.[13] The analogy of plant and child resulted in an educational theory that emphasized the passive function of teachers; they should provide only those conditions necessary for normal growth and should interfere, direct, and guide as little as possible. In the twentieth century, the exponents of Progressive Education attempted to revolutionize schools by employing just this assumption.[14] The child's interests should form the basis of curriculum, for interests are natural manifestations, and their development in children will lead to adults who will be intellectually curious and whose interests will be many-sided. Since children's activity is natural, and since what is natural is good, the Progressives emphasized activity in their curriculum. Similarly, children's expressions were naturally good, and thus Progressives encouraged expression. The teacher was to act as coordinator, to facilitate the learning process by building on children's purposes. The teacher was definitely not to be a policeman or any other kind of authoritarian. Discipline problems, it was hoped, would be rare, for children doing what they naturally wished to do would have no need to misbehave.

Progressive Education waned and tended to become discredited in the 1930's and 1940's. But many of the assumptions of Progressivism about children, growth, development, and education blended into educational theory to become part of the "conventional wisdom." It did not, however, displace previous practice and theory.[15]

Hence while art, music, and creative writing are recommended for all primary-school children—on the assumption that it is good for children to express themselves—at about the middle elementary level, children learn to draw according to rules and to appreciate the "right" music. Dramatics is either dropped from the curriculum or reserved for only a few. This sharp transition may be defended by asserting that at this age children change their intellectual appetites and capacities, and that a constantly modified social role and developing socialization requires a change in educational method. This may be a valid argu-

[13] The term "kindergarten" is Froebel's. Kindergarten means literally "a garden of children."

[14] It is admittedly risky to generalize about Progressive Education, since it was far from a single, unified movement. But these assumptions and practices were fairly common and were endorsed by many.

[15] The history and practice of Progressive Education are treated in considerable detail in Lawrence A. Cremin, *The Transformation of the School* (New York: Knopf, 1962). The theory of interests is analyzed in Charles Brauner, *American Educational Theory* (Englewood Cliffs: Prentice-Hall, 1964), "General Method From Six Practical Traditions," and the analysis of the relationship between John Dewey and Progressivism is found in Ernest E. Bayles, *Democratic Educational Theory* (New York: Harper and Row, 1960) in Chapter 15, "John Dewey and Progressivism."

ment, but we doubt it. If it is valid, then it should be a simple matter to answer the following questions: What is there about the growth and development of children that makes activity and expression essential at an early age but undesirable later? Why is active participation thought to be valuable at an earlier age and passive observation desirable later? Unless these questions can be answered satisfactorily, the conclusion must be that the curriculum is based on two opposite and irreconcilable theories of human nature!

Superiority and Inferiority The educational implications of the theory that human nature is bi-polar have been fairly well worked out. Plato and Aristotle conceived of superiority as a combination of moral and mental traits which, if nurtured by a proper education, would create a noble individual. His nobility would be manifested not only by an unselfish, generous, courageous character, but also by a lifetime interest in activities of the mind. The two philosophers conceived of a plan of education that would harmoniously develop the young child in character, mind, and body and create a superior man. It was assumed that certain subjects and certain activities would yield the desired person, but that other subjects—and most certainly Plato and Aristotle had in mind what we would now call vocational or practical subjects—were completely inappropriate. Vocational training was fit for a lower type, for no vocational study would ever liberate the mind or soul.[16]

The Socratic and Aristotelian philosophical positions, as we have seen in a previous chapter, became part of the thinking of Western Civilization. In particular, the dichotomy between the superior and the inferior person, or the dualism between a liberating education and an enslaving one, has been enshrined as doctrine. During the Middle Ages the conception of a highly developed intellect lost strength. Superiority was identified with hereditary nobility. The moral and intellectual superiority of the Greeks was replaced by superiority of aristocratic manners and virtues such as military prowess, valor in battle, and self-sacrifice for a noble or supernatural ideal. It is now difficult to know whether "superiority" refers to what is conferred by membership in a higher class or what is associated with character, with intelligence, or with all three.

In the writings of John Locke the theory that a certain pattern of

[16] The words "liberal" and "liberating" have an interesting history. *Liber* is Latin for "free." But it is not clear whether a liberal education is one designed for a free man: that is, one not born a slave, or whether it is an education that is to free someone. If it is the latter, it is not clear whether it is to free one *from* or free *for*. These distinctions are important but they are usually absent from most discussions of "liberal education."

formal education is appropriate to innate superiority found full expression. Locke, who was himself a tutor in a wealthy family, described a fairly complete educational plan for a young aristocratic boy. The plan combined a somewhat Spartan physical existence with vigorous play, study of the classics, and rather sophisticated character training.[17] This is still the regimen of most of the preparatory schools in England, such as Harrow, Winchester, and Eton. Such an education is usually deemed appropriate to a few, those who will become the governing class. The masses are thought to require only the basics and either manual or technical training.

Neutral-Interactive   The implications of the theory that human nature is essentially neutral have yet to be worked out in great detail. This is partly because the view is quite recent and partly because it is not easy to understand.[18] John Dewey attempted to trace the implications of this position in a number of his works, and some of his followers have continued his line of thought.

If human nature is neutral—neither actively good nor actively evil —then it follows that teachers need not "make" children good, nor need they stand by passively and allow children to develop "naturally." What is assumed is that children ought to develop a trained intelligence so that they can decide for themselves what is and is not good. The development of good character is a matter of teaching one to discriminate between different moral positions.

It is also assumed that the development of one's potential depends on the quality of interactions at every stage. Depending on the kinds of experiences one has, one may develop into many different kinds of adult. These experiences should be provided both to act on the unfolding potential of a child and to prepare the way for future experiences. An educational experience is desirable to the extent to which it can make the best use of a child's present aptitudes to prepare him for future experiences.

The emphasis on experience is derived from an important postulate of those who believe that human nature is neutral. Man, say Hunt and Bigge, is "fundamentally purposive; he continuously generates wants which he then sets out to satisfy." [19] From this standpoint, all

[17] A good discussion of English preparatory schools is in Frederick Eby, *The Development of Modern Education* (Englewood Cliffs: Prentice-Hall, 1952), "Locke and the Philosophy of Empiricism." The discussion of Locke's educational theories is in his *An Essay Concerning Human Understanding.*

[18] Apparently because "neutral-interactive" is a nondualistic term, and it is difficult for people habituated to thinking in an "either-or" sense to begin thinking in "both-and" terms.

[19] *Psychological Foundations of Education,* p. 51.

education must take into consideration inherent purposiveness.[20] Specifically, this position means that teachers must discover the purposes and goals of students and attempt to see that what is done in the classroom becomes part of their purposes.

Another postulate of this position is that human nature is not fixed or static. Human beings are assumed to change as growth, maturity, experiences, and wisdom change them. This postulate becomes important when it is realized that many regard human nature as fixedly competitive or aggressive. An important theory in our culture is that competitive man is a part of competitive nature—that *all* nature is characterized by constant struggling for survival and success. Education, therefore, is designed to make people develop the natural competitiveness that is "in" all of us. The position we have been describing does not hold that human beings are either naturally competitive or naturally cooperative. It holds that competition and cooperation are learned from the culture, and that they may be taught.[21]

It should be seen that assumptions about human nature are a fairly important part of any set of assumptions about the teaching process. It may also be seen that all the theories of human nature described here are equally viable. It would appear also that they are all likely to be incorporated into the unrecognized body of assumptions of any one teacher. Unfortunately, each theory of human nature carries with it implications for practice that are not consistent with other positions. To believe, unaware that one is doing so, that each position is just fine—in its place—is to operate in a classroom with methods and techniques that are unharmonious and self-defeating.

Rights

The topic of rights is related to the theory of Natural Law; indeed, it is implied in that theory. We have noted that Natural Law is the

[20] Much educational psychology in this century seems to be based on the assumption that human beings are not purposive; rather that they are essentially passive reactors. It follows that education is essentially a matter of presenting the right stimuli for students' reactions. The paradox is that, although there is much talk about needs, interests, goals, and so forth, the psychology underlying educational practice is largely one that does not allow for goals or purposes.

[21] As mentioned before, this theory is based to a large extent on the findings of such social sciences as anthropology. Ethnologists have discovered an extremely broad range of personality types throughout the world. A much cited comparison is between the gentle, cooperative, pleasant Arapesh of New Guinea and their close neighbors, the Mundagamoor, who are hostile, aggressive and combative. It may be seen that our own culture emphasizes both competitiveness and cooperativeness. It is not clear when each trait is desirable.

philosophical position that the world is divided into two realms, the physical and the moral. These two realms are obedient to unchanging and certain regulatory principles. The regulatory principles create a fixed and static universe in which there are inescapable responsibilities for all creatures. In addition to responsibilities, there are certain rights which are inherent in what has been called the "human condition." The usual way of saying it is that all human beings, whatever their age, class, race, or condition, are guaranteed certain rights. These rights have usually been thought of as absolute and inalienable: absolute because they are affected by no condition or exception, and inalienable because they cannot be taken away. It is usually said that all human beings (sometimes infrahumans are included) have certain rights which cannot (or perhaps "should not") be removed.

Discussion usually centers around these questions: What are these rights? Whence or from whom do we derive them? Generally, religious philosophers have held that rights are given to man by God. Non-theologically oriented philosophers have often held that rights are given to man by Nature—that in the very scheme of things, man has certain rights.[22]

In our culture the existence of absolute rights has usually been taken for granted. Each historical era has tended to interpret rights differently, but their existence is usually assumed to be absolute. For example, the political foundations of our country were based on the belief in absolute rights. Democratic philosophers in the eighteenth and nineteenth centuries assumed that self-government was one of these rights. In the mid-nineteenth century, the economic theories of Adam Smith were buttressed by the position that the right to own property and to make a profit was absolute. When the central government made efforts to control organized industry, it was held that industrialists could do as they wished "with due respect to the Ten Commandments and the Penal Code," [23] and that it was unnatural and immoral for the government to regulate the marketplace in any way.[24] In the twentieth century, particularly after the coming of the

[22] Seemingly this was the approach of Jefferson, who talked about rights coming from "nature" or "nature's God" and listed them as "life, liberty, and the pursuit of happiness." See the Declaration of Independence. Jefferson's position is not unique, for many intellectuals of this period were deists, a philosophical position that God is not separate from Nature, but is co-terminous with Nature—that is, with the totality of existence.

[23] Quoted in Walter Lord, The Good Years (New York: Harper and Row, 1960), p. 64.

[24] While it was held that government should be a neutral referee, it was also held that organized labor had no right to legal protection. This may seem unbelievable today, but state supreme courts and the United States Supreme Court,

New Deal, it was assumed that government had the responsibility to protect the rights of the politically and economically weak.

The question of rights is far from simply an academic or speculative topic. The entire civil rights movement in this country is based on the belief in rights—that all minorities have civil, political, and economic rights equal to those of the majority. The concern with such issues as self-incrimination, search and seizure, freedom of speech and press also springs from the belief that rights naturally devolve upon all men.

A more recent position has risen to challenge the older assumptions about rights. The newer theory, often indentified with humanists and relativists, is that rights are human inventions and are neither absolute nor inalienable.[25] Rights do not appear to be inalienable because all rights may be taken away under certain conditions. The right to life may be taken away by the state on conviction of a serious crime. Liberty does not appear to be either unqualified or inalienable, for one's liberties may be modified or even removed. Thus one may not address a crowd on a city street if by so doing he impedes the movement of others. Economic rights are not grounded in nature, as reflection on economic practices throughout the world will reveal.

Rights are not held either to be granted by God or "built into" nature. This position is denied because it is difficult if not impossible to determine precisely what rights are supposed to be granted by God —even admitting His existence. One may find a wide range of rights alleged to be derived from a higher power. To argue that rights inhere in Nature or human nature provides the same counter-argument: How does one know precisely what rights inhere in human nature? A large number of rights have been asserted to inhere in human nature, ranging, as we have seen, from the right to make a profit to the right to vote.

If rights are neither inalienable nor unqualified, what are they? Rights apparently reflect extremely important values, usually determined by cultural consensus. Rights exist in relation to other rights. The right to freedom of speech is relative to the right to privacy. The

---

prior to the mid-1930's, consistently struck down limitations on hours, regulation of working conditions, minimum wages, regulation of child labor, establishment of courts of arbitration, and other measures designed to protect the laborer, on the grounds that these were injurious to the employers' absolute contractual rights. Hence, one can infer that, strictly speaking, this theory of rights applied to employers but not to employees.

[25] Humanism is a position that the center of human concerns and interests ought to be exclusively human beings and their activities. There are many forms of humanism—literary humanism, existential humanism, scientific humanism—but most forms are opposed to theism.

right of freedom of the press is relative to the right to protect reputations against slander. The right of a country to protect itself against subversion, internal or external, is relative to a number of civil rights. Rights appear always to be in conflict. This is so because man has plural values, many of which, taken together in a given time and in given circumstances, are incompatible. It also seems clear that, because rights are usually phrased as abstractions, they need constant clarification and redefinition. The context of a given right changes constantly, and if rights are not to become real obstacles in the way of human welfare, the culture needs constantly to redefine their meaning.[26]

Educational Implications

Each of these views of the meaning of rights carries with it certain implications for education. Since the traditional position that rights inhere in nature or come from God is the dominant theory in our society, the implications of the position are somewhat easier to grasp. Teachers, while recognizing that it is inadvisable to stress the theological origins of rights in public schools, have nevertheless placed rights in a quasi-religious context. This is usually stated in the following form: Our rights have been assured for us by inspired men who struggled to see that posterity should enjoy what is necessarily its due. This approach celebrates the efforts and sacrifices of the Founding Fathers, of Washington, Lincoln, and other great men.

These men, it is held, intuitively recognized that certain rights were due the American people, who were uniquely blessed, and they fought to see that we would possess them. The end product of this approach is supposed to be an emotional commitment to certain rights —that is, students must respect American heroes who secured our rights and realize that we must protect these rights against all incursions.

If rights are as described in the second position—important cultural values which may be expected to conflict constantly—then teaching procedures must be much different. Students must discern the particular conditions and meanings attached to each right; for example, they must attempt to understand the meaning of the right of free speech as it relates to other values. What are these other values? With what does free speech conflict? What has been the history of free expression

---

[26] For a more complete discussion of this meaning of rights, see S. Samuel Shermis, "A Redefining of Rights," *The Phi Delta Kappan,* 47 (May, 1966): 515–517.

in our country? What are the dangers *of* free expression? What are the dangers *to* free expression? How does one decide which right takes precedence when, as often happens, free speech comes into conflict with another right?[27]

Although the second approach may well seem coldly intellectual, it is argued that a better and more enduring emotional commitment comes with an intellectual understanding of a right. This seems to be the assumption of a social studies curriculum study group composed of attorneys, professors of law, and high-school teachers.[28] This group argues that the teaching of civil rights in this country has always been weak and that much can be done to strengthen it; that the teacher must first understand the history of civil rights. Students should then be taught to understand the meaning of rights in the context of historical conflict. They must be helped to see that a changing conception of rights accompanies changed conditions.

Freedom, Order, and Control

If asked to define the word *freedom,* most Americans say that it is the right to do as one wishes as long as he does not infringe on the rights of others. If pressed to explain what rights freedom may infringe on, the respondent shifts the discussion to innate rights. Then, if requested to define how a *freedom* can be a *right,* the person usually replies by equating it with *liberty.* Liberty is then identified with absence of control. Absence of control, of course, is regarded as a very good thing.

The preceding account, much abbreviating the process but still faithfully reflecting the usual perception of freedom and control, describes an extremely muddy and inadequate conception of freedom, liberty, rights, and control. The terms are equated with each other, the reasoning is circular, and the position is little more than an abstract and vague expression of our dislike for control and affection for freedom.

There are really a number of meanings of *freedom.* In a negative sense, *freedom* means "freedom from"—that is, absence of coercion, force, or restriction. One may be free in the sense that he can do as he wishes without fear of unpleasant consequences. In a positive

---

[27] A recent and most interesting illustration of this point may be found in an article by Henry Steele Commager, "Should Historians Write Contemporary History?" *Saturday Review,* 49 (February 12, 1966): 18–20; 47.

[28] This position was presented in a discussion on "The Role of the Law in the Social Studies Curriculum," before the National Council for the Social Studies on November 26, 1965.

sense, *freedom* is "freedom to"—a perceived opportunity to make a decision and carry it out. These two concepts of freedom are not mutually exclusive: freedom *from* may imply freedom *to* and freedom *to* may imply freedom *from*. For instance, when one is free *from* the fear and expense of sickness, he may be free *to* invest his energy and zeal in interesting or creative ways. By the same token, when one is free *to* speak his mind or worship as he sees fit, he is also free *from* the fear of being jailed or fined for criticizing the king or other officials or free from being harassed and persecuted by those of other religions.

Freedom also has another, very different, meaning. In one philosophical sense *freedom* means knowledge of and obedience to absolute truth. Thus the free man is one who knows what the conditions of existence really are. Knowing these conditions, he bows to the inevitable and does what he must do. Similarly, *freedom* may be treated in the context of obedience to divine will. God, it is alleged, has made certain requirements of man. Some of these requirements are quite clear, but some of them are not and require that man attune himself to God's will. When man understands what the Lord demands of him, perfect freedom consists of obedience to His will. This conception of freedom is particulary important in the light of our Puritan heritage.[29]

In another philosophical sense, *freedom* has been used in connection with one who has mastered his own impulses successfully. The position is that no one is less free than one who is driven by his own unconscious desires and wishes. As some of the ancient philosophers would have it, a person who is prey to his every wish and desire is a slave. In this century, Freudian psychologists have added a slightly different emphasis. The free man is one who understands his unconscious urgings and has learned to find a balance between his natural demands and the requirements of his conscience or censor (the Freudian term is "superego"). *Freedom* in this sense is something like a mixture of self-control and inner balance.

There are, of course, other meanings of *freedom*, but the most important meaning in our culture seems to be freedom *from*. Throughout our history freedom has been opposed to control. Control is seen as an ever-present danger, something that a central government—usually called "they"—wishes to fasten on "us." The grounds for perceiving control as evil must be understood within the context of the history of emigration to this country. Historically, control has been associated with repressive and often cruel overlords. Emigrants from Europe in the last three hundred years came to this country, in large part, to escape from the repressive control of kings, emperors, czars, and other

29 See Gaer and Siegel.

governmental functionaries. On the frontier, where control was often difficult to exercise, the antipathy against control was nourished. Eventually there arose the American myth about freedom and control: freedom must be absolute and is always good, and control is always evil.

The social reality, however, is quite at odds with this conception of freedom and control. Urbanization and industrialization have led to greater interdependence among people and more complexity of organization, a situation requiring more and more pervasive control by the federal, state, and local governments. No one has come up with any substitute for increased control at all levels. And it is true that controls have modified many traditional freedoms. Consequently, there is a cultural paradox: while controls are demanded, they are also resented.[30] This has meant that the traditional perception of freedom and control is not in line with the actual conditions of our society.

Part of the problem lies in an inability to understand what controls are and how they function. Control means little more than direction. To be controlled means that a particular behavior is made to flow into a certain channel. To control water means that the flow is directed along a particular route; it is not free to go in any and all directions. To control a person's behavior is to direct it along a certain line. Thus control itself is essentially neutral—it may be either desirable or undesirable, harsh or mild, destructive of values or helpful to them. Control may or may not involve force, for one can exercise control with great subtlety.[31] Control may be perceived—the Berlin wall, for example—or may be unperceived, as, for instance, the cultural pattern that tells us to shake hands when we are introduced to someone.

Order is related to but somewhat different from control. Order, in the sense that it applies to society, means a patterning of stable organization. All societies are characterized by some kind of order. All societies have patterns which regulate economic, religious, artistic, familial, and other kinds of behavior. Order appears to be inherent in the very term *society*.

Order and control may be discussed in a *qualitative* or *quantitative* sense. We may ask, qualitatively, "What *kind* of order or control?"

[30] Although it is widely believed that controls have been thrust on the populace by power-hungry bureaucrats in Washington, this interpretation is far from the truth. All federal controls, even the controversial agricultural controls, came into existence because of the stated wishes of an influential part of the citizenry.

[31] B. F. Skinner, psychologist and advocate of a position called "operant conditioning," is especially proud of the fact that his system allows one to exercise control so subtly that no one but the conditioner is really aware of it. See "Freedom and Control of Men," *The American Scholar*, 24 (Winter, 1955–1956): 47–65. Needless to say, he has not gone unchallenged by those who worry about "Big Brother."

Or we may talk, quantitatively, about *how much* control. Although control and order have been historically regarded as opposites of freedom and liberty, they are, in fact, nothing of the sort. Control may enhance liberty or may destroy it; often it does both. The regulation of the speed of automobiles in a residential district is a limitation of liberty. On the other hand, one feels safer when there are traffic controls: one is more free from fear.

When an old liberty is removed, emotions are high and there is usually talk about tyranny or oppression. It makes more sense to ask whether what has replaced the older liberty is better or worse. The Pure Food and Drug Acts did indeed take away freedom—the freedom of manufacturers to sell unsafe, dangerous and contaminated products —but there is little talk now about recovering this freedom. Unless one asks specific questions about individual issues, there is great danger of becoming rigid and unrealistic.

The problem, then, is not freedom *versus* control or order, but rather what kinds of freedom and what kinds of control. The issue is not to be seen as an irrestible conflict between two forces, one desirable and the other necessary but vaguely evil. It is rather to be viewed as a weighing or evaluation of what kinds of freedom for what purpose, and what kinds of control for what consequences.

Educational Implications

There are educational implications in the different positions concerning freedom and control. First it should be said that our entire educational system is a response to the belief that education should liberate human potential: the educated person, by virtue of his education, has a greater chance—enlarged freedom—to maximize and develop his potential and talents. The assumption is that more knowledge enables one to make a wider variety of choices.

There is also widespread agreement that schools should transmit to the younger generation a disposition to prize freedom. Schools, it is felt, should make students esteem liberty by dramatizing the benefits of democracy. The customary way of doing this is to celebrate the American heritage by teaching about folk heroes and important events. The outcome is supposed to be an appreciation for our legal procedures, our social and political traditions and, it is hoped, loyalty to what is called, loosely but with great conviction, "our way of life."

As long as freedom is treated as vague abstraction, then all schools can be interpreted as enhancing freedom. Indeed, many believe that American schools have kept us free. But if freedom is defined in somewhat more specific terms, as we have attempted here, then the belief that our schools have kept us free is open to question. William Boyer has argued: if freedom requires that individuals understand their society and be intelligently critical of it and that they defend institutions necessary for the maintenance of unrestricted social criticism,[32] American schools cannot be said to have kept us free. For, he says, American schools have consistently backed away from allowing students to investigate or criticize certain beliefs. Teachers have been most reluctant to criticize—that is, evaluate—differing positions, philosophical beliefs, historical events, economic theories, widespread attitudes and values.[33]

If Boyer is correct, one of the first imperatives for schools is to teach students to become critical of our way of life. The assumption is that, as students grow in the capacity to distinguish among different positions, they will become more skilled in making decisions that will enhance freedom. This assumption should be examined in the light of two rather long-standing theories, the German concepts of *lehrfreiheit* and *lernfreiheit*.

Lehrfreiheit means, roughly, the freedom to teach. It suggests that any subject that a competent teacher chooses as appropriate for inquiry or discussion should be allowed. Even if the subject is distasteful to a majority, or even if the teacher's position is regarded as radical or eccentric, he has a right to inquire, study, or comment without fear of dismissal or any other unpleasant consequences. The assumption is that the freedom to teach will yield benefits to the community at large. By his opening important subjects to dispassionate scholarly inquiry, the community will receive a fund of information and knowledge.

Lernfreiheit, the freedom to learn, is the correlate of the freedom to teach. *Lernfreiheit* means that students have the right to inquire into any topic of their choice. Together, the freedom of teachers to teach and that of students to learn comprise academic freedom.

To the extent that students and teachers are free to inquire into important and relevant issues, ideas will be open for criticism and examination. When ideas are open to criticism, men become better

---

[32] "Have Our Schools Kept Us Free?" *The School Review*, 71 (Summer, 1963): 222–228.

[33] The reason for the moral neutrality of schools, argues Robert Mason, is that the public school teachers and administrators of the early and mid-nineteenth century fought to gain support from a pluralistic society, and in order to keep this support tried to avoid anything that would antagonize any part of the public —hence exclusion of controversial issues. See Robert E. Mason, *Educational Ideals in American Society* (Boston: Allyn and Bacon, 1960).

able to decide what beliefs are to be preferred, what courses of action are open, what consequences are to be desired. Academic freedom, an implication of an open and free society, is designed to perpetuate the society. It is, of course, entirely true that freedom is dangerous, that people will use freedom to do foolish things or think heretical thoughts. But the assumption that most people will use freedom in an intelligent and responsible way is as good a counter-argument today as it was for Thomas Jefferson. When schools are going to feel secure enough to allow teachers and students to exercise the freedom that seems so clearly to be essential to learning is, at present, an open question.

Equality

One of the most persistently troublesome tenets of democratic social philosophy is our idea of equality. When Jefferson penned the phrase "All men are created equal," he started a controversy that has lasted to our own day.

The official democratic dogma that all men are created equal was re-emphasized with the election to the Presidency of Andrew Jackson in 1828. With a Tennessee backwoodsman sitting in the White House, the doctrine of equality evolved from an abstraction to a literal truth. The fully formulated dogma went somewhat like this: despite differences in social class, education, and talent, all men are basically and essentially equal. In all important respects, one man is as good as another.

But though the equality of man may make a stirring slogan, it is denied by physical evidence—men obviously are not equal. Some are more intelligent than others; some have natural aptitudes and energy that lead them to positions of command. Some are lazy, slothful, unambitious, and undeserving. Physically, mentally, morally—and in every other way—inequality, not equality, is a fact of existence. Thus the paradox of our democracy: a slogan that attracts verbal affirmation but is denied, allegedly, by common-sense understanding. The way out of the dilemma may involve examining the various dimensions of equality.

Theories of Equality

From the point of view of Christian theology, there is a spiritual equality among man: in the eyes of God, the souls of all men are of equal value. No matter what the conditions of life on this earth are, no matter how unequal men may be in wealth, endowment, or status, in His eyes, all souls are equal. This certainly is one meaning of the term *equality,* but because it is a theological concept, it is not completely acceptable as a doctrine for public schools.

In recent times certain democratic theorists have attempted to interpret equality as a statement, not of literal fact but of desirable conditions. The desirable conditions are that no one should have unfair barriers placed before him in his quest for achievement, success, or self-actualization. Conditions of existence are likened to a race in which it is unfair for any runner to suffer barriers or obstacles not provided for any other runner. If the basic conditions are equal for all, then talent, effort, and ambition will be the only factors in deciding who wins the race.

In another variation, the competitive race context is unimportant, and equality is made the pre-supposition for a political and social democracy. Thus the bounties of a democratic life should be equal for all, and no one should be denied them because of race, religion, or any other factor. This is the assumption behind many of the judicial rulings and legislative actions of the last ten or fifteen years. The rejection of racial inferiority by the Supreme Court in 1954 (*Brown vs. Topeka Board of Education*) is based on the tenet that racial inequality is incompatible with democracy. The considerable increase in federal aid to education is premised on the belief that it is fundamentally unfair for persons to suffer from unequal educational opportunity. The drive within the last few years to protect the civil rights of Negroes is predicated on the theory that no one should be deprived of a fundamental Constitutional right because of the color of his skin.

Implications for Education

Despite the emphasis on spreading equal opportunities in the areas of education, civil rights, vocations, and housing, some fundamental questions remain. First, what is the aim of equality? To say that we require equality to achieve national goals raises the question of which national goals. Debate about the value of national goals is conspicuously absent, in part because as a culture we are not given to abstract speculation, and in part because national goals seem to be self-evidently desirable. But the question remains: What is the goal in the quest for equal opportunity in housing, vocations, education, and civil rights?

In part, the answer is that equality is an end in itself. This is a tenable position. There should be equality of opportunity because equality is in itself desirable. It is easy to believe that it is inherently wrong for anyone to suffer deprivation because of poor environment, because he does not have access to good schools, or because he is a member of a minority. But suppose we phrase the question differently: To what *end* is equality a *means?*

The answer "Everyone should be equal to achieve the good things of life" is no answer at all if the "good things" are left undefined. What are the "good things" for which equal educational opportunity is a means? If we assume that we all possess equal opportunity to secure an education, what should be the goal of this equal opportunity? Or if we assume that there is no job discrimination—that anyone has a chance to get a job as long as he is qualified for it—what should be the objective of equal vocational opportunity? Without a reference point, an end, means become most unclear and obscure. Equal opportunity in our democracy might come sooner if we were clearer about the end or ends sought through it.

Another problem inherent in our philosophical attitude toward equality is the conflict between our notions of excellence and equality. A serious consequence, assert some, would be for the drive toward equality to produce schools that are no longer concerned with excellence. Schools must concentrate on excellence by giving the talented few an opportunity to enjoy a very high-grade education. If schools are overconcerned with equality, it is felt, will they not neglect the excellent few in favor of the mediocre many? This question is discussed by John Gardner in *Excellence: Can We Be Equal and Excellent Too?* [34] Gardner maintains that our schools can be committed to both excellence and equality if we but redefine what we mean by the terms. He advocates a plural definition of excellence: there are many ways of being excellent and we ought not overlook any of them.

Equality of educational opportunity for all entails still another problem. While it is fairly easy to see what equality of political opportunities means—every qualified person able to vote, run for office, and so on—it is much less simple to define "equal educational opportunity." Does it mean providing the "same" facilities for all? If so, how is this possible? Does it mean simply some kind of uniform financial support for schools throughout the nation? [35] Does it mean

[34] New York: Harper, 1961.

[35] At present individual states, through what is known as foundation plans, are attempting to equalize educational opportunity in this manner. A minimum per-pupil expenditure is established throughout a state, and no school district is allowed to fall below this figure. School districts that are less affluent are granted state aid to raise them to the established average. This procedure, adapted to a nationwide plan, may be one method of implementing equal educational opportunity.

that there should be a set of uniform requirements concerning curriculum, teacher preparation and certification, and school construction? If education exists, as many maintain, to release the potential of each child, since potentials vary greatly, how can schools deal equally with such variation?

Thus the concept of equality, with its apparent present-day meaning of equal opportunity for all, does not itself provide a complete plan of action. What equality is, how it is to be realized and implemented, to what end it is a means, and to what extent it works against the development of excellence—these are problems arising from the context of what has been democratic dogma for more than a century and a half.

10

Social
Philosophy
(CONTINUED)

How Men Are To Be Ruled

After many thousands of years of experimenting with different kinds of governments, man, it would seem, should have decided which government is best. In fact, nothing could be further from the case. How men should rule themselves seems almost as unclear as it was two or three thousand years ago. Whether "common" men are basically capable of ruling themselves or whether a few strong, talented, or well-trained persons should rule, is still a moot point. Even when it is agreed that men should rule themselves, it is still not clear how this should take place.

Rule at the Top

Through most of the history of organized society, the favored governmental form has been either monarchy or aristocracy, in any of various guises. Primitive societies are usually governed by a council of elders, often males. Most ancient societies were governed by one man—a monarch, king, or tyrant—usually assisted by a council of lesser rulers. Rule by a limited number of men, often families, was another common form. When rule is in the hands of a few families with hereditary powers, the government is known as an aristocracy. In an aristocracy, a privileged class, often a nobility, may coexist with a monarch and share powers with him. An oligarchy—rule by a very few—may be government by a hereditary aristocracy, a priestly class, or simply a limited number of men who form an inner circle of decision-makers. Usually oligarchies are concerned with preserving their own privileges and getting for themselves more and more power.

The assumption underlying both monarchy and aristocracy is that the masses are incapable of ruling themselves wisely, so that some one person or a limited number of persons must make decisions for the people. The decision-makers are assumed to have the necessary energy, intelligence, ability, and perhaps knowledge to rule. The masses are assumed to be so unstable, divided, short-sighted, and driven by passions that they are totally unable to rule themselves wisely. Only chaos and disorganization would prevail were it not for the firm rule of the vigorous and decisive leaders, who alone know what is best for the people.

Democracy: Government by the Governed

The foregoing assumption is challenged by the socio-political theory called democracy.[1] The term and original forms of democratic theory came from Greece, but most modern democratic theory and practice originated in England and, to some extent, in France. After the initial phase of theocracy in New England in the early seventeenth century, the colonies slowly acquired skill in democratic self-rule.[2] Our own experience, together with that of European democracies, has generated a considerable fund of theory about what a democracy is and how it should function and toward what ends.[3]

Although the forms of political democracy[4] differ from country

[1] It confuses Americans to be told that a democracy may easily coexist with a titular monarchy. England and the Netherlands, for instance, combine reigning monarchs with effective self-government.

[2] Two important points about self-rule: First, it may be either direct, as with the New England town-meeting or the Swiss *langsgemeinde* governments; or it may be indirect, as with most representative governments. Second, self-rule in the original thirteen colonies was self-rule only in the sense that we ruled in the absence of England. In fact, throughout most of the colonies, government was in the hands of an oligarchy. Democracy grew only slowly and with many setbacks.

[3] For a discussion of democratic theory and the problem of defining democracy, see E. E. Bayles, Chapter 10, "A Definition of Democracy"; Henry B. Mayo, *An Introduction to Democratic Theory* (New York: Oxford Press, 1960), "The Problem of Defining Democracy."

[4] By "forms" of democracy is meant the procedures, mechanics, or techniques of a particular democratic government. For instance, the United States Constitution separates legislative, executive, and judiciary powers. In Great Britain rule is essentially by parliament. Voting by secret ballot, election of representatives, holding of office for a stipulated length of time, and instruments of some direct and popular control, such as initiative and referendum, are other forms of democracy. These forms, it must be emphasized, are not inherent in or absolutely essential to a democracy. It is erroneous, as is often done, to confuse democracy with a two-house congress, with a president, or with any other particularized form.

to country, there is consensus on the essential meaning of the term. A political democracy is based on the assumption that those who are ruled must have some say about how and by whom they are ruled— although how much say is always a moot point. There is an implied egalitarian assumption here: there should be equality among the electorate in reaching decisions. There is also, insists Bayles, a further implication of democracy: not only should there be equality of opportunity in decision-making, but there should be equality of obligation to carry out the decision. Once a majority has decided on a course of action, it is incumbent on all to abide by the decision. A minority may, of course, work toward rescinding a majority decision or modifying it. The main point is that there must not be two sets of rules, one for a privileged caste and the other for the masses.

The assumption which supports a democracy is that the people are capable of ruling themselves, of making their own decisions. This assumption implies that the people are able to choose decision-makers wisely and rationally rather than having decisions made on their behalf by someone who is not responsible to them. Whether or not this is so cannot be determined by facts. It is very much like any other philosophical assumption in that it cannot be proven with finality by supporting evidence. It should be pointed out that a very large number of thinkers—from Aristotle to H. L. Mencken—have been opposed to democracy and have been certain that when the people direct their own destinies they invariably make a mess of things. Many have believed that a democracy must be corrupt, that it is a producer of mediocrity, or that it is nothing but incoherent rule by the masses.[5]

For many centuries democracy has had its supporters and detractors. Many thinkers have attempted to define the distinctive characteristics of a democracy. We can only mention these characteristics and arbitrarily state that the most essential is representative self-rule. Other alleged characteristics generally considered valuable are essential fairness, higher standard of living, encouragement of people to learn by experience, lack of class antagonism and strife, and the likelihood that people will be awarded according to merit.[6] Argu-

[5] H. L. Mencken, the American humorist, was at his sarcastic best in discussing democracy. For instance, "Why should democracy rise against bribery? It is itself a form of wholesale bribery. In place of a government with a fixed purpose and a visible goal, it sets up a government that is a mere function of the mob's vagaries, and that maintains itself by constantly bargaining with those vagaries." *Notes on Democracy* (New York: Knopf, 1926), p. 180.

[6] These are all highly debatable, especially the points about the reduced class strife and the higher standard of living. There are certain Middle-eastern sheikdoms with very high standards of living and certain South American democracies with low standards. And though there is much less class hatred and strife in our country than there was in eighteenth-century France, class friction is by no means absent.

ments against a democracy are that it is too slow and cannot act in a crisis, that it does not work well in a complex society, that it elevates mediocrity to rule, that it involves the tyranny of a majority and that, in fact, it does not exist because the actual ruling is in the hands of a small political and economic oligarchy.[7]

Implications for Education

Whether democracy does or does not have flaws is not really the point. We live in a democracy, and a more useful question therefore is: What are the implications of a democracy for education?

If democracy is essentially a socio-political system characterized by equal opportunity to participate in the decision-making process, then the schools in a democracy should function to improve the electorate's ability to make decisions. Students should be taught what a decision is and should be educated in the skills of decision-making. Since self-rule and decision-making necessarily involve a high degree of independent thinking, the ultimate goal of education in a democracy should be to improve the ability of all to think independently about the life of which they are a part.[8]

Some believe that the best way to improve decision-making skills is to use as subject matter the problems that will actually require decisions on the part of an electorate. Another way of saying this is that the social studies curriculum ought to consist of the problems inherent in our democracy.[9] These problems need not be the current ones only, but may well include those which have been long-standing, pervasive, and troublesome. The problems or issues that clearly require examination for their solution are usually called "controversial." Although it may be objected that schools should not handle "hot" controversial issues because they may make trouble for teachers and administrators, the objection is shallow. These issues "make trouble" in large part precisely because they persist, and it may be that they persist because schools have persistently ignored them.

If excessive power is thought to lie in the hands of economic and

[7] The following works treat the points made here: C. Wright Mills, *The Power Elite* (New York: Oxford U. Press, 1956); John Dewey, *The Public and Its Problems* (New York: Holt, 1927); Alexis de Tocqueville, *Democracy in America* (1835, revised edition, New York: Knopf, 1945); James Bryce, *The American Commonwealth* (New York: 1910).

[8] E. E. Bayles develops this point in a number of places in *Democratic Educational Theory*.

[9] Maurice Hunt and Lawrence Metcalf, *Teaching High School Social Studies* (New York: Harper, 1955).

political oligarchies within our own system, then schools should deal with the issue by raising for discussion and research such questions as these: What effect does concentrated wealth have on democratic forms and functions? Is it the government's right or responsibility to limit an individual's wealth to prevent undue political power, or ought one to be free to make as much money as he can? Since economic oligarchies are often accused of abusing democratic functions, it may be worth while to discuss what the limits of permissible power are in a democracy. Too, how is political power actually wielded in our democracy—what is the theoretical and what the actual distribution?

The current dispute over proportional representation in state legislatures is really a part of the continuing debate over the distribution of political power. Students should study the issue by trying to answer such questions as these: What led to the original bi-cameral mode of representation? [10] Is the bi-cameral legislature effectively representing the population at present, or is it obsolescent? If it is obsolescent, how should it be changed?

It is being alleged that the courts are presently usurping the rights of legislatures by creating rather than interpreting public policy. The function of the courts has been controversial since the time of John Marshall. This topic may be treated by asking the following questions: How well has the distribution of powers really worked? Is conflict between the three branches of government inevitable? What does it mean to "make" and what to "interpret" public policy? Why have courts been arrogating more and more power to themselves—if indeed they have? What effect does class status have on the administration of justice at the local level? At the national and state level?

The presence of a rather large lower social class, consisting in part of racial and ethnic minorities, constitutes an important social problem. This lower class is essentially outside the mainstream of the body politic and is probably culturally deprived. What is more serious is that isolated enclaves of the lower class, jammed into slum ghettoes, threaten constantly to explode into violence. Since the official cultural belief is that we are a classless society, schools typically do not study the nature and problems of a class structure. But students would do well to examine some of the sociological literature on this issue and wrestle with such questions as: How should we deal with pockets of poverty in a generally affluent society? Is democracy compatible with any sort of class structure? How does our class structure compare with a caste system?

[10] Part of this problem *is* studied. Students learn about the compromise between the various large and small states at the Constitutional Convention. What is not discussed is whether a compromise reached in 1789 is appropriate today.

At present, international problems are generating vigorous controversy everywhere—except in public-school classes.[11] Since the electors must make decisions about foreign policy, schools should study these questions: What should be our role in an international body like the United Nations? How should we deal with societies which have social, economic, and political systems very different from our own? What is the difference between "world leadership" and "world domination"? What has made it difficult to formulate a viable foreign policy? How should the United States, the most powerful nation in the world, use its power?

If our forefathers had adopted a totalitarian form of government, there would not be any logical reason for studying social issues. Really important decisions in a totalitarian society are made at the top and do not require the formal consent of the populace. In a democracy, however, the premise that public policy is made by and for the people carries the implication that the public requires training both in political decision-making and in acquiring adequate information. The place where all, or nearly all, the people can receive experience in decision-making is the public schools. Yet evidence exists that the public schools have historically backed away from really serious examination of national issues and social problems. The social problems for study by students in the public schools—only a partial list, of course, has been given here—demand thoughtful consideration for their solution. But if schools continue to behave as they have traditionally, these problems will either be solved in undemocratic ways or continue to persist—with consequences that may be disastrous. We can do no better than conclude with a quotation by John Dewey: In an analysis of the relationship between academic freedom and democracy, Dewey hoped for a new education whose goals would be to "investigate truth; critically to verify fact; to reach conclusions by means of the best methods at command, untrammeled by external fear or favor, to communicate this truth to the student; to interpret to him its bearing on the questions he will have to face in life." [12]

Toward What End?

What is the proper end of government? This is an ancient philosophical query, but it has never seemed a problem to the American people, who have assumed that our national purposes are self-evidently clear. The prologue to the Constitution proclaims the preservation of

[11] Discussion of "current events," though a staple in schools, tends to be little more than a contextless coverage of unrelated happenings.

[12] "Academic Freedom," *Educational Review*, 23 (January, 1902): 3.

liberty for posterity as an inherent aim of our government. Another aim, though not hallowed by an official document, is the provision of enough material possessions to make life decent and enjoyable.

These two ends have always been extremely important in our history, for it was precisely freedom and material comfort that emigrants to our shores lacked in their native countries. Those who suffered under czars, aristocracies, emperors, police states, or—in the nineteenth century—under factory owners, saw in the United States a country where people could live without fear of a brutal police force, without legal meddling in their religious beliefs, and without a pervasive network of restrictive laws. This absence of coercion, as we have seen, was identified with freedom. A low level of material comfort—degrading poverty—also impelled emigration to this country. Land, a job with good wages, a better standard of living, an opportunity to "make something of oneself" appeared to be worthwhile goals. Over the years, freedom and plenty have been enshrined as national goals, and even more, are widely regarded as the unique contributions of the United States to man's aspirations and accomplishments.

But freedom and a decent standard of living are, in a sense, almost minimal goals. Although there has always been tension between the demands of freedom and those of order, we have succeeded in realizing a high degree of freedom,[13] at least in the sense of freedom *from*. And as the nation has become increasingly middle class, we have achieved a level of affluence unimaginable in previous times. Yet the mere possession of objects has come to have a rather hollow meaning.[14] Consequently, the expression of our national goals has undergone modification and sophistication. Perhaps our goal may now be phrased in

[13] This is a controversial assertion. Many believe that our freedoms are in imminent danger from either the extreme right or the extreme left. However, there is evidence that we actually have quantitatively more freedom than we have had in the past. See John P. Roche, "We've Never Had More Freedom," *The New Republic*, 134 (January 23, 1956): 12–15; January 30: 13–16; and February 6: 13–15.

[14] At least the deluge of sociological essays and fiction would indicate this. For analyses and criticisms of middle-class life, acquisition, status symbols, conspicuous consumption, and so on, see the following works: Sinclair Lewis, *Main Street* (New York: Harcourt Brace, 1948), Gunnar Myrdal, *Challenge to Affluence* (New York: Pantheon Books, 1963), Paul Goodman, *Growing Up Absurd* (New York: Random House, 1960), A. C. Spectorsky, *The Exurbanites* (Philadelphia: Lippincott, 1955), Thorstein Veblen, *The Theory of the Leisure Class* (New York: Macmillan, 1908) and Vance Packard, *The Status Seekers* (New York: David McKay, 1959). A recent and vigorous objection to the drive for material possessions is Jules Henry, *Culture Against Man* (New York: Random House, 1963).

this way: our government exists to provide opportunity for all to realize their inherent potential to the end that there will be created a society that is spiritually rich and materially prosperous.

This goal—if indeed it is our goal—is not a sharp break from the two goals discussed above. It takes cognizance of the importance of material prosperity, but it involves a change of emphasis: freedom *from* toward freedom *to*. The freedom *to* is the freedom to realize one's inherent potential.

Realization of the potential of *all* citizens is a function of a society which is structured very differently from the rigid, class or caste-bound societies of the past. In such a society, one's role was fairly well determined in advance of his birth. One's vocation, position in the social hierarchy, privileges, perquisites—one's destiny—lay within rather rigid confines, determined by birth. But in the mobile and relatively free society in which we live, there are far fewer restrictions on self-realization: the Jacksonian dream that one should be allowed to go as far as he can, restricted only by ambition and a talent, is a reality for many.

The formulation of a national goal of opportunity for self-realization is largely an outgrowth of pluralism in our society. Multiple philosophies and differing dreams and aspirations have merged to create here a culture in which one man's aspiration is not only as good as another's, but often quite possible of accomplishment. The study of vocations in schools assume great importance because there are so many occupational opportunities. Our rapidly accelerating technology and increasing wealth have also widened opportunity. Not only are there more vocations possible, but the rising standard of living has made commonplaces of such terms as "professional opportunity," "travel," "recreation," "creative leisure time," "hobbies," "satisfaction."

Thus the sum total of wealth, technological advance, pluralism, and freedom have made it possible for the hypothetical average person to realize a great many possibilities in himself and to do a great many things. It is not an exaggeration to say that the creation and maintenance of opportunity for the realization of individual potentialities has become the assumed and expected function of our government. The important underlying assumptions are: (1) that individuals are unique, with important potentialities that can be realized in a variety of ways; (2) that as individuals realize their potentialities, the entire nation is enriched.

Understanding this goal is not as simple as it may seem. First, the term "potentiality" lacks clarity. What kind of potentials are to be realized? Certainly not all potentials are equally desirable. One may have potential for becoming a safe-cracker. If the answer is that safe-cracking, for instance, is not a socially desirable function, then the next question is: How does one determine what are socially desirable potentials? If this question does not seem serious it is because one may not realize that lurking behind generalizations about "socially desirable potentials" are a host of unrecognized ethical assumptions.

Second, quite apart from the problem of meaning, how are so many potentialities to be realized? Does this nation have the educational facilities to handle an almost infinite range of potentialities? Colleges, junior colleges, technical schools, graduate schools, correspondence schools, and private, special interest schools exist to deal with a wide spectrum of educational potentialities. This situation may seem gratifying to some; but to others it simply indicates that education has attempted to take on too many responsibilities and, having tried to do too much, has done nothing well.

But if we assume that the aim of government is the development of each individual's potential, what does this imply for education? First, it means a revolutionary change in our entire culture. Evidence indicates that there are many potentials that are culturally undervalued, just as Goodman points out that there are many socially valuable functions that are undervalued and ignored.[15]

Those with talent in art, literature, and music often have difficulty in acquiring necessary training, in supporting themselves financially, and in finding sufficient encouragement. To develop artistic potential, our culture would have to change its basic value orientation. It is highly unlikely that our schools will develop artistic potentials if the culture ignores them.[16]

Another implication of a national goal of self-realization is that there must be a change of emphasis in the preparation of teachers. It is relatively easy to find teachers who are well-trained in the sciences and mathematics, less easy to discover well-trained social studies teachers, and the number of well-prepared teachers in the humanities and fine arts is disturbingly inadequate. One often finds elementary teachers who know no more literature than is presented in the textbook and teaching manual. High-school teachers without sufficient preparation are often assigned dramatics, speech, or English classes. It is pointless

[15] Paul Goodman, *Growing Up Absurd.*

[16] The author recently participated in an accreditation visit to a new high school, the pride of the community. There were eight teachers of mathematics and one of fine arts. One fine arts room in the school contrasted with several well-stocked laboratories and science classrooms. There was no orchestra or musical ensemble—except for a pep band. How common such a situation is, of course, is debatable. But it is clearly not unique.

to expect teachers to develop students' potentialities in fields about which the teachers themselves have only the most superficial knowledge.

Third, the development of a wide range of potentialities logically implies a change in the methods of teaching. Although educators have talked about "individualizing instruction" for years, not enough has been accomplished. The textbook, covered methodically chapter by chapter, is still the staple. While many schools have a multiple-track or grouping program, this often means simply covering the same material at different rates of speed. Individualizing instruction would mean asking two questions: What should this child know? What is the best method of teaching it to him? Neither question can be answered easily, but both are worth asking. To answer them would involve an imaginative reconstruction of education: larger and better libraries and instructional media centers, more contact with stimulating personalities, better facilities, more appropriate texts, administrators with a better grasp of teaching, and greater dissemination of research about learning and teaching.

This last point is crucial. Much valid and reliable data has been secured by researchers about the characteristics of different kinds of learners and about the most effective teaching methods. Indeed, one is amazed to see the vast number of research projects at universities dedicated to discovering newer and more effective ways of teaching. But—with certain gratifying exceptions—the information gained through this research is not being utilized by teachers. It is easier to teach all students the same way.

The development of human potentialities requires, too, that all education be financed far more adequately than at present. Better financing for education is not a sufficient condition, but it is clearly a necessary one. At present, the quality of education one receives often depends on such theoretically irrelevant factors as one's race or ethnic background, one's residence, or the state in which one happens to live. For the goal of realizing individual human potential to be realized in fact, there must be a more uniform and better financing of education.

Finally, to say that one should realize his potential raises two questions: What is human potential? How can we realize it? At present, psychologists traditionally concerned with measurement of one aspect of potential—that is, intelligence—are attempting to devise measurements of other kinds of potential, such as creativity.[17] When reliable research can help us answer questions about the meaning

[17] See Nathaniel L. Gage (ed.), *Handbook of Research on Teaching* (Chicago: Rand McNally, 1963), Part II, "Methodologies in Research on Teaching."

and measurement of potential, we will be in a better position to fulfill potential.

There is no accusation here that our educational system has done nothing to help students toward self-realization. One respected critic of American education, Dr. James B. Conant, has recognized that our educational system has probably made more effort to deal with more kinds of potential than has Europe.[18] Extracurricular activities, such as special interest clubs, student government, athletics, and band and choral groups, are attempts to deal with such dimensions. But much more remains to be done before American education can claim that it systematically seeks to develop each individual's potential.

Economic Theory and Educational Practice

In the nineteenth century a number of economic theories were transplanted from Europe to this country, where they were hospitably received and subtly blended with theological positions and certain scientific dogmas. This seemingly odd mixture has become part of our culture and has influenced our theory and practice of education.[19]

The basic economic concept was the tenet, advanced by the Scottish philosopher Adam Smith in the late eighteenth century, that the most dependable of all human motivations is self-interest. Men, Smith thought, are more likely to respond to their own personal, selfish interests than they are to vague, altruistic motives. What affects any person most directly, what has the most intimate connection with wants, wishes, and perceived self-interest, is just what will motivate him most dependably.

Around this theory there developed the notion of the "economic man." Man, according to this position, is essentially acquisitive. Implanted in man, somehow, is an urge to acquire possessions—land, animals, money, whatever. This view and other facets of it advanced by David Ricardo, John Thomas Malthus, Alfred Marshall, and Herbert Spencer were received in this country most hospitably and became the "conventional wisdom" of capitalistic economic theory.

[18] Conant makes this point in *The American High School Today* (New York: McGraw-Hill, 1959) and *Recommendations for Education in the Junior High School Years* (Princeton: Educational Testing Service, 1960).

[19] The reader may get some idea of how this mixture of beliefs affected education by reading of William Torrey Harris in Merle Curti, *The Social Ideas of American Educators* (Patterson: Littlefield, Adams, 1965). Harris was an immensely influential American educator whose actions and writings literally shaped American education in the second half of the nineteenth century.

But such theory needed to displace the more ancient Christian belief that man should not store up treasures in this life, that cooperation and not competition was God's desire for man, and that business and finance were somehow un-Christian.[20] The new position was that God, who had chosen certain men to be saved, would certainly not punish his elect on earth: he who became prosperous did so because of God's grace. Thus resulted the merger of economic theory and theology: God had blessed, and not damned, acquisitive man, and things of this world are really not opposed to Heaven but are part of the Eternal Plan.[21]

It seemed to follow that the truly good society was one which produced enough wealth for all to be comfortable—that this world was not merely an unimportant antechamber to eternal life, but a place where people should gather the fruits of hard work and shrewd judgment. There was some sort of equation of moral superiority and material possessions. By the twentieth century it seemed to us that Americans were morally superior to Europeans and were therefore blessed with a much higher standard of living; or perhaps we were morally superior because we had a higher standard of living. At any rate, there was an identification of the moral life and a productive society.

The marriage between industrial technology and science also tended to support the notion that the only worthwhile reality was the one that could be quantified. Character, education, taste, and other intangibles are all very good, but if one wanted to get the real measure of a man, the best way was to find out how much he owned, how large a house he possessed, how much he earned a year. The question "How much is he worth?" is not a query about a man's character.

In short, the nineteenth century saw an emerging value structure which emphasized production, material goods, and the supreme worth of the quantifiable.[22] Of course, while this value structure was being built up, the older, more traditional values emphasizing asceticism, the

[20] R. H. Tawney, *Religion and the Rise of Capitalism* (New York: New American Library, 1958).

[21] John Dewey was much interested in this amalgam of religion, economic theories, and scientific method. See his *The Influence of Darwin on Philosophy*, (New York: Peter Smith, 1910), *The Public and Its Problems* (New York: Henry Holt, 1927), and *Individualism Old and New* (New York: Minton, Balch, 1910). See also Curti, *The Social Ideas of American Educators*, and Henry Steele Commager, *The American Mind* (New Haven: Yale U. Press, 1950).

[22] For an excellent analysis of the relationship between education and theories of efficiency and quantification, see Raymond Callahan, *Education and the Cult of Efficiency* (Chicago: U. of Chicago Press, 1962).

worthlessness of material good, and the priority of the things of the spirit did not suddenly die out; they simply existed side by side with the newer set of values.

Although most Americans greeted the new industrialism and affluence with enthusiasm, a few entertained serious misgivings. Henry Adams, the historian, was unhappy not only with democracy but with the commercial civilization that had developed by the end of the nineteenth century.[23] In *The Gilded Age* Mark Twain expressed his disappointment with the shallowness of American life, and William Dean Howells described the conflicts of a capitalist in *The Rise of Silas Lapham*. But perhaps the most sharply worded criticism of nineteenth-century American life comes in Walt Whitman's *Democratic Vistas*. "Society in these States," says Whitman, "is cankered, crude, superstitious and rotten. Political, or law-made society is, and private, or voluntary society, is also." Further, Whitman asserts, "The depravity of the business classes of our country is not less than has been supposed, but infinitely greater. The official services of America, national, state, and municipal, in all their branches and departments, except the judiciary, are saturated in corruption, bribery, falsehood, maladministration; and the judiciary is tainted." [24]

But Whitman, Howells, Twain, and a later generation of so-called "muckrakers" did not reflect the feelings of the majority. For most, a benign providence had supplied America with scientific and technological know-how, with business acumen, and with a religion that sanctified the acquisition of material goods.

It could have been predicted that education would begin to reflect this amalgam of scientific positions, economic theory, and theology. The schools, it was held, have a responsibility to enhance economic efficiency. Not only should arithmetic be taught for business use, but other subjects too must be concerned with the production of better workers. Indeed, it was held that secondary schools should even teach trade and vocational skills.[25] This is remarkable only in the light of the ancient European tradition that education was concerned with intellectual development, with character building—with anything but

[23] Henry Adams, *The Degradation of the Democratic Dogma* (New York: Macmillan, 1919).

[24] New York: The Liberal Arts Press, 1949, p. 9.

[25] For instance, Theodore Roosevelt wrote on the necessity for a new education in secondary schools: "[I]n a general way I feel that the nation should, by making appropriations, put a premium upon industrial, and especially agricultural, training in the state schools. . . ." "The Emancipation of Education," in William H. Lucio (ed.), *Readings in American Education* (Chicago: Scott, Foresman, 1963).

economic efficiency. So important was economic efficiency as a cultural value that Americans chose not to emulate the European tradition of providing separate apprenticeship training. For us, apprenticeship training smacked of a European class orientation. We would be able, it was hoped, to integrate vocational education in the mainstream of secondary education.

Translating this newer doctrine into viable educational method was the next step. At the turn of the century, vocational training was strengthened by such legislation as the Smith-Hughes Act and the Smith-Lever Act which, in effect, made secondary schools responsible for teaching home economics and vocational agriculture. Schools also added secretarial training, bookkeeping, and other courses intended to increase general business skills. Eventually automotive mechanics, woodworking, electricity—almost the whole range of vocational skills— were included in the secondary curriculum.

The belief also developed that schools were essentially like any business institution and should be governed by the same standards, values, and procedures as business. This meant, in practice, that schools were to be judged by the criterion of efficiency. Administration was to be efficient. A particular subject was valuable only to the degree that it could be shown to be efficient. Teachers were exhorted to be efficient. While the emphasis was extremely heavy, it can be shown— as we have come to reflect on this period in the last few years—that the conception of efficiency was anything but clear. It may be possible to determine efficiency in a business—the most or the best produced at the least expenditure—but this criterion can not easily be applied to learning. In effect, yardsticks held up as measurements of efficiency were little more than value judgments treated as self-evident standards.

Accompanying the developing cultural value of efficiency was emphasis on measurement. Intellectual performance, it was held, could be measured with the same procedures as the measurement of ball bearings or any other material object. One could establish norms —averages based on a large sample—and then apply these norms to handwriting, spelling, arithmetic, or any other academic task. Thus came the widespread use of nationwide testing instruments designed to measure the performance of students.

The practices introduced at this period have become ingrained. And the defense of efficiency as an educational goal and of measurement as an educational practice has been eloquent and meaningful. Yet the entire theory and practice is very much open to question. As we have noted, one can rate the efficiency of a business or industry, but it is by no means clear that education is amenable to the same kind of measurement. It may well be that one reason teaching is an under-compensated profession is that it has been difficult to measure and quantify.[26]

The application of business values to education is, Callahan points out, extremely unfortunate, because there are inherent differences between business and education. The application of the standards of one in judging the other is, he says, fundamentally wrong. The products of an educational system are not only knowledge—which is to some degree capable of measurement—but also intangibles—values, attitudes, appreciations, understandings—which are not capable of precise measurement. Because there has been so strong a drive toward measurement in our schools, we have witnessed an increase in emphasis on the measureable and a decrease of interest in the intangible but still important values.

Finally, the fundamental assumption of capitalism—that self-interest is a primary motive and that men are by nature acquisitive—may have yielded a profound dislocation in our entire culture. It is becoming obvious to a number of observers [27] that our overemphasis on private property, on production and consumption, and on the acquisition of material goods is subverting other cultural values. For instance, at its inception, television was hailed as a magnificent tool for educating a large populace. But as the years go on, it seems clear that television is developing primarily as a vehicle to sell merchandise and only secondarily as an educative instrument.[28] Schools are doing little to bring about an awareness of this value conflict in American culture, for by exposing television to critical scrutiny, teachers may come dangerously close to criticizing the basic assumptions of capitalism.

[26] That is, if we accept the assumption that one ought to be rewarded according to how much one produces or how well one can perform, and if this assumption is applied to education, problems arise. While it is easy to decide the worth of a car salesman—by how many cars he sells—how can quantitative measurement be applied to a teacher? Should we reward a teacher on the basis of how many students he passes, how many he fails, how many correct responses his students make, how many of his students go to college, or just what?

[27] For example, Max Lerner, *America As a Civilization* (New York: Simon and Schuster, 1957). See also John Kenneth Galbraith, *The Affluent Society* (Boston: Houghton Mifflin, 1958) for a discussion of certain effects of economic theory on our culture.

[28] Says Louis Kronenberger, "The presentation of the program is worse, and far more uniform. Whatever the pros and cons for commercial television generally, there can be no argument about how uncivilized, how rife with crudities, timidities, imbecilities sponsored programs tend to be." As for educational television: "[It] remains a kind of sop that under the present system will never become a sufficient offset." "Uncivilized and Uncivilizing," *TV Guide*, 14 (February 26, 1966): 15–19.

At present the argument seems to be between those who criticize schools for failure to indoctrinate "spiritual" values and those who criticize schools for failure to educate students to adjust to a technological, acquisitive society. Since educators have not thought seriously about the assumptions behind the criticism leveled at them, they have responded by doing a little bit of what all critics want.[29] The attempt to make all critics happy has made no one happy and has simply increased the divisions within public education.

The World Order

Since ancient times, philosophers have expressed concern for positive and peaceful relationships among all peoples of the world. While certain thinkers have believed their country or culture or religion immeasurably superior to any others, other thinkers have stressed the oneness or the community of men and have envisioned a future when all men would be united. The Stoics, for instance, believed that a desirable world order would stress the commonality of men and not their differences. This same belief is to be found in Judaism and Christianity, as well as in some of the Asian religions and philosophies.

In the Renaissance and the Enlightenment, some philosophers conceived of a legal and moral code that should govern international relations. Hugo Grotius, the Dutch jurist and philosopher, tried to persuade nations to adopt rules that would govern them in peace and war.[30] Immanuel Kant's *Perpetual Peace* (or *Eternal Peace*) is another effort to describe the ground rules for world peace.[31] Other philosophers since have analyzed the conflicts separating men and have advocated a framework that would lead to a world order. The term "world order" is a difficult philosophical term, but it seems to describe a particular conception of how men throughout the world ought to arrange their lives so as to live in peace and accord.

Those who argue for teaching all children a conception of a world order point to the increasingly suicidal nature of war and conflict in this century. Technological advancements in communications have not

[29] For an analysis of different criticisms of contemporary American education, see Mary Ann Raywid, *The Ax-grinders: Critics of our Public Schools* (New York: Macmillan, 1962). For an evaluation of what happens when a school system attempts to placate critics without analyzing the values involved, see James G. Stone, "Teacher Education by Legislation," *Phi Delta Kappan*, 47 (February, 1966): 287–291.

[30] *De Belli Ac Pacis*, usually translated as *The Rights of War and Peace*.

[31] Both Grotius and Kant lived during particularly warlike eras. Grotius found himself involved in the fratricidal struggles between religious factions in Holland, and Kant saw Europe become a battleground for the Napoleonic Wars.

facilitated peace and concord—as it was thought in the nineteenth century that they would—but have made it easier for men to quarrel and war. Differences among cultures, conflicting national ambitions, economic competition for raw materials, and territorial needs for expanding populations have turned the world into a tinder box. Thus during this century world wars, limited wars, "wars of liberation," nationalistic wars, revolutions, and rebellions—in short, conflict within and among nations—have greatly increased the concern for establishing peaceful and orderly international relations.

But neither our nation nor most others have done much to spread the philosophy that international cooperation is a prerequisite for world order. Indeed, the history of our country reflects the problems inherent in adopting a world outlook. We have generally thought ourselves superior to all other nations. We have looked with suspicion on "entangling alliances." Our attitude toward international organizations is ambiguous: it is proper to join them as long as joining does not conflict with our sovereignty. At the same time that we have assumed the position of world leadership thrust upon us after World War II, there are still large pockets of isolationism in many parts of our country. Even though there is a strong verbalized desire for peace, it is still thought proper to meet all international crises with an arms increase and a military build-up. Our attitude—and again it must be emphasized that we are not unique—is a mixture of a verbalized longing for world peace, isolationism, military commitments to countries in all parts of the world, and reliance on might as a means of realizing international goals.

Many who have thought about the problem phrase the question as follows: What kind of world order would allow social change to come about without either constant brushfire wars or an admittedly suicidal nuclear war? Specifically, how can nations throughout the world achieve political stability and also acquire the technology and raw materials and skills that will enable them to survive and prosper in a world that must remain peaceful?

If this question expresses the issue accurately—and many would deny it—then what implications exist for education, both in this country and throughout the world?

First, there must be a qualitative change in the curriculum. Since economic problems are central to world conflicts, students will need a basis for understanding how men produce, distribute, and consume goods. This suggests that economics should be introduced into the social studies curriculum and should be studied at least as carefully as the history of the country. And since nations have adopted political systems based on very different assumptions, early study of political theory and comparative government also appears necessary. It is clear that peoples of the world will interact in the future on yet more intimate levels. Some understanding of culture and cultural differences can be provided by the discipline of anthropology.

Second, there should also be a change in one of the long-standing functions of education. Education in most countries has been essentially a tool of nationalism. Nationalism is characterized by the feeling that one's own country is unique, favored, and pre-eminent, and that all other nations are less worthy. This feeling has undoubtedly been extremely useful in supplying the national *esprit de corps* necessary for internal development. But at present the attitude appears to be inimical to progress. To cooperate with other nations on the basis of mutual respect is scarcely possible if the peoples of each nation regard others with contempt and indoctrinate this contempt through their school systems. Thus nations will have to discard the practice of inculcating unfavorable stereotypes of other peoples. Nations will also have to stop teaching history in such a way that students learn only interpretations favorable to their own country.[32] In the past, history has been taught by eliminating unfavorable material, mythologizing national heroes, and presenting other nations as either inferior or threatening. It has been indoctrination in patriotic values and, conversely, inculcation of negative attitudes toward others.

Third, nations will have to give up some cherished notions about the nature of conflict. Our own country in particular has a nostalgic fondness for violence and physical aggression. Although schools do not tend to overemphasize violence, other educative institutions in our culture certainly do. For instance, one of the most persistent motifs in popular literature and television is the hero who deals with conflict by fists and guns. The belief that things can be set right by a good, strong man who triumphs in the end through superior physical force does not comport with the need for a legal framework wherein disputes and conflicts are worked out peacefully. It is hard to believe that a people being habituated to violence will come, at the same time, to prefer arbitration, mediation, and compromise.

Two other educative institutions require scrutiny in the light of the assumed goal of a peaceful world order. The mass media—which

[32] A recent article on the subject of biased and unscholarly history textbooks is Ray Allen Billington, "History is a Dangerous Subject," *Saturday Review*, 49 (January 15, 1966): 59–61; 80–81. This is a summary of an extensive report on the subject. See Billington and others, *The Historian's Contribution to Anglo-American Misunderstanding.* Report of a Committee on National Bias in Anglo-American History Textbooks (New York: Hobbs, Dorman, 1966).

clearly function educatively—have traditionally assumed that conflict between persons or between nations makes news. People, it is alleged, wish to read about conflict and, conversely, people find un-newsworthy the slow process of mediation and conciliation.[33] Until newspapers and periodicals become more responsible and attempt to educate their readers in the ways and means of arbitration, the popular taste for violence is not likely to be attenuated. This is not to call for another kind of biased reporting, nor to suggest that mention of conflict should be omitted. What is needed is simply more objective and dispassionate reporting of *all* the news.

Government, the other educative institution, appears to assume that the public is not intelligent enough to understand the complexities of world events. Our own government, for instance, has often refused to popularize anything but an "official" point of view, has censored news felt to be demoralizing or upsetting, and has used its extensive control over information to propagandize *a* position. Thus it has abetted the national tendency to believe that we are an island of purity in a world inhabited by evil men. Theoretically at least, it should be possible for governments to use their extensive power to educate the public in many points of view. It would require a considerable change in philosophy for governments to stop propagandizing and persuading their constituencies, but there is no reason why they cannot undertake the education of their populaces in the aspiration, viewpoints, and feelings of others—even those in opposition to their own national policies.

Some may view this argument as misguided liberalism which seeks to indoctrinate an un-American concept of One Worldism. That is not intended. Changing international conditions have forced all countries toward more frequent and intimate contact. This contact, occurring at a time when many nations throughout the world are attempting to satisfy their own aspirations for a more decent and plentiful life, has resulted in frequent conflict. If nations are to survive without debilitating small-scale or suicidal large-scale wars, peaceful methods must be established to solve conflicts. The only answer is a world order in which established legal channels assist in the arbitration of conflicts. Education can help bring about this kind of world order, not by inculcating any one position but by honest teaching of what others are and what they want. This position would not commit a teacher to propagandizing any view but rather would free him to direct an honest, open, and objective inquiry into international issues.

[33] For instance, the fighting between Turks and Greeks on the island of Cyprus was front-page news for weeks. The successful attempt of the United Nations to end fighting and mediate the conflict went without extensive coverage.

Conclusion

In these two chapters on social philosophy we have attempted to define important concepts in our culture by seeing how they are currently employed. This is scarcely a unique approach, but it is a departure from the usual practice of (1) defining terms as they were used in the eighteenth or nineteenth centuries, and (2) behaving as if the terms had no relationship to current goals or practices. These critical terms have then been examined to see what implications exist for educational practice.

Any reader may legitimately object to either the definitions or the assumed implications. This is to be expected. Such terms as *equality* and *rights* are and have always been subject to various interpretations. The real issue is not *how* these terms are analyzed but *that* they *be* analyzed. The object of this analysis is to provide a sounder and more intelligible basis for practice. The assumption is that one cannot function effectively in a democratic school system unless one understands what is unique about our way of life and how our political and social beliefs can function to guide educational practice.

Currently important concepts in our democracy are used much the way many say prayers: with appropriate solemnity but little understanding of meaning. Thus democracy becomes simply a very nice way of life, freedom is doing what you want, and a right is something no one can take away from you. Verbalizing in this way can only perpetuate the separation of theory and practice. If in fact we are a democratic society with important freedoms and rights guaranteed to everybody, then *what* are these freedoms and rights? If in fact we want each person to realize his unique potential, then logically we must reflect on the meaning of potential and the educational method by which it may be realized. If in fact we believe that democracy is a unique and desirable way of life which ought to permeate educational practices at all levels, then it behooves us to understand what we want and how we should attain it.

The only alternative to hollow verbalization separated from practice is for all teachers to acquire the ability to think discerningly about the larger social life of which schools are only a part.

QUESTIONS FOR DISCUSSION

1. Ask a few friends to define such terms as *rights, equality,* and *freedom.* Compare their definitions with those given in the text.

2. Why are Americans typically vague in their understanding of important political beliefs?

3. How would one go about verifying the assertion that all men, or some men, are naturally inferior, naturally good, or naturally evil?

4. Do you agree with the thesis that the checks-and-balance system of government is a logical outgrowth of the belief that human nature is weak and corruptible? Explain your answer.

5. Boyd Bode holds that Jefferson, Paine, and others of their time were attempting to combat a theory of rights that was rooted in a feudal and aristocratic society and, in doing so, created a theory of rights that in its own way was just as absolute. How would you evaluate this thesis?

6. Ask the following persons what they mean by *free* or *freedom:* a ten year old child; a member of a social minority group; a Catholic priest; a teenager; a school administrator; a professor of political science. Can you draw any conclusions from the definitions?

7. Can one legitimately argue that the local district *should* lose control over education? Discuss.

8. Ask any five persons you know what is meant by the expression "government control." Did they, at some time, say that *government* means *federal government,* and did they imply that control means "taking some liberty away"?

9. Can you frame your own statement of national goals?

10. Why do communists and socialists in Europe call their countries "People's Democracies"? Are they ignorant of the true meaning of the term? Are they hypocrites? Or is there some other answer?

11. What does democracy imply for classroom discipline?

12. Read the essay, very popular at the turn of the century, called "Acres of Diamonds" by Russell Conwell. How does this essay illustrate the points made on pp. 236–241?

SUGGESTED READINGS

CALLAHAN, RAYMOND. *Education and the Cult of Efficiency.* Chicago: U. of Chicago Press, 1962. In the second decade of this century, says Callahan, the assumptions and methods of the science-of-management movement were applied to education, with the result that a completely inappropriate set of values has seriously harmed education.

COMMAGER, HENRY STEELE. *The American Mind.* New Haven: Yale U. Press, 1950. Assuming that Americans are a distinctive people with unique thought, character, and conduct, Professor Commager uses a wide variety of sources to illuminate his subject.

CREMIN, LAWRENCE A. *The Transformation of the School.* New York: Knopf, 1962. This is the best work on the rise of Progressive Education in this country. The author treats in much detail both the philosophical background of the movement and its history after 1915.

CURTI, MERLE. *The Social Ideas of American Educators*. Patterson: Littlefield, Adams, 1965. Curti, a historian, describes the social philosophies of a number of important educators in our country. Note especially his essay on William Torrey Harris, who combined German absolute idealism with nineteenth-century laissez-faire beliefs.

DE TOCQUEVILLE, ALEXIS. *Democracy in America*. (Originally published in English, 1835–1840.) There are many editions of this work, which is a series of related essays on America of the Jacksonian era. De Tocqueville's descriptions are extremely astute, his analysis very keen, and his predictions amazingly accurate. He combines a detached and critical view of Americans with admiration of our successes.

DEWEY, JOHN. *Individualism Old and New*. New York: Minton, Balch, 1910. In this work Dewey analyzes the reality and the myth of individualism in our society. Our vaunted individualism, he asserts, is usually restricted to *economic* individualism and so ignores other important dimensions of the term.

GALBRAITH, JOHN KENNETH. *The Affluent Society*. New York: Boston: Houghton Mifflin, 1958. In readable prose Galbraith elaborates on the theme that contemporary America is operating with economic theories that were designed for an economy of scarcity and are inappropriate for conditions today.

LERNER, MAX. *America as a Civilization*. New York: Simon and Schuster, 1957. In a very lengthy work Professor Lerner presents a detailed and penetrating analysis of our culture. Note his assertion that a civilization may destroy itself by treating its most important cultural value as an absolute, and then note his warning about American economic values.

PARRINGTON, VERNON L. *Main Currents in American Thought*. New York: Harcourt, Brace, 1927. Two Volumes. Although ostensibly an analysis of literary movements from 1620 to 1860, this work, now a classic, provides a most complete analysis of American intellectual history of that period.

TAWNEY, R. H. *Religion and the Rise of Capitalism*. New York: New American Library, 1958. Somewhat dry and detailed, this work explores the conflicts between the religious ethic and the rise of capitalist theories.

11

Two Trends
in Contemporary
Educational
Philosophy

Since World War II, interest in the philosophic foundations of education has increased considerably, and with increased interest has come an expansion of the field. In the past, those supporting a particular philosophical position have been concerned with developing an abstract statement of their position, emphasizing traditional philosophical categories. More recently, many educational philosophers have shifted their attention to implementation of a position. Thus they have written about creativity, curriculum reform, teaching machines, problems of slum dwellers, educational financing, academic freedom, educational television, and similar concerns. Nevertheless, traditional philosophical analysis has not disappeared.

The first contemporary trend we shall examine is idealism, a mode of philosophizing that began in ancient Athens.[1] In the United States idealism was the dominant philosophy until fifty years ago and, though it has been challenged recently by other schools, such as relativism, existentialism, and realism, its influence remains significant. Idealism

---

[1] Some commentators would say that the ancient Hebrews contributed much to the historical development of idealism in their emphasis on the value of the individual, on universal law, and on personal freedom. See I. B. Berkson, *The Ideal and the Community* (New York: Harper, 1958).

has been an important element in the way we think about values, goals, and ultimate matters.

The second philosophical trend we shall examine is linguistic analysis—more simply, analysis. Analysis is a twentieth-century movement, as different from idealism as a philosophy could possibly be. The contrast between the two movements will afford some insight into the direction of philosophy in this century.

Idealism

Idealism is an ancient philosophical tradition asserting, in various forms, that spirit or mind is the primary fact of existence. In contrast with materialism, all forms of idealism emphasize that the world is not inert matter without purpose. In contrast with realists, idealists maintain that external reality—whatever its nature may be—must be understood through the medium of the human mind. In contrast with relativists, idealists believe that, in some sense, reality is absolute. Idealism is, therefore, an absolutistic philosophical position asserting that the world, of which man is an organic part, is essentially spiritual.

The position that man is a part of a spiritual existence—and hence himself spiritual—carries with it certain educational implications. Idealism has developed a set of traditions with regard to content and method of teaching, the goal of education, and the role of the teacher. A teacher who is a consistent idealist may be expected to teach in a manner distinctly different from that of teachers in another philosophical tradition.

The first clear statement of idealism which we have came from Socrates and Plato. Though subsequent idealists differ from them, they share the Platonic belief that the idea (the words *idea, ideal,* and *form* are roughly synonymous in Platonic idealism) is in some sense more real and more permanent than what is known through the senses. This philosophical position was expanded in eighteenth- and nineteenth-century Germany. German idealists—often called "classical" idealists—such as Fichte, Hegel, Kant, Lotze, and Schopenhauer elaborated on such philosophical categories as the absolute, man, nature, mind, morality, knowledge, ethics, history, and the State. Philosophers from other countries, in particular Descartes and Rousseau from France and Spinoza from Holland, also contributed to philosophical idealism.

German idealism has been especially important in American education. It was carried to this country by a number of American educators, in particular William Torrey Harris, who became one of the most influential American educators of the nineteenth century. Harris was United States Commissioner of Education between 1889 and 1906, editor of the *Journal of Speculative Philosophy,* and Superintendent of Schools of St. Louis. He exercised great influence on many American philosophers, professors, and teachers. In the hands of Harris, the Hegelian idealistic position was blended with certain social, political, and economic theories; the combination affected many kinds of educational practices in this country.[2]

Another extremely influential idealist was Josiah Royce, professor of philosophy at Harvard from 1880 to 1916, whose teaching and writing spread a modified Hegelian idealism. In the twentieth century, Herman H. Horne, teaching at New York University, persuaded a large number of his students to embrace idealism, among them Donald Butler and Louise Antz. We shall use Horne, Butler, and Antz as exemplars of modern idealism as it applies to education in this country.[3]

The Tenets of Idealism

The Mental and Spiritual   What do idealists mean when they say that the universe is constituted of ideas or is essentially mental? They do not mean that matter is spiritual, but rather that the world is understandable only by means of mental activity—that is, *underlying* matter is a spiritual reality. "Mind," says Horne, "is the explainer." [4] Only through the operations of mind can reality be made comprehensible. To say, as other philosophers do, that there is a reality above mind is to misunderstand the idealist's point. "For," says Horne, "this supposed [reality] other than itself (mind), supposed to be more real than itself, is *itself a conception of mind.*" [5] Whatever may be said about the world is always a construct of mind. Idealists do not deny that things may exist independently of man, but, they hold, when man comes into relationship with whatever exists, his mind functions to grasp the nature of reality. "Mind or its many synonyms"—reason, thought, spirit, soul— "... somehow accounts for things and renders their operations intelligible." [6]

A contrast with philosophical realism will make this position more

[2] This amalgam has been discussed in Chapter 10.

[3] More information on idealists in this and other countries may be found in J. Donald Butler, *Idealism in Education* (New York: Harper and Row, 1966).

[4] "Idealistic Philosophy of Education," in Nelson B. Henry (ed.), *The Forty-first Yearbook of the National Society for the Study of Education, Part I, Philosophies of Education* (Chicago: U. of Chicago Press, 1942), p. 142.

[5] *Ibid.*

[6] Louise Antz, "Idealism as a Philosophy of Education," in Hobert Burns and Charles J. Brauner (eds.), *Philosophy of Education: Essays and Commentaries* (New York: Ronald Press, 1962), pp. 237–252.

meaningful. In philosophical realism, reality is held to be external to man, who is simply a passive observer. This "spectator" theory—so called because man is a spectator of external events—is seen by idealists as reducing the universe to a set of mechanical operations and man to an unimportant entity. Idealists would say that the world is an expression of a moving spirit, that the apparently mechanical laws which appear to regulate the universe are themselves expressions of a higher spiritual reality. This is extremely significant, for the world is thereby made personal and thus permeated by purpose. In the words of one idealist, ". . . all that is real is ultimately mental, and accordingly personal, in nature." [7] When the world is viewed as essentially friendly to man, teleological, and personal, one behaves differently than when the world is regarded as impersonal and indifferent to man's fate.

The Self That man is part of a spiritual world carries with it certain implications for persons—or, to use the idealist's term, "selves" —since most idealists assume the existence of a higher power. [8] Though this higher power may be called God, the deity, the first cause, or even the underlying spiritual reality, most idealists conceive of a Being, a Self, who in some sense is a shaper of events. Man is like this Being— that is, he has certain characteristics found in the Being. Urban asserts that we are still trying to decide whether we are merely biological entities or

whether we are sons of God—in more philosophical terms, whether our intelligence, reason, and all that these terms connote, are merely biological adaptations or have also a transcendental meaning and *status*. [9]

Since most idealists would assume that the self does have a transcendental meaning, the problem is to decide what that meaning is—in other words, to determine how man relates to the Supreme Being.

Even though man has a complex and intricate growth and development, "The growth of the person, or the spirit, in man is even more marvelous." [10] The self, says Horne, is capable of unlimited capacity for growth in

[7] Butler, p. 47, quoting from Mary Whiton Calkins, "The Philosophical Credo of an Absolutistic Personalist."

[8] Even though most idealists are theologically oriented, there is considerable range of belief. Some reflect an orthodox Protestant position, some call themselves "pantheists," some are "deists," and there are other variations.

[9] Butler, p. 41, quoting from Wilbur Urban, "Metaphysics and Value."

[10] Horne, p. 154.

the attainment of knowledge and wisdom, in the production of an enjoyment of the beautiful, and in the acquisition of the ideal virtues of understanding, sympathy, cooperation, forgiveness, and self-sacrifice.[11]

The Supreme Being, the Ideal Person, has these virtues in infinite amount. The individual human being needs to incorporate these virtues into his personality. He does this essentially by growing toward an image of the most desired and desirable personality—that is, he imitates the Supreme Being.

Growth, imitation, and *maturity* are three key words in idealism. By imitating a model of behavior, we mature and grow toward an ideal, who contains the perfection of virtues. Adults who have modeled themselves after the Supreme Being have reached further toward that perfection than children. Thus adults function as a kind of intermediary model, exemplifying in their own behavior what should serve as an inspiration for children.

Knowledge and Values   In modern forms of idealism, the separation of knowledge and values that we usually see in realism or other philosophies is absent. True knowledge, the idealist holds, is a coherent, systematic, man-made interpretation of events. This brief definition contains most of the idealist's epistemological position: the emphasis on man as the creator of knowledge and on true knowledge as always systematized.

This last point is critical. An idealist would say that we have knowledge when the supposed object of knowledge somehow fits into a pattern—that is, any given truth must fit into a mosaic in which it is organically related to other—perhaps all other—truths. An historian might say, "This event must have happened in *this* way because we have definite knowledge of these other events and they mean only thus and such." For instance, we have excellent reasons for stating that there was a Battle of Lexington in 1776 because subsequent events could not have happened unless there had been such a battle. Other kinds of knowledge are yielded in this manner. We know that a given chemical reaction occurs in a given way because other pieces of information already possessed form an organized pattern into which the new knowledge fits in a certain way.

Similarly, other kinds of knowledge are yielded by this approach. It is widely believed, for example, that people work better when they have a goal and when they have a reasonable chance of succeeding. It is also known with some certainty that excessively punitive teachers,

[11] *Ibid.*

who scold students and emphasize only their errors, do not have much success in the classroom. Given this pattern, it is possible to state that teachers should provide goals which are within the reach of most students and should encourage them to reach these goals. That is, the judgment that teachers should encourage students fits in logically with the two other judgments.

Because the idealist has this approach to knowledge, he does not, like believers in certain other philosophical systems, trust only knowledge which is empirically verifiable.

The idealist's approach to knowledge has been very adequately summarized by Antz. The mind organizes material by relating parts to wholes. Mind selects the material which constitutes knowledge. In the same sense that mind creates knowledge, it also creates values, "practical and artistic . . . scientific, moral, social, religious, philosophical." [12] Finally, mind becomes enriched and expanded as it performs these tasks. In a real sense, "The active subjective mind creates itself." That is, "It identifies itself as self." [13] In short, knowledge is not a passionless, absolutely objective representation of external reality. Knowledge exists only insofar as a mind—your mind, my mind, or many minds—reads meaning into the universe and actively constructs what men agree is dependable truth.

Because individual selves are organically related to the spiritual universe, knowing is essentially an act whereby finite man attunes himself to infinite reality. To "attune" oneself to infinite spiritual reality is to come into harmonious relationship with real spiritual existence. If it is objected that this is an intuitive process and hence unreliable, an idealist might reply: "Certainly it is an intuitive process. But unless you care to believe that man is a mechanical reproducer of reality— a flesh-and-blood Thermofax—the only other alternative is that man intuits reality, that he knows in an inner and really somewhat mysterious way." Thus idealists would hold that knowledge is a coherent, conceptual structure selected, organized, and related by a self who employs his cognitive faculties to attune himself to a higher spiritual reality.

Values are like any other kind of knowing in that they are about real things. Values, says Butler, "are real existents . . . because they . . . are rooted in existence." [14] Something is not good because you like it, but rather good and evil are what they are because of the way the world is. Goodness and evil inhere in the universe. An evil act is not

[12] Antz, p. 244.
[13] *Ibid.*
[14] Page 74.

thought to be evil: it *is* evil. But, Butler insists, there is another element of this formulation: "Values are largely what they are because of the individual persons who possess and enjoy them in their experience." [15] While this may appear to contradict the first point, it does not really, Butler hastens to say. The apparent contradiction is dissolved when we attempt a synthesis between the belief that values inhere in reality and that they exist only in individuals. Such a synthesis, Butler says, would state that while values are realized only within the lives of individual human beings, there is a ground for values. This ground for values is God, and only in Him is there the perfection in which "positive values are fully realized and enjoyed." [16]

Most idealists would say that we must learn to distinguish among values. Some values are matters of personal preference, but others are absolute and to be held by all regardless of time, place, and circumstance. Probably most idealists would hold that absolute values are God-given and hence coercive. Most idealists would probably also hasten to say that, since man intuits his values, it is quite possible for him to be incorrect in his apprehension. But as history is revealed and as man gathers experience, man sees clearly what actions yield evil consequences and what enhance his spiritual growth. Hence, when idealists say, "We must" or "It is good to . . ." they are not expressing merely personal and dogmatic opinions: they are stating what man's best intuitions have revealed.

The Over-Arching Goals of Idealism

Herman Horne, who often expressed himself in felicitous prose, wrote:

Our philosophy dares to suggest that the learner is a finite person, growing, when properly educated, into the image of an infinite person, that his real origin is deity, that his nature is freedom, and that his destiny is immortality.[17]

We can do no better than explain each phrase in this remarkable statement of an idealist's position.

The "finite person" grows—that is, matures—into an image of an "infinite person." Here is the microcosm–macrocosm duality discussed earlier. The infinite person contains within himself, perfectly devel-

[15] *Ibid.*
[16] *Ibid.*, p. 75.
[17] "Idealistic Philosophy of Education," p. 155.

oped, the absolute virtues. A proper education makes one develop into an image (not, of course, an absolute likeness) of the Infinite. That the origin of the person is deity means that the person (and note here the choice of "person" and not "individual") has a divine origin. Persons are not simply biological existents with no dimensions beyond what can be charted by a zoologist. Persons are continuous with the spiritual, with God: they are children of, or created by, God.

That human nature is freedom is a reference to the idealist's belief that freedom is built into personhood. We do not do what we do because we must do it, or because of some biological, automatic mechanism, or because economic or other forces inevitably destine us to behave in a certain way. Our freedom means precisely that we can make choices. This freedom is part of our being.

The notion that our destiny is immortality is somewhat more difficult to understand, for immortality is always a complex subject. Horne's reasoning is as follows: Man's intuition that he was not born to die implies that the world is spiritual. In such a world, the destruction of selfhood would be impossible. If this argument does not convince, "But if the death of the body, which is itself a creature of mind, meant the death of the mind, too, then mind would not be the reality after all." [18] In a universe in which the ultimate reality is mind, it would be inconceivable for individual minds to be destroyed.

Other idealists do not state the position precisely as Professor Horne does, for they choose to emphasize different elements, but Professor Horne's statement does summarize the overarching goal of idealism: Education is the process by which the individual selves become more and more like an absolute ideal. The end of this process is not dissolution but immortality.

With this background, we can discuss some important educational implications.

Idealism and Education

To understand how idealism has influenced American education is difficult for two reasons. First and most obviously, the intermixture of different philosophical traditions in this country makes it risky to isolate certain practices and label them as belonging to one or another tradition. Second, there is always a gap between the writings of the philosopher and implementation into practice by students and disciplines. Most philosophers, if they could be resurrected, would look

[18] *Ibid.*, p. 149.

at what had been done in their names and say, "I didn't mean that, really. You haven't quite got my point." [19] Notwithstanding these two real barriers, we shall attempt to see how philosophical idealism has influenced the practice of American education.

First let us consider certain practices that have been clearly identified with the idealistic tradition. Then we shall cite some contemporary idealistic philosophers on such topics as the nature of learning, curriculum, the role of the teacher, and so on.

The Great Man Probably no aspect of educational practice is so distinctly idealistic as the use of great men as models for student imitation. The truly great man, it is argued, contains within his soul more of the divine aspirations than most. The noble character of a Washington, the scholarly ambitions of a Lincoln, the heroic self-sacrifice of an Arnold Winkleried,[20] to mention only three often-used historical heroes, may be employed by teachers as models. Students learn of their deeds to the end that they may become inspired to lead higher and better lives. Obviously, the use of great men also serves patriotic and nationalistic aims, for the heroes may well be selected largely from the roster of one's own nation.

The Teacher Idealists see the teacher as key to the teaching-learning process, that it is the personality, intelligence, training, and character of the teacher which determines the effectiveness of learning. Perhaps the most important requirement of the idealist teacher is that he have a mature and well-developed personality. Since the teacher is to be the model after whom students pattern themselves, he must possess those characteristics which students will incorporate into their personality. In Butler's words, "For the immature, the teacher is the universe made personal." [21]

The idealist teacher recognizes that imitation is the primary mode by which children learn. One can observe children imitating their elders—scribbling to imitate writing, using the same words and inflections as their parents and teachers, growing into the value model provided for them. Since this is so, the idealist is most concerned with the basic personality patterns of teachers. The teacher must be the kind of person who commands respect, who inspires pupils to learn, who

---

[19] The most unhappy recent example is John Dewey, who lived long enough to see his own ideas deformed and distorted.

[20] The Swiss patriot, not usually studied now, but held up often in the past as a supreme example of self-sacrifice.

[21] Page 99.

truly communicates his subject matter to them. To the extent that the teacher realizes that he is, in Butler's words, a "co-worker with God" in perfecting man, to that extent will he himself grow into a "master in the art of living." [22]

The idealistic teacher is not only a personality, but a finely trained technician. He not only knows his subject matter, he appreciates it. That is, he understands the meaning and significance of it and how it fits into the lives of his students. He is a master of teaching techniques—he understands testing, the principles of psychology and the laws of growth and development. Further, he knows how to combine his knowledge of method, of subject, and of students.

Perhaps the most important fact of learning the idealist knows is that education is ultimately self-education. Rather than saying that teachers teach, it is more correct to say that students learn. Teachers merely provide the best possible environment for learning. Ultimately it is the self-activity of students that constitutes learning. In Horne's words, "The development of mind is from within out, not from without in . . ." [23] One learns when he can somehow view the necessity of an idea or a skill. When a person realizes that a given body of knowledge is necessary to complete himself, he exerts the required energy and effort to learn it. Learning therefore is a life-long process of self-completion and self-realization.

It is probably this idealistic belief that the teacher functions as a model for his students that has led to the traditional practice of requiring teachers to behave according to standards higher than those usually expected of others. In the past, teaching contracts in small towns specifically forbade teachers to drink, dance, or develop romantic interests. Today the stipulation is seldom stated, but in small towns it is still generally expected that the teacher will celebrate out of town and, in general, comport himself in such a way that he will not attract attention.

The emphasis recently in idealistic writings is less on conformity to a specific moral code than on the development of interesting, warm, well-balanced personalities. Idealists recognize what has become obvious to many: that the specific teaching method or perhaps even extensive grasp of knowledge is less important than the person; that in the hands of a person who is not dedicated and alive, any method fails; and that a committed, intelligent, sensitive person makes the best kind of teacher.

[22] *Ibid.*, p. 100.
[23] *The Philosophy of Education*, Rev. ed. (New York: Macmillan, 1927), p. 273.

Curriculum   Idealists are concerned with all aspects of the curriculum, but they tend to feel it is in the aesthetic that the best evidence of man's spiritual kinship to the divine is found. In both the production and appreciation of the beautiful, selfhood becomes enlarged. For this reason, idealists have always emphasized art, music, and literature, and many include theatre and ballet. Idealists strive to combine the two aspects of a work of art—the communication of an intuited truth embodied in an aesthetically pleasing form.

Mathematics and science, too, are imbued with the spiritual, for both go beyond the too often stressed computational and mechanical. Mathematics and science are keys by which the universe may be partially unlocked. In them are glimpsed the richness and harmony, the simplicity and unity of the universe.

The actual content of the subject is less important than the intent of the teacher or the purpose for which it is taught. Any subject, properly conceived, can serve the idealist's aim of education. Whatever the nature of subject matter, its true value is not as an external something, a body of facts or skills to be added on. Subject matter is rather man's conception of the universe, selected by mature persons as appropriate for study. Whatever the particular form of a subject matter, its aim is to enlarge the self and bring it closer to ultimate spiritual perfection.

Symbols   Beginning with Plato, idealists have always emphasized the importance of knowing and using symbols. Language and mathematics have been emphasized because of their symbolic content. Implicit in the writing of many idealists is the belief that by mastery of symbols, man can come closer to an understanding of spiritual reality. The very heavy emphasis on grammar, literature, languages, and higher mathematics in Western education for many centuries reflected the belief that the spiritual universe is apprehended only by those who can manipulate symbols.

The Parent of Another Philosophy   Pragmatism (experimentalism or relativism) owes much to idealism. As a student Dewey not only studied Hegelian idealism, but he came under the personal influence of William Torrey Harris, one of the principal exponents of idealism in this country. Although much has been made of Dewey's criticism of idealism, a careful reading of his writings will reveal his debt to the idealists. The emphasis in Dewey's writing on self-initiated activity, interest, and growth is essentially a rewording of idealism. In a real sense, the influence of idealism in schools is double: as a tradition it has directly shaped American education; as the parent of another philosophical tradition, it has indirectly influenced school practices.

An Assessment of Idealism

That idealism is an incredibly rich tradition is admitted by all philosophers. From Plato to the present, idealism has attracted many profound thinkers. Idealistic philosophy is often written with great subtlety and brilliance, and many philosophical and educational innovations can be traced to idealists. Often these innovations have been assimilated by other philosophical traditions and have become part of the intellectual *Weltanschaüung* [24] of the West. For instance, Hegel's dialectical synthesis became part of Marxism, which has itself formed official Communist philosophy; the emphasis on introspection yielded phenomenology.[25]

Idealism can also claim to be a most comprehensive philosophy. Although it is not a systematic position because there is so much variation, there is little of importance that idealists have not developed. Idealists can claim an epistemology, a vast corpus of metaphysical writings, extensive comments on ethics, a large body of social philosophy—in short, a wide-ranging and well-developed philosophical tradition.

The idealist's emphasis on personality has added an important dimension to teaching. The idealist's definition of personality proceeds logically from the assumption that human beings are not simply biological organisms, but are continuous with—are part of—the spiritual universe. Thus the logical implication: human beings are persons who possess divine attributes and because of this are entitled to respect and consideration. In recent years, this belief has permeated counseling theory, psychology, psychiatry, and education.[26] It has resulted in a new and fresh look at human relationships in teaching. In sum, ideal-

[24] *Weltanschaüung* is literally "world conception" or "world view." It means, approximately, the generally accepted conception of the world held by most persons at a given time.

[25] Phenomenology is a branch of psychology once quite influential in Europe. It originated in the writing of Immanuel Kant, and it was developed by Husserl and Brentano. Phenomenology is essentially reducible to the belief that we can learn more about the world by starting with the experiences of the knower rather than by categorizing the known. There seems to be some evidence that phenomenology is reappearing, particularly in counseling psychology. A good brief explanation of phenomenology is in Harold Titus, *Living Issues in Philosophy,* fourth edition (New York: American Book, 1964) p. 304.

[26] See, for instance, Richard Detering, "Philosophical Idealism in Rogerian Psychology," in Burns and Brauner, pp. 415–424.

ists would probably insist that to elevate human beings to the status of the divine provides a superior rationale for deciding what is ethically good and pedagogically desirable.

It is often felt that an important function of a philosophy is to provide psychological comfort to its adherents.[27] This may well be one of idealism's strengths, for it has provided such support in its assertion that we are all part of a spiritual universe. We are not regarded as having been set adrift in a completely mechanical universe which is unconcerned about human welfare. Rather the cosmos is friendly to human aspirations. Human life is not a "watch in the night" but an essential part of a Grand Design; death is not the end, but only the beginning of a new existence. Thus psychological strength is derived from the feeling that we are one with the universe.

We may say that idealism has been an historically important philosophical tradition that has attracted some of the greatest thinkers in the Western world. It has been most hospitable to rich diverse philosophical conceptions. Its influence on educational practices in Europe and this country has been incalculable. Its emphasis on personality and on the cosmic support inherent in its spiritualism has been of inestimable comfort to millions.

On the negative side, idealism may be criticized for being out of tune both with the prevailing scientific *Weltanschaüung* and with recent events in education. Research in all sciences, it has been alleged, does not support the idealist's assertion of a spiritual universe. Any spiritualistic theory reduces to mystical and subjectivistic feelings which do little to explain the objective world of biophysicists, chemists, and astronomers. In this view, the idealist is merely substituting his wistful hopes of a "friendly" universe for a careful view of the way things really are. Nor, as has been mentioned, do the idealist's traditional concerns have much to do with teachers' organizations, merit pay, the newer biology, school architecture, teaching machines, or a hundred other important events and problems that really do occupy the thinking of teachers.

Idealism, both the classical idealism of Kant and Hegel and some of the present-day positions, has been attacked as vague and unclear.[28] An example of such writing is Hegel's *Philosophy of Right:*

[27] This is emphasized by the psychologist and philosopher Carl Jung. Jung felt that the empiricism and logical positivism of the last two centuries have cheated men of spiritual comfort and have alienated them not only from their fellow men but from the universe.

[28] See Brand Blanshard, *On Philosophical Style* (Manchester: Manchester Press, 1954) for a discussion of the philosophical styles and a critique of Hegel's writing.

The universality of this consciously free will is abstract universality, the self-conscious but otherwise contentless and simple relation of itself to itself in its individuality, and from this point of view the subject is a person.[29]

A philosophy that abounds in grand abstractions—spirit, mind, soul, person, the cosmos—is often in danger of losing the reader amid a welter of brilliant but most unclear metaphors. The distance between Hegel's "abstract universality" and the understanding of ordinary, or even gifted, men is so great as to defy comprehension. This fault in idealism—if it is a fault—may be due to the nature of the idealist's constructs: concepts that simply will not lend themselves to simple descriptions and understandable terms.

At least one cultural trend has cast considerable doubt on idealism as a rationale for public-school educational philosophy. As we have seen, idealism in this country has historically been allied with Protestantism. The secular nature of public schools, re-emphasized by a number of recent Supreme Court decisions, raises serious questions about a God-centered philosophy. Idealists themselves have been hard put to suggest exactly how a theistic rationale can function in an educational system in which, legally at least, all sectarian beliefs must be kept out.

In sum, idealism has been an extremely important philosophical tradition in this country. The writings of classical idealists, brought here by American scholars who visited Europe in the late eighteenth and nineteenth centuries, have exercised considerable influence in shaping educational theory and practice. In recent years, however, idealism has been criticized as irrelevant to contemporary educational issues. It is difficult to understand, assert some, how a metaphysical belief in the continuity between a spiritual universe and spiritual man has any serious meaning for education in this century. In reply, idealists may well assert that in time of spiritual crisis, in a country threatened by materialism, nothing could be more relevant than a philosophy that offers modern man philosophical consolation, a plan for living, and justification for existence.

Linguistic Analysis

If you can conceive of a philosophy that has no cosmology, no binding body of beliefs about ethics, that is firmly opposed to meta-

[29] Georg Wilhelm Friedrich Hegel, *Philosophy of Right*, First Part, Abstract Right, in *Great Books of the Western World* (Chicago: Encyclopaedia Britannica, 1952), Vol. 46, p. 21.

physical speculation, and that has said very little about aesthetics or social organizations, then you have a picture of linguistic analysis. If you conclude that this is not a school of philosophy, you are right. It is not. Linguistic analysis is a name for a movement within twentieth-century philosophy that conceives its function not to create a "body of propositions, but to make propositions clear." These words, from Ludwig Wittgenstein, one of the founders of the movement, summarize the point of linguistic analysis: the true occupation of philosophers is to enable all of us to use language in such a way that our meaning is always sharp and clear.

Although linguistic analysis is a contemporary movement, in a sense its roots stretch back to the Greeks. Aristotle was always extremely concerned that his terms be precisely defined. But the immediate antecedents of this position are in positivism, English empiricism, and the contributions of a group of philosophers known as the Vienna Circle. Positivism contributed a concern with science and the scientific method, in particular with scientific interpretation and the meaning of verification. Although one can relate linguistic analysis to much of eighteenth- and nineteenth-century British philosophy, the three names most associated with the movement are G. E. Moore, Bertrand Russell, and Alfred North Whitehead. Russell's and Whitehead's three-volume work, *Principia Mathematica*, written between 1903 and 1914, was essentially an exploration in a new set of logical propositions. Finally, the activities of the Vienna Circle, a group of thinkers who assembled in post-World War I Austria, helped popularize the movement and bring it to the attention of American philosophers.

A rather unusual German philosopher, Ludwig Wittgenstein was perhaps most instrumental in developing the movement. Wittgenstein set the philosophical "style" at Cambridge University, and today analysis continues to be the dominant philosophy in England. His successors, Gilbert Ryle and A. J. Ayer, continue the movement that is often called "ordinary language," for its emphasis is on language as it is used by "dentists and shopkeepers." [30]

The Position of Linguistic Analysis

The essential position of linguistic analysis is that the vast majority of what are called philosophical problems are not truly philosophical problems but the result of linguistic confusion. Philosophers have been tricked by their own language to think that they are dealing

[30] What is asserted here is that linguistic analysis arose from this background. Linguistic analysis as such is not synonymous with positivism, empiricism, or logic.

with profound philosophical issues when, in fact, they are merely unable to use language in a meaningful way. Philosophical problems as such, asserts Wittgenstein, arise when "our language has gone on vacation." [31] In other words, philosophical problems are a kind of sickness the cure for which is better use of language.

By "better use of language" analysts appear to mean an understanding of how language is used, of when statements communicate and when not, and of which misuses of language make for blockage in meaning. If we illustrate with a statement used to epitomize meaningless language—How high is up?—we can see what the analysts are saying. "Up" is a direction and "how high?" asks for a magnitude. We cannot meaningfully ask for a magnitude of direction. The problem arises because the sentence appears to make sense but does not. And here is the crux of the problem: We may ask questions or make statements which appear to communicate, but which on analysis do not.

The verb *to be* is a prime source of the confusion that analysts would like to expunge. We may say "The pen is black" and also "John is my friend." In both cases the predicate is *to be*. But in the first case the verb denotes an attribute—that is, *black* is an attribute of *pen*. But in the second case, *to be* is a copula, a link or connection. The longstanding habit of confusing the two meanings of *to be* is responsible for the production of pseudo-problems. And the chief repository of confusion and pseudo-problems is metaphysics.

Philosophers who engage in metaphysics, like poets, usually write nonsense. Here linguistic analysts are not being insulting or denigrating poetry. The term *nonsense* is used in a special sense. Some statements are meaningful; they "make sense." For example, "John is six feet tall." This sentence makes sense in that it communicates a proposition which can be shown to be either true or false. But much of metaphysics is nonsense—it does not make sense. In what conceivable way can we show such statements as "to be is to be perceived" [32] or "empirical events are essentially delusive" to be either true or false? Metaphysics and poetry make assertions like these, which in no manner known to man can be demonstrated either true or false.

If the linguistic analysts are correct that "It is the business of philosophy to settle which statements are meaningless and which have meaning," [33] then the question arises, "How does one determine what is meaningful?" The answer is that we must provide a theory of verifiability. How? By admitting as meaningful only those statements for

[31] Quoted by Abraham Kaplan, *The New World of Philosophy* (New York: Random House, 1963), p. 61.

[32] This is the cornerstone of the subjective idealism of Berkeley.

[33] Kaplan, p. 64.

which there is the possibility, even if a weak or only theoretical one, of proving it either true or false. This verifiability theory appears to be an implication of the scientific method. Philosophy *per se* can never prove anything true or false. Such proof is the province of the empirical sciences. What philosophy can do is to see that we use our language in a proper and meaningful way. And that is *all* philosophy can do.

But for linguistic analysts, that is quite enough. By gaining skill in the correct use of language and by building up a more adequate logic, linguistic analysts feel that they have dissolved several thousand years of pseudo-problems—for instance, the mind-body "problem." The mind-body issue has concerned philosophers for centuries. Some philosophers have theorized that mind is a function of body, while others have taken the opposite position—that mind is dominant and body a function of mind. Others—in particular, Descartes—have postulated an "interactionism" in which there is a mind within a body. Gilbert Ryle ridicules this last proposition, calling it the "ghost in the machine" fallacy, for it is simply an absurd combination of a mystical mind in a mechanistic body.[34] A better solution of the problem is to ignore the traditional formulations and simply take a leaf from behaviorism: talk only about what can be observed as visible, verifiable behavior. In so doing, we see that the traditional mind-body quarrel is simply one more hoary and insoluble argument that has plagued philosophy. In effect, conceiving of mind and body as philosophers have traditionally done is to set up a problem about which nothing meaningful can be said. The cornerstone of Wittgenstein's philosophy is that "Whereof one can not speak, thereof he must remain silent." The corollary is, "What can be said, can always be said clearly." To understand the limits of language and logic and the findings of experimental science enables one to free himself from metaphysical speculation to say something useful about the world.

But once one is free from pseudo-problems and verbal snares, what that is "useful" can one say about the "world"? What is "useful" and what is the "world"? "The world," says Wittgenstein, is "whatever is the case." This short and cryptic statement means apparently that the world is whatever discloses itself, even if very partially and incompletely, by experience. We ask ourselves, what would the world be like *if* this or that were the case. Or, put another way, we ask what conceivable difference it would make if what is asserted were actually true.

[34] "The Ghost in the Machine," in Israel Scheffler (ed.), *Philosophy and Education* (Boston: Allyn and Bacon, 1958). See also Nancy Gayer, "How to Get the Fly Out of the Bottle." *Phi Delta Kappan,* 43 (April, 1963): 281.

As to "useful," there is yet another problem. One would think that, after divesting oneself of false and misleading beliefs about language and learning how to communicate precisely, the linguistic analyst would then go on to construct truly useful theories that would guide practice. But no. This is not the concern of analysts. One educational philosopher who is a linguistic analyst writes at great length on the impossibility of using theory to direct practice.[35] Theory does not direct practice, asserts Newsome, and to say that it does is to misunderstand both theory and practice. This position (much at odds with the one presented in this book in Chapter 2) reflects the linguistic analyst's distrust of grand theoretical systems and his tendency to reject the conventional wisdom in educational philosophy because it is insufficiently precise. If philosophers bend their energies to enabling others to communicate, to pointing out unexamined assumptions, and to exposing errors in thought, this alone is adequate. This analytic activity, rather than the prescription to others of what should or should not be done, is the justification for philosophy.

Analysis and Education

If educational philosophy is not to be used as theory for the guidance of education, what other use has it? This is difficult to answer, for analysts are by no means in agreement as to the proper use of philosophy. For instance, with regard to the basic question of whether philosophers should propose appropriate moral guides for educators, Elizabeth S. Maccia says, "Undoubtedly Scheffler is wrong when he states that the philosopher 'must in all modesty resist the role of expert moral guide.' "[36] Much of the writing of analysts would not likely be used by laymen as sources of guidance, for it is dry and technical and hard going for the non-expert. This statement would probably not dismay the analysts, who take the position that philosophy may very well be technical and dry, but is not much important scientific work also difficult to read? As Philip Phenix puts it,

... the history of ideas shows time and time again ... that many of the most important advances stem from persistent attention to apparently minor technical problems.[37]

[35] George L. Newsome, Jr., "In What Sense is Theory a Guide to Practice in Education?" *Educational Theory*, 14 (January, 1954): 31–39.

[36] "Analysis and Philosophy of Education," *Proceedings of the Fifteenth Annual Meeting of the Philosophy of Education Society*, 1959, p. 62.

[37] "An Analytic View of the Process of Generalization," *Proceedings of the Twenty-First Annual Meeting of the Philosophy of Education Society*, 1965, p. 118.

In recent years many educational philosophers have taken an active interest in linguistic philosophy, and the journals and meetings of philosophers of education have more and more come to include analytic papers. George E. Barton, Jr., indicates what he takes to be the true relationship of at least one form of analysis to education:

In this type of analysis, we insist that terms be univocal, that inferences be rigorous, that matters of value be sharply separated from matters of fact, that scientific knowledge properly purged is the best knowledge—and all this seems to amount to an insistence on precision which differentiates the emphasis of this type of philosophy from that of other types.[38]

If this is the purpose of linguistic analysis in education, what specific implications are there? Newsome asserts there are none—if by "specific implications" one means a set of propositions that are to direct curriculum, teaching methodology, and so on. Instead, analysis can function for educators by assisting them to clarify their thinking about education.

For instance, analysts might give attention to such typical statements as, "Teachers should provide real-life experiences for their students" or "The curriculum should be based on lifelike situations." First, these statements should be recognized as prescriptions, statements of what someone ought to do, rather than descriptions. Second, the descriptive terms "real-life experience" and "lifelike" should be examined to determine their meanings. The term "life" is a description of all the activities of living human beings. One of the activities of living human beings is conjugating verbs. Yet as this statement is usually employed, conjugating verbs is not what is meant, for grammatical exercises are not considered "lifelike." But if grammar is part of "life," why would it not be included in the prescription? This kind of statement, an analyst would say, is an example of the substitution of an ambiguous, emotive slogan for a meaningful and precise term.[39] Since the literature of education abounds with nonsensical statements like these— prescriptions dressed up as descriptions with no meaning whatso- ever—analysts feel that they can render a service to practitioners in ed- ucation by pointing out the real nature of statements. An analysis such as this, while it does not provide a useful substitute for "real life,"

[38] *"De Principiis Non Disputandum Est:* The Effects of Varying Types of Philosophic Analysis on Educational Theory," *Proceedings of the Sixteenth Annual Meeting of the Philosophy of Education Society,* 1960, p. 23.

[39] See B. Paul Komisar and James E. McClellan, "The Logic of Slogans," in B. Othanel Smith and Robert H. Ennis (eds.), *Language and Concepts in Education* (Chicago: Rand McNally, 1961), pp. 195–214.

is valuable, analysts claim, insofar as it clarifies the meaning of a frequently used dictum.

In clarifying the meaning, the analysis has dissolved it. While this may seem entirely negative, dissolving problems that are pseudo-problems is clearly an important service. To the extent that teachers need not worry about doing the impossible—in this case "providing" "lifelike" experiences—to that extent can they ask themselves questions which really make sense.

Linguistic analysts can also provide theoretical models for use by teachers. Scientists often construct a theoretical model before they engage in a particular task. For instance, in Mississippi a group of scientists constructed an entire model river system, complete with locks, levees, canals and dams, to see how water behaves under certain conditions. The completed model provided a basis for constructing the actual dams, locks, canals, and dikes for the real river system.[40] Similarly, those concerned with teaching may be helped to construct accurate models of what is wished. Unfortunately, constructing a model is not a simple matter. Emotive and ambiguous statements intrude. Terms are not defined with sufficient precision. Assumptions are not examined. And most important, how a particular model would be validated or confirmed is not often precisely specified. Thus, by helping teachers and those engaged in experimenting with education prepare adequate theoretical models, analysts can perform an important service.

Models for meaning and verification are most essential in education. Often there is a sharp disjunction between a model and the means designed to verify the model. That is, a model may be set up in one way and the verification procedures may actually be designed to verify something quite different. A case in point is some of the current research on creativity. Do the tests for creativity actually measure creative persons? Analysts might say that first one must specify operationally what a creative person does—that is, construct a model of a creative person. The verification process should flow logically from the assumptions that one makes about creativity. If, for instance, a test actually measures what turns out to be intelligence and not creativity, then the verification procedure is at fault or the model of creativity is not sufficiently precise to be tested.

Here the analyst feels he may make an important contribution by

---

[40] Recently computers have been pressed into service providing models. Information, based on a proposed model, is fed into machines. The machines provide data on the probable consequences of this or that part of the model. The model may then be modified. For a good, non-technical discussion of this innovation, called simulation, see Dorothy L. Meier and C. H. Bradford, "The Study of Man," *Transaction,* 3 (March, April, 1966): 37–39.

removing elements that cause confusion and difficulty. By clarifying terminology, examining the logic of assumptions, attempting to specify outcomes, and providing a reliable method of verification, analysts can enable us to use language with such precision that we free ourselves for truly creative enterprises.

Critique of Analysis

There has been comparatively scant criticism of analysis as a philosophical position. It is seemingly impossible to criticize a position which claims to have no tenets. Nor is it clear how to criticize educational practices that flow from linguistic analysis when no claims are made for any practice. However, in a stinging criticism of linguistic analysis, John Paul Strain rejects the analysts' assertion that they can provide no implications for education. "Educational consequences are implied in these assertions," argues Strain. "When educational theory is not allowed, when, in effect, students are not permitted . . . to form ideas in their general significance," how are they to carry on the enterprise of education? The answer is that they "should be conditioned for learning practices, techniques, and skills." [41] That is, instead of theory as a guide to practice, analysts are simply substituting common usage as a basis for practice.

The end result of this is to glorify technique and usage. Students who are trained in this fashion are "only highly skilled technicians." Such students have a "decided fear of having their own interpretations," [42] for so much emphasis is placed on the proper use of linguistic skills that the analytically oriented teacher ignores beliefs and attitudes. The tendency today for students to avoid committing themselves to any position "highlights a basic theme among students today—prodigious thinking, i.e., without believing." [43]

Further, the influence of linguistic analysis is felt in a tendency to reject scholars who attempt to relate their own specialty to many other related fields. So much emphasis is made on narrowing the range of knowledge and on mastering techniques, that the broadly educated person with wide interests is immediately suspect. Analysts assert, says Strain, that no one can know that much about so many fields and any man who claims to is obviously an impostor.

Some philosophers are irritated by the tendency of analysts to be

[41] "A Critique of Philosophical Analysis in Education," *Educational Theory,* 14 (July, 1964): 187.
[42] *Ibid.* p. 188.
[43] *Ibid.*

most enthusiastic about picking apart others' positions and engaging in destructive criticism. Analysts are "at their teaching best when attacking a position rather than defending one." [44] Because analysts claim they have no philosophical position of their own, they have none to defend; and because they are committed to a fairly narrow conception of philosophy as purification of language, they can freely criticize others without supplying any viable alternative of their own.

The writings of analysts are usually highly detailed and technical explanations of why we must not use a certain term in a particular way, or why it is impossible to maintain something. In so writing, analysts, it is charged, succeed only in talking to each other. Little interest is shown in the pressing problems of teaching. Linguistic analysis, it is alleged, is of no help to teachers who might profit by the insights of educational philosophers but who cannot understand the analysts' writing, or if they can, could not possibly apply them to classroom activities.

Perhaps the most serious criticism that can be made of linguistic analysis is that it conceives philosophy too narrowly. Values and those traditional philosophical categories dealing with values—ethics and aesthetics—are seen as outside the realm of philosophical interest or competency. Abraham Kaplan writes:

But note how great is the preoccupation here with purely intellectual goals and standards—the emphasis is on science, truth, belief, observation, and inference. But art, beauty, morality, politics, and religion apparently lie outside the scope of this powerful method, if not outside the scope of philosophical interests altogether. [45]

In their eagerness to achieve clarity, precision, and vigor, analysts have divorced themselves from the really important political, social, and economic issues of this century. In their distrust of sweeping systems and grand abstractions, they have refused to concern themselves with the perennial philosophical problems—what is man, toward what end should life be lived, how should man govern himself?

One educational philosopher has asserted that linguistic analysis reflects a retreat from the world. [46] Intellectuals have usually held that ideas make a difference, that ideas can somehow change the world. Linguistic analysts are so preoccupied with technique and so chary of

[44] *Ibid.* p. 189.
[45] *The New World of Philosophy,* p. 89.
[46] The author is indebted to Bruce Hood of The University of California, Los Angeles, for this criticism.

using ideas as tools that they have simply retreated from the testing of ideas to the minute dissection of propositions.

In the relatively few years that linguistic analysis has captured the attention of educational philosophers, it has had nothing like the effect on education of pragmatism, existentialism, or Thomism. This is scarcely to be wondered at since analysts do not conceive of philosophy in the same terms as do adherents of other positions. And this perhaps is the problem in rendering an evaluation of analysis. It does no good to criticize a philosophy on the grounds that it ignores certain tasks if the reply is, "Of course we ignore these tasks. Such tasks fall outside the realm of philosophers. Such tasks involve speculation. If we wish to know what the facts are, we turn to scientists. Our only job is to see to it that language about education communicates clearly." Obviously any criticism of this philosophy—or, better, philosophical method—must be made with relation to another conception of philosophy.

If one conceives of philosophy as solely a technical analysis of language the goal of which is to dissolve pseudo-problems, clear up misconceptions, and sharpen terminology to the end that all will be assisted to think more clearly, then linguistic analysis is the proper conception of philosophy. If, however, philosophy is an attempt to understand the widest possible meanings in life so that one may develop for himself theories with which to cope with human problems, then linguistic analysis is far too narrow. That a tool designed to help us employ language in a precise, meaningful way is philosophically useful is obvious. But that language analysis is the sum total of philosophy is by no means acceptable to all as the purpose of philosophy.

Analysis

Both linguistic analysis and philosophical idealism reflect two ancient traditions in the history of philosophy. In one tradition, philosophers have attempted to define terminology as sharply as possible. The goal of this philosophy is precision, and one need only consult the writings of Aristotle—especially the *Metaphysics* and *Politics*—to see how concerned he was with words and their use. The other tradition is reflected by Socrates, the conscience of Athens, who, without fear of consequences, insisted that each person examine the meaning of his life. Socrates asserted that no human life is defined only by the limits of one's environment or by events in one's own lifetime. Rather, human beings are continuous with a reality that transcends time and space. The key to right living is understanding this reality.

It appears, then, that both idealism and analysis reflect two persistent, perhaps complementary, modes of philosophizing. Apparently philosophy necessitates a concern with both broad issues and technique and method. That idealism and analysis are only part of the total picture is evident from our previous discussion of other philosophical positions. Perhaps we can now generalize about the activities of contemporary educational philosophy.

Since education is not a self-sufficient activity but one inseparable from a social matrix, educational philosophers have attempted to explore the social matrix. They have addressed themselves to such questions as: What values in our society have what meaning for education? What values in our society are harmful to education? How should education respond to particular movements within our society? For instance, how can education supply the demand for more technological training and yet retain certain humanistic values?

A major task of educational philosophers is thus simply to ask the *right* questions. Just as in science, where the real difficulty may lie in asking the correct questions, the problem in education is often to formulate the question that gets to the heart of the issue. To the layman, an educational practice is likely to be self-justifying: whatever is, should be. But to the educational philosopher, practice does not justify itself. The fact that a particular subject has been studied for many years does not mean that it *should* be studied. Hence one may find such questions as these: What value is there in the study of ancient languages? Are the traditional rationales for the study of ancient languages still valid? Does the fact that education in this country has largely been under state or local control necessarily mean that this pattern should continue? Granted that objective examinations lend themselves to rapid scoring, may there be any damage in them to students? The significance of these questions is that they go beyond the obvious, external appearances. They are attempts to explore the hidden and elusive implications that are not likely to appear unless one searches for them.

Educational philosophers engage in a similar analysis of educational issues and meanings. In much of the writing today there are efforts to get at the meaning of practices, to assess the relevance of goals, to evaluate the merits of new proposals. The procedure involves a question: What, exactly, is being proposed? For instance, with regard to the much-heralded recommendations of James B. Conant regarding high schools, some educational philosophers have asserted that these are essentially retrogressive, reactionary proposals. In effect, they say, Conant is simply asking for more of the same—more language, more mathematics, more science. He has not addressed himself to the important questions: What kind of language? What is the purpose of science-teaching? How does one best teach these subjects? Despite the attention attracted by Conant's proposals, these critics say they are not what they appear.[47]

Philosophers often question the unspoken but important assumptions underlying a proposition. For instance, it is usually held that psychological research is so important that almost any method to gather information is acceptable, no matter what rights of subjects are violated. Recently some philosophers of education have pointed out that a well-documented experiment, while seemingly impeccable, required the investigator to lie and deceive the subjects, who were treated merely as dupes. The question thus raised concern what rights all subjects in psychology experiments possess.

In the last sentence is a clue to another function of educational philosophers—the deliberate, often harsh criticism of educational theory and practice. In our culture, criticism, especially negative criticism, is undervalued.[48] However, such criticism is apparently warranted, if for no other reason than to check the blind passion for novelty that often seems to be so disruptive to education. It has happened, for instance, that the same school system will simultaneously install teaching machines and advocate that teachers encourage creativity. It is at this point that the concerned philosopher will raise relevant questions, provide analyses of the assumptions that underlie both teaching machines and creativity, and then point out the consequences for practice.

The dampening of ardor for misconceived or unexamined projects is only half the goal of criticism, of course. The other half is the stimulation of both further thought and experimentation. By suggesting promising leads, recommending improved designs or models, providing a wider view of the issue, or exhorting consideration for neglected tasks, educational philosophers may also stimulate change.

---

[47] For a rather detailed analysis of Conant's recommendations and the reaction to them, see the March, 1964, issue of *The Journal of Teacher Education* for "A Symposium on James Bryant Conant's *The Education of American Teachers*." See especially the analysis by Robert Beck, pp. 41–44. Beck is a philosopher and historian of education.

[48] "Destructive" criticism is regarded in our culture as a very damaging thing. What is overlooked is that some criticism must necessarily be destructive. There appears to be no reason why all criticism must be constructive in the sense that it must supply a viable alternative. Edmund Burke did not provide substitute interpretation for Rousseau's theory of the origin of government. His criticism was largely destructive and, in view of the utter lack of evidence supporting Rousseau, furnished a very desirable addition to political theory.

QUESTIONS FOR DISCUSSION

1. What is the essence of idealistic philosophy?

2. What accounted for the nineteenth-century mixture of idealism, social Darwinism, and economic theory? What effects did it have on education? What effects remain?

3. What would a realist find to criticize in idealism?

4. If we accepted Professor Horne's position outlined on pp. 254, what difference would it make to education in this country?

5. How convincing is the idealist's conception of curriculum?

6. What is your reaction to the idealistic practice of requiring a high standard of behavior of teachers because they are to function as models?

7. How clear is linguistic analysis?

8. Can you suggest some philosophical problems that are not genuine problems but the result of incorrect use of language?

9. Should linguistic analysts feel some responsibility for applying their theories to educational practice? Discuss.

10. What tenet or tenets of analysis should all teachers understand? Why?

11. What are the similarities of idealism and analysis?

12. What would be a relativist's criticism of analysis?

SUGGESTED READINGS

ANTZ, LOUISE. "Idealism as a Philosophy of Education," in Hobert Burns and Charles J. Brauner (eds.). *Philosophy of Education.* New York: Ronald Press, 1962. In this brief introduction to idealism by an idealist, the author discusses the idealist's theory of knowledge.

BERKSON, I. B. *The Ideal and the Community.* New York: Harper, 1958. This is both a criticism of Kilpatrick and Dewey and a summation of the idealist's position. The author also develops the idea that the ancient Hebrews were quite important in the historical growth of idealism.

BUTLER, J. DONALD. *Idealism in Education.* New York: Harper and Row, 1966. This is a complete but brief development of the history and tenets of idealism, its relationship to education, and a summation of criticism of the position.

GAYER, NANCY. "How to Get the Fly Out of the Bottle." *Phi Delta Kappan,* 43 (April, 1963). This is a brief and simple explanation of linguistic analysis written for the layman.

HORNE, HERMAN H. "Idealistic Philosophy of Education," in Nelson B. Henry (ed.), *The Forty-first Yearbook of the National Society for the Study of Education, Part I, Philosophies of Education.* Chicago: U. of

Chicago Press, 1942. Horne was one of the leading idealists in this century. In this well-written essay there is an exposition of the position and a criticism of other philosophical positions.

KAPLAN, ABRAHAM. *The New World of Philosophy.* New York: Random House, 1963. This book is a description and criticism of a number of contemporary philosophies, including analysis. The author was himself a student of several analysts, but this has not prevented him from giving a remarkably objective treatment of the strengths and weakness of the position.

STRAIN, JOHN PAUL. "A Critique of Philosophical Analysis in Education," *Educational Theory,* 14 (July, 1964). This is one of the few works quite critical of linguistic analysis in education. The author takes the position that analysis, despite its assertions to the contrary, does have concrete implications for education.

Epilogue

Forces pointing in different directions and having their origins in many parts of our culture pull and push a teacher. As a result, instead of possessing sufficient knowledge to select a goal, an appropriate set of methods to reach that goal, and a means of evaluating the goal, the teacher often either perceives no goals, methods, or means of evaluation, or perceives them in such numbers that their meaning is likely to be unclear. The body of theory that is supposed to guide teaching practice is crowded with contradictions, often unperceived by practitioners and teachers of practitioners alike.

Such contradictions can lead to serious problems. A teacher at any time has his choice of assuming that children are passive objects whom he is to "shape" by mechanical means, or that they are essentially goal-oriented beings with purposes. He can believe passionately in democracy and yet preside over the classroom as an authoritarian. He can know that, because of the structure of our society, individuals must unite effectively and enforce collective demands before they can get what they want, and yet feel that collective action and demands seem unprofessional. At any given time he may read and accept the fact that *the* most significant value of education is a social value that can be satisfied only when all children learn what they must know. Or he can choose to believe that the most significant value in education is the individual development of persons and self-fulfillment of individuals. Or he can prefer to believe that the goal of education is met only when students become proficient in a certain subject matter.

What happens when all these attitudes—and many more—overlap in the teacher's consciousness? The results are ambiguous and difficult to evaluate. Perhaps it is the strain of incompatible beliefs that generates a vitality in American education unmatched in the world. But education is also pulled in different directions, energy is dissipated, support is difficult to obtain,[1] and the quality and quantity of education vary enormously through the country. Some of the consequences of theoretical confusion include the following: teachers who verbalize in one way and practice in quite another; teachers who undergo internal conflict because they do not really know what to do;[2] teachers who engage in mutually conflicting practices for dimly perceived goals, alternating between "strict" and "permissive" classroom control for the goal of "self-discipline"; teachers who require aimless busywork of their students—filling in page after page of workbooks, watching movies and filmstrips only distantly related to the matter at hand; school systems which vaguely sense that the curriculum is meaningless and attempt to compensate for curriculum inadequacies with grades, prizes, material bribes, punishments and rewards; students who, sometime after the fourth grade, miss the joy of learning and bend all their energies to preparing for an acceptable college; parents who willingly collaborate by first talking about the importance of self-fulfillment and then force their children to take courses toward a college major or an occupation seen as appealing only by the parent;[3] schools and colleges that require courses in art appreciation and then build a campus in an architectural style that can only be called Early Penitentiary;[4] high-school superintendents and teachers who verbalize about the necessity for something called "meeting needs" and then wonder why three-fourths of their lower-class minority students drop out in the sophomore year.

What Can Philosophy Do?

This list could be expanded almost indefinitely. The point is that the many self-defeating, ineffectual, and superficial educational prac-

[1] There is evidence that communities are becoming more and more reluctant to pass school bond issues.

[2] This is seemingly most evident about grading time. The teacher who believes in the stern dictum that grades are objective measures of a student's progress agonizes about giving a failing grade to the pleasant, cooperative, hard-working, but dull student. Duty pulls one way but personal feelings push another.

[3] This is illustrated by the parents who tell their child, "We want you to choose an occupation that will make you happy. We feel you will be happiest as a doctor, a lawyer, or a CPA."

[4] In almost all institutions of higher education can be found verbalizations about the need for teaching students to appreciate beauty. But the architecture is ugly because the trustees fear the wrath of citizens who will object to spending public money on "frills." The implications for the students about the "value" of beauty are clear.

tices in our culture are the result, ultimately, of lack of understanding at the theoretical level. Improvement will come only when those responsible for education understand the philosophical meaning of what they do. It is a fallacious notion that all educational problems can be solved or lessened if we but spend more money, offer more courses in college, or load classrooms with more sophisticated machines. Better financing, more education, and better use of technology may be necessary conditions, but they are clearly not sufficient. The complex process of education will be improved only when we begin to understand the nature of the complexity involved. And whatever useful information psychologists, sociologists, and financial experts may tell us about education, all educational issues are ultimately philosophical.

What is needed are teachers, principals, curriculum consultants, boards of education, parents—those who make decisions about education—who understand, at the deepest level, what the problems and the decisions are really about. Certainly part of the responsibility for developing this understanding devolves on those who call themselves educational philosophers.

Educational philosophers can teach how to ask the right questions. What *is* it that is being proposed? What assumptions support the proposal? What evidence supports the proposal? What consequences are likely to flow from the proposal? What alternatives are there?

An important intellectual skill is the realization that theory is not divorced from practice. When those responsible for education stop belittling theory as irrelevant abstraction and pay attention to the consistency and adequacy of their theory, the first step to the improvement in practice will be taken.

One critical skill is the development of sensitivity to conflicts. Any educational practice ought to be evaluated in the light of the following questions: What values does this particular practice enhance? What values does it tend to endanger? In the light of the values enhanced and the values harmed, is the practice worth it? It is important to realize that values are not easily seen or measured. Whatever the cost of a certain program, class, or building, what kinds of values can be expected at what time in the future? How will we know if these values have come about? What instruments or means exist to evaluate the results? The assumption here is that only to the extent to which one's theory—one's map of the future—is clear and coherent will one be likely to realize the desired values.

Educational philosophy ought also to teach tools of understanding, not just in the sense of comprehending structure and process, but in the sense of seeing what lies beyond the immediate. No teaching method, school architectural plan, extracurricular activity proposal, textbook, or test is a self-sufficient, independent entity. To choose a book or give a test commits one to a range of values that go beyond the classroom or the school environment. When one makes an educational decision—any kind of educational decision—one is, in a sense, affirming or denying a universe of values. For a teacher to station himself in a classroom during an examination for the purpose of erecting barriers against cheating is not merely for him to conduct an examination. It is to commit himself to a certain position regarding human nature: that human beings need constant guarding to repress their natural evildoing. Similarly, for him to refuse to deal with a controversial issue in class is to commit himself to a theory of human nature: that students are not capable of reaching a decision on important matters.

To teach a subject is not simply a matter of presenting subject matter to a class of live bodies. One does not learn merely by being in contact with something. Effective teaching requires that one possess a theory of learning, a body of conceptual tools concerning the definition of learning and beliefs about how learning takes place, about the meaning of motivation, and the meaning of forgetting or non-learning. This statement appears to be beyond serious doubt, and all departments of education teach learning theory in some sense. But what must also be realized is that any learning theory presupposes a philosophical position. To make an assertion about learning commits one to a theory of reality, a theory of knowledge, and a theory of human nature. Fully to understand one's own learning theory requires understanding the philosophical foundations on which it rests.

More specifically, as we have tried to point out, a learning theory involves beliefs about the meaning of knowledge. When one becomes acquainted with theories of knowledge, it becomes fairly obvious that the verb "to know" includes a large number of meanings—that knowing the multiplication tables is not the same as knowing that crayfish moult, and that neither of these kinds of knowledge is the same as knowing that good children do not push or shove in lunch line. When the teacher begins to see the implications of this, he is in a better position to improve the learning process in the classroom.

Finally, anyone who has ever engaged in fruitless argument with another or who has ever failed to teach a child is in a position to appreciate the insights of metaphysics. Apparently, opposites in a dispute must be perceiving reality somewhat differently. The same must be true of the non-learning child and the teacher. If so, matters might be helped if the disputant or the teacher understood how the other perceived reality. If this position is valid, then theories of reality may be a conceptual tool of use in understanding. What we are suggesting here is that an extremely abstract subject—metaphysics—has considerable practical use.

That education is necessary for the constant renewal of a culture is granted by all. That education is an enterprise which can enrich the lives of all who engage in it is equally conceded to be true. But before a teacher can derive the immense satisfaction from teaching that many have claimed, he must first know what he is about—what teaching is and how best to teach. To this end, he will spend his life asking questions. This book provides data sufficient only for a beginning.

Index

281